Best Wishes
Sam aka
Ahmykah

SWEET LIBERIA
LESSONS FROM THE COAL POT

by SUSAN D. PETERS

Sunrise Consulting
Chicago, Illinois

Sweet Liberia: Lessons from the Coal Pot ©2010 by Susan D. Peters

Sunrise Consulting books may be purchased for educational, business, or sales promotional use. For information please write: Special Markets Department, Sunrise Consulting, 11834 S. Normal, Chicago, IL 60628

ISBN-13: 978-0-9827125-0-4
LCCN: 2010926461

Original artwork and Cover design: Barron Steward
of www.barronsteward.com
Editorial Team: Erica Weber & Lissa Woodson
Interior Book Design: Lissa Woodson of www.macrompg.com
Photos from the private collection of Susan D. Peters

Distributed by Ingram Book Group

Sunshine Consulting trade paperback edition May 2010

10   9   8   7   6   5   4   3   2   1

Manufactured and Printed in the United States of America

For information regarding discounts for bulk purchases, please contact us at 773-401-4570 or sunriseconsultingonline@gmail.com.

DEDICATION

I dedicate this book to my mother and my sister Yvonne who allowed me to go on my journey trusting in the Universe to bring me safely home. And to my brother Godfrey who is among our ancestors and whom I have loved through time and space.

My thanks and appreciation to my five wonderful children for living this dream with me. I hope that they will understand why we shared this journey and forgive me for any mistakes I made along the way that may have affected their lives.

ACKNOWLEDGMENTS

I wish to acknowledge the contributions and thank the many people that have assisted me on the journey to tell my story.

They are many but I'd like to begin with Dina Elenbogen at the Gleacher Center-University of Chicago, who took the first deep dive into my rambling manuscript and gave it to me straight between the eyes, with respect.

To my wonderful family, I want to thank you. Sarah Anderson-Lambert, my mother, my friend and my rock. Thanks for believing in me when I didn't believe in myself. Yvonne, my Angel sister, who had my first published pamphlet on her dresser for years, and who prayed me out of Africa, I love you. Thanks to my five children, Tonya Peters, the most devoted big sister and elder daughter in the world. Thanks to my eldest son, Gyasi Mwewe, for always making me feel that I'm a VIP in his life. Thanks to you Muasa Mwewe, for showing me, seriously, how to raise you. Thanks to Zevah Johnson our family's rudder, steady as she goes. Thanks to my youngest daughter, Hope Peters, for showing me that everything God gives you is good and for bringing me so much unexpected joy. Thanks to my eldest grandbaby Yahanna, for always keeping me down to earth.

Thanks so much to my editorial dream team-Supreme thanks to Lissa Woodson, the hardest working woman in self-publishing! Lissa has truly been God's hands, feet, and master editor/consultant on this project. Your passion for the written word and your willingness to help me share my story has taken my skills to another level. "Never could have made it without you."

Erica Weber, you are a fine editor. I love your spirit. Thanks for your frank and probing questions about my manuscript. I appreciate you so much. To Debra Mitchell and Anna Moore, thank you so much for your assistance! Barron Steward, your cover design astounded me. It is nothing short of fine art. Jeremy "J. L." Woodson, much respect for "putting your foot" in my website!

Thanks to all my friends for listening to me talk about my Liberian experience and helping me move forward. Angela and my Blank Canvas sisters, I am biting through my cocoon!

Last but very importantly, thanks Jill Zimmerman, my former colleague and friend, for rummaging through your war wounds and searching for the beauty and the hope and sharing it with us.

THE LIBERIAN NATIONAL ANTHEM

All Hail, Liberia Hail
All Hail, Liberia Hail
This glorious land of liberty shall long be ours
Though new her name green be her fame
And mighty be her power, And mighty be her power,
And mighty be her power,
In joy and gladness with our hearts united
We'll shout the freedom of a race benighted
Long live Liberia, Happy Land
A home of glorious liberty by God's command
A home of glorious liberty by God's command

INTRODUCTION by Jill Zimmerman

Meaningful connection. When I think about Susan Peters and how she entered my life, this is how it feels. I remember staring at her resume and realizing that we had both lived in Liberia--a small, but significant country in West Africa. I had now been back for almost ten years and it had been a long time since I had spoken to anyone about my life then. I called her, and we talked for almost an hour, not about the job she was applying for, but about living in Liberia. There was an instant connection. Ultimately I hired Susan and while she clearly met all the criteria for the position, it was really the bond I felt to her through our mutual experience in Liberia that led me to hire her.

Susan and I lived in Liberia during two profoundly different times in the country's history. I was there working for The Taylor Institute and UNICEF-Liberia during the height of the civil war. Susan enjoyed a more peaceful time--full of richness and vitality--a time that her book shares with you more explicitly than I could. Susan and her family fled Liberia on August 8, 1990. I arrived in Liberia three years later on a hot afternoon in August of 1993. I was only going to be there for four months and ultimately ended up staying a year. Our task was to work with former child soldiers and children in displaced camps

There are many stories from my life in Liberia. But one I remember vividly is working with ECOMOG (Economic Community Monitoring Observer Groups--a the West African peacekeeping force) to free captured child soldiers. The children, ranging in age from nine-to-sixteen were held in a make-shift prison at an old French school in Sinkor. We negotiated their release and a rehabilitation program that would help re-integrate them back into their communities. The relationships we developed with the young combatants-some of whom were not much older than my seven-year-old son-were deep and significant. They came to rely on us and in a strange way--we relied on them too--to see that, in a country deep in pain-hope and change were possible.

Over the years Susan and I have shared many stories about living in Liberia. It is the telling and re-telling of these stories that has helped me realize that these powerful experiences have shaped who I am today. While my time in Liberia was relatively short, it was life-changing. We all have experiences that are life-altering, Susan's book reminds us how important it is to learn from them.

--Jill Zimmerman worked for UNICEF-Liberia and the Taylor Institute (Chicago, IL), which had a contract with UNICEF-Liberia. Founded in 1975, the Taylor Institute is rooted in advocacy and committed to influencing public policy for people in the United States and around the world.

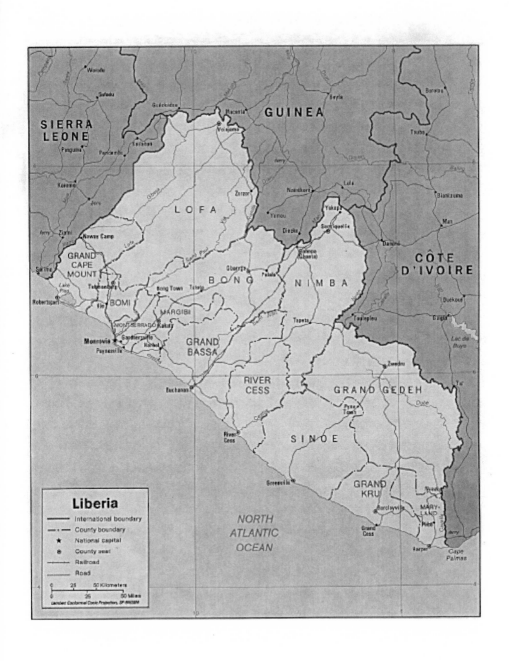

"Bear in mind that you should conduct yourself in life as at a feast."
--Epictetus *Roman (Greek-born) slave & Stoic philosopher*
(55 AD - 135 AD)

THE COAL POT
AS A METAPHOR

The coal pot is both an icon and a metaphor for God's most basic gift to all of us- life. It stands at the center of Liberian life and culture. When I reflect on my sojourn in Liberia, my thoughts inevitably return to the feelings of the warmth generated by the cooking and sharing of meals prepared on a coal pot.

PART I

JUMPING WITHOUT A PARACHUTE

"Sometimes it's necessary to go a long distance out of the way in order to come back a short distance correctly."
--Edward Albee, American Playwright

Susan D. Peters in late 1970's

"Sweet Liberia" by Liberian recording artists Zach and Gebah felt like an anthem! It was popular in the 1980's and has a strong nationalistic strain urging Liberians to work together, to love, and to treat each other fairly and to accept the responsibility of electing their own leadership.

"Sweet Liberia, land of liberty is our home. Let us keep it standing. It's the one and only home that…"

It is a playful upbeat tune and contrasts the national anthem, "All Hail Liberia," which is more austere in tone. The words of this song were the background music for my life between 1982 and 1989.

For me, it was a period of intense productivity, hope and change.

BEGINNING AT THE END

August 8, 1990, Liberia West Africa

Massive Embassy gates clanged shut behind us. My heart filled with joy. In several weary steps, my family and others with the good fortune of surviving the trip to the American Embassy in Liberia, had instantly been transported from the barbaric civil war in West Africa, to the United States of America. Throngs of starving, ragged, and terrified Liberians, along with Africans from various tribes, clamored outside the gates. I could only say a prayer for them.

I am not sure what made me—maybe the adrenaline from fear and anxiety—but I looked up, and out of a dozen faces, I focused keenly on one particular marine perched on the perimeter wall of the Embassy. I was struck that he looked more like a red-faced teenager than a soldier. In the next instant, I saw him transform from a relaxed young man into a man preparing for battle. A shrill alert blared from the siren, his eyes widened and jaw hardened. The sound of speeding jeeps and machine gun fire permeated the air. The rebels were boldly attacking the Embassy of the United States of America!

Instinctively we hit the ground. Crawling along the concrete walkway toward the U.S. Consulate's office was no easy task. The sound of machine gunfire assailed our eardrums. When all was quiet, only the coppery smell of spent ammo prevailed, we received the "all clear" and rose cautiously.

"Ms. Rahm!"

I spun around coming face to face with Ray, a Peace Corps worker once assigned to the Liberian National Red Cross. Today, he was dressed in civilian clothes, but wore a sidearm and the hardened gaze of a man accustomed to killing. Secretly, I had always believed he was CIA. Grinning, he revealed the familiar cracked front tooth as he waved a quick hello. Dazed at seeing him out of context, but relieved at the renewed feeling of safety, I feigned a smile.

Once inside the U.S. Embassy Consulate's office, he lingered, personally expediting our group's paperwork. His rank spared us the bureaucratic cruelty of repatriation, ordering that my children and I were not to be separated under any circumstances. *Good never loss.* I reflected upon the Liberian adage which, simply put, means the good you do comes back to you.

Ray had been a complete asshole as a Peace Corps worker. Supposedly, he had been stationed at the Red Cross Headquarters in Liberia to help develop additional revenue flow to confront our ever-growing financial problems. He came in like a whirlwind and was quickly promoted to Senior Staff where his brashness and lack of tact wreaked havoc on everyone's nerves. Yet, whenever he visited the Red Cross Day Care Center, he seemed to transform into a softie, displaying a gentle, patient attitude. I was the Director of the Center, and during the children's naptime, he would often stop by my office to sit and express his frustration with Liberia and its people. We would chat about the things we missed about good ole America, a place I had secretly vowed to leave behind forever. Today, Ray's face and squinting brown eyes brought a feeling of relief and gratitude for his influence.

Ray, with my youngest daughter in his arms, led my bedraggled family to the ocean side of the Embassy.

"Well, now I know the answer to why you aren't married, dude," I quipped.

"Yep, war is what I do."

"So what now?"

"I'm on my way to Somalia," he said instinctively, feeling for his holster. Our final words were clipped short as two C-130 military helicopters landed, making the palm trees bow low and our clothing blow against our bodies. As we boarded, I looked back one last time and thanked him from the bottom of my heart.

The copter crew was swift, outfitting us with helmets to protect our ears from the deafening sound of the propeller blades slicing through the humid air. Relieved and unafraid, I peered through the portals as we took off, looking down on the ground and then the ocean below.

It was unlike any experience my children ever had, but then the last few months had been full of uncertainty, most of it terrifying. My youngest son, Zefron, dressed in a yellow and black Haywood Academy uniform that complimented his honey hued skin, sat wide-eyed, scanning the inside of the copter. The gunner, positioned to squelch enemy ground fire, added to the surreal effect.

In moments, we were flying over the Atlantic Ocean. A crewmember mentioned that two rescue copters would be making multiple trips to airlift delinquent refugees out of Liberia that day. I was grateful that Ray had used his influence to enable my family to leave together since that was not always the case. A woman and her son were huddled across from me, he seemed like just a baby compared my children. The child gagged, then vomited, perhaps from motion sickness, but more than likely from fear; while my girls, EliTikvah and Zevah, sat poised. I could only wonder what they were thinking.

This morning they had risen, like any other day, with the sun shining through their window of our cozy home on Chubor Road. Would that be the last time they slept in their beds in the place they had called home for so long? Where would we go from here? What was in store for our futures? War had changed us. War had changed everything.

Occasionally one of my children would look around, anxiety in their dark brown eyes, and in the tense set of their young shoulders.

"Are you all right, baby?" I would ask. They would nod and all would be fine until their next anxious moment.

Sitting in the copter, I bore the full burden of my decision to remain in Liberia when all other American citizens, including my eldest son, daughter, and granddaughter, had been evacuated two months prior. How had it come to this? Amidst the relief I felt for my family, I also harbored deep feelings of remorse and shame for leaving friends behind, including "Ma Seeton" who had been like a mother to me; my granddaughter's father; my business partner; and Chris, who was so much like a son to me.

Several months earlier, Liberians listened by candlelight to a man describing the fate of their beloved country. Rumors abounded that a U.S. submarine was harbored off the coast of Liberia. The people hoped and prayed that America would intervene in the war and spare their country, colonized by free Blacks from America in 1821, from a Civil War that would catapult it backwards fifty years. However, trouble had erupted in the Middle East and America rushed to protect its oil interest in the Persian Gulf, turning its back on its friend, Liberia.

Now months later, I closed my eyes and thought of the ancient Ghanaian symbol, 'Gname,' that means, "No one knows the beginning or ending of anything except God." For the remainder of the helicopter ride, I repeated the mantra over and over, trying to find a sense of peace, which would take years to come.

Ahnydah, Elrahm
and Zevah

REMEMBERING A GOOD THING

Before we disembarked the C-130 helicopter, we were told to head directly to the lower deck of the submarine that would be taking us to Sierra Leone, the next leg of our escape to America. I listened to their directions but felt as if I was completely numb, my spirit hovering slightly above my body. The curly haired woman and her sick son climbed down first, followed by a group that had traveled with my family for most of our journey toward freedom and safety. Together, we had safely passed through half a dozen armed checkpoints. My children were next and then, finally, it was my turn.

I inhaled deeply, allowing the smell of the ocean to fill my lungs, basking in the sun's warmth on my back. I remember looking up and seeing the faces of African American sailors peering over the sides of the boat, cheering when they saw us climb the ladder toward them. Words of "Glad we got you and the kids, Sis. Welcome aboard!" and "Y'all are safe with us now" abounded.

I looked into the dark brown eyes of the men, any of whom could have been my brother or my husband, and my heart swelled, until the tears fell uncontrollably. Nothing that had happened as we attempted to flee Liberia had made me cry, until now.

Our very survival had depended on my strength. We had lived through months of uncertainty and rising fear, living close to starvation, sleeping to a lullaby of machine fire, and terrorized by the violence all around us. But it wasn't until this moment, when I felt the sincerity exuding from the sailors I reconnected with my own tribe—African Americans who shared my experience, and I gave myself permission to finally unleash the frayed emotions I had used to fuel our escape.

I have always been very emotional. My mother noticed this in my early childhood and being the patient and understanding woman that she was, she never devalued my tears. Instead, she taught me that it was perfectly all right to cry, but only after you have done what needs to be done, and in this case—I had. *Her grandchildren were safe!* We were alive, and had managed to escape a war characterized by the British Broadcasting System as, "The worst Civil War since the Biafran War in Nigeria" where hundreds of thousands had been killed and mutilated.

Finally, as the sailors carried my little ones on their shoulders to the cafeteria, I heard constant reassurance, and I finally felt safe and welcome.

How had my sojourn in Liberia come to this? My rescuers must have been curious as to why I had chosen Liberia over America in the first place. My family always questioned my decision to relocate to the Motherland, and I never seemed to have the right words to provide an answer. Explaining my reasons for moving in the first place, let alone describing the happiness I felt in Liberia was difficult. My mother and sister, and my Uncle Pete, a detective with the Chicago Police Department, and his wife, Connie, always looked at me as if I were just a bit off my rocker. My letters to them over the years shared trials and tribulations, but also constantly reassured them that I was happy, fulfilled, and doing work that I loved. I was directing what was arguably one of the best day care facilities in the country; I had worked on project to develop Liberian women; I had been a fundraiser; and I had finally branched out with Essie, my Liberian partner, to found our own school, "First Steps Child Development Center."

How did I expect my family to understand why I had remained with my children in a country where a coup, fueled by suppressed tribal hatred, had quickly escalated into full blown Civil War? The last time I spoke with my sister by phone, she literally begged me to come home. While she was praying that we would leave Liberia, I was fervently praying that the violence would stop so that we would be able to stay. During our last conversation, she detailed the nightly news' footage of the Civil War, which showed the heads of beheaded civilians sitting on wooden market tables like cabbages. My brother-in-law had pleaded with me to accept airline tickets for my children and me. Why hadn't I seen that I needed to get the hell out of Liberia and come home? Perhaps it was that I remembered the beauty of the country before all the turmoil, what I consider the sweet beginning.

Over the years, I had overcome so many barriers in between and was no longer struggling for acceptance. I wasn't the same 'qwee' (as in green) American woman who, when overwhelmed by the sheer magnitude of her mission, would steal into her office, close the door, put her head on her desk and cry like a lost child. I was Ahnydah Rahm in Liberia. People knew and respected me and my work. My family had a diverse and expanding social circle, and I could see the fulfillment of my passion in addition to a comfortable life for my family looming on the horizon. After all the challenges and struggles, I could finally have my mom and sister visit my home, Liberia, and show them all the reasons why I loved the country as much as I did.

My life in Liberia had not been easy, but the way the journey had unfolded was prophetic. No matter what hardships I encountered, I was never tempted to turn back. I was walking inside my purpose.

In the summer of 1975, I had a fate filled encounter with a pair of fortune-tellers. As I recall, it was a lazy, hot Saturday and my husband and I decided to spend the afternoon browsing the 53rd Street Art Fair on the grounds of Kenwood High School in Chicago's Hyde Park. An amazing array of oil paintings, photography, and handcrafted silver jewelry were sandwiched between dozens of tables displaying the jewelry, each piece more striking than the next against the purple and black velvet cloth. I quickly located my favorite jewelers: Seka, Babatunde, and Eomat. I flitted like a bumblebee, going from one display to the next, eyeing their creations in gold, silver, and semiprecious stones. It was artful window shopping, nearly as good as buying the beloved artifacts. We didn't have much disposable income while my husband was attending University of Illinois-Circle Campus, but nevertheless, we would typically purchase something small to assuage our desires and our expensive taste.

The sky provided the perfect brilliant blue backdrop for the afternoon. Walking through the crowd, relishing the company of creative people, I felt rejuvenated. The very air around them felt lighter, more energized. As we strolled through the fair, a couple dressed in African garb piqued my curiosity. Their table display proclaimed them as fortunetellers, and as an aspiring student of the things unexplained and supernatural, I was immediately drawn to them.

"How much?" I eagerly questioned.

"Seven dollars for a psychic reading, seven dollars for your astrology chart, Sista." I couldn't pass up on either, especially at that price! I sat down, and because I had memorized the time of birth on my birth certificate, he was able to quickly prepare a natal chart.

"You have a very masculine chart for a woman."

Although irritated by the remark, inwardly, I knew he spoke the truth. I had always wanted to be the kind of woman men take care of, yet I had a knack for picking the ones that realized I did such a good job of it all by myself.

After he completed my astrological chart, I moved on to his wife feeling content that my reading had not foretold doom. While her mate had been efficient and matter-of-fact, the woman's aura was truly mystical, and her gaze was so intense that I felt embarrassed at the intimacy of our eye contact. She gently held my hand, closed her eyes, and just as her silence became uncomfortable, she spoke.

"Both your mother and your father have drinking problems... alcoholics, but your mother is not drinking anymore."

She had my attention. It was true that my father, who lived in California, drank a fifth of whisky a day, and that my mother, who had been a drunk through my pre-teen years, woke up one morning, and simply stopped drinking. The brown-skinned woman also saw that I had both a brother and a sister, but that my brother had moved onto the next world.

"He died violently."

How could she know? I wondered. *Did she also know that he died on his wedding day?*

I could only nod my head, chills running up and down my body at her accurate insight.

She had quickly built my trust and esteem by knowing so many details of my past. Having done that, she continued in an upbeat tone. "You will travel abroad and you will stay for a long, long time. I think you will go to Africa."

Then her words took on a detached, rambling quality and her psychic information flowed.

"My sista, we all have a karmic debt, something that our souls came here to accomplish. Your karma is not bad and you can clear it in this life." I asked what it was and she leaned over as if conspiring with me. "In a previous life, you were a wealthy, very selfish, and arrogant person. Your karma in this lifetime, is to learn to serve and to serve willingly."

She then became very still and quiet, as if she was seeing a lot but weighing how much to share with me.

"I see a son coming next for you," she grinned. Then she signaled that my reading was over.

My husband, who had been looking at framed black and white photographs, came over as we finished, and I relayed my reading with him. I know that some "fortune tellers" are frauds, but the fact that she *knew* about my parents' alcoholism and my brother's murder made her words resonate with me, leaving me breathless at the future she had foretold for me.

Several years afterward, I became pregnant and miscarried. Broken hearted from my loss, I was determined to fill the emptiness with laughter, and after two months, I became pregnant again and gave birth to a robust son that tipped the scales at well over eight pounds. His father chose the name Gyasi, which means *wonderful* in the Akan dialect and began with the first letter of my murdered brother's first name. Gyasi was the first of the many joys to come. Following behind him were two daughters, and another son. Eventually, our children would top out at five.

I kept my natal chart for years. It became yellow and dog-eared from my occasional references, and the words the psychic spoke to me with such quiet authenticity have never left me. I have lived to see everything she foresaw on that Saturday afternoon come true.

I thought of this and other things as I sat aboard the submarine that carried us from Liberia, my home for eleven years, to Freetown, Sierra Leone.

Ahnydah and the children at Peace Villa

LOVE IT OR LEAVE IT

In the late 1970's, my husband and I were embittered over the inequalities of the life of Black people in America. Like many young activists, we sought an organizational affiliation to address the discrimination and to feel as if we were doing our part to fight for equality and justice.

After investigating the Black Panthers and the Nation of Islam, we decided against both. In the National Islam the person who was "recruiting" us kept putting emphasis on how subservient the women needed to be when they joined. The Black Panthers had so much violence surrounding them, that it put me off some. There was always an air of being ready to launch an armed defense, but I felt that we, as a people, at that time, couldn't win a war. Equally, on either front, I didn't want to dress in clothes that make me a target of a nation that was unfriendly to counter-culture activists. I told my husband if he wanted me to dress in traditional clothing, he would have to take me to Africa where the motherland was open and receptive to us.

Finally, my husband joined, and I tagged along, the Institute of Positive Education (IPE), a Southside Chicago organization founded by noted author, Haki R. Mahdbuti, then known as Don L. Lee. The well-respected, well-organized IPE subscribed to the doctrine of African Nationalism and the popular Nationalist tagline at the time, "Africa for Africans at Home and Abroad." After several years with the Institute, my husband legally changed his name from Walter Allen to Muasa Mwewe. I selected the African name Sijui, which loosely translated means, "I don't know," for its lovely sound and because it was an accurate depiction of where I was in my life at that time—a seeker, not knowing what I was seeking, but open to the journey.

During our affiliation with the Institute, Muasa's friend and mentor, Kwesi introduced him to a group of Hebrew Israelites that flourished in Atlanta, Washington, D. C, and a number of other cities including Chicago. Hebrew Israelites claim ancestry with the lost tribes of the Bible who inhabited Israel long before the migration of European Jews—with the looks and features which most identify as Jews today. The organization and its leadership were intriguing to us, offering what none of the other Nationalist groups did. The Original Hebrew Israelite Nation of Jerusalem had settlers in three cities in Israel and were recruiting for their missions in Liberia and Ghana. While many African American activists claimed philosophical alignment with Africa, doing so from a distance in order to enjoy the securities and pleasures of America, the Original Hebrew Israelites were actually 'walking the walk.'

The Hebrew Israelites were especially appealing to Kwesi for one particular reason. He had a mistress, and rather than dissolving his marriage and breaking up his family, he wanted to bring her into his family. The climate between Black men and women in the Nationalist community during the '70's was tumultuous, and discussion of the preservation of the Black family was a topic of serious concern, often resulting in heated debates. Black women complained bitterly that there were no suitable mates to marry and build families with—thousands of men were lost during the Vietnam War, incarceration rates for Black males were increasing, and some black men had begun crossing the color line and choosing Caucasian women as mates. Progressive groups discussed ways to keep the Black family viable and a movement developed that discouraged the one man, one wife norm, and instead, encouraged an alternative lifestyle of polygamy or "man-sharing."

Like many other Nationalist groups at the time, the Hebrew Israelites also weighed in on the issue and shared their system of 'divine marriage,' which is a union consisting of a man and one or more wives operating under specific guidelines created to provide support and fairness for the women involved and accountability for their husband.

Muasa and I discussed the pros and cons of joining the Hebrew Israelites. With growing pressure from Kwesi, who had already been recruited along with his family, my husband seemed more and more set on joining the group as well. I argued that I wanted to finish college and urged that we wait two years, but none of that seemed to matter. Suddenly, everything seemed to boil down to who wore the pants in the relationship and when Muasa issued me an ultimatum, I acquiesced. Ultimately that meant I didn't finish college and it was more due to my fears and insecurities that I gave in. At the time I was so in love with my husband, and he was so enthralled with the group, that I was afraid I might lose him. I feared that he would join and leave for Africa without me and find another woman to replace me. As I lay in my bed in America and my husband left for a mission in Liberia, I conjured up images of him with someone else that sent me into a spiral of, "Well, I've always wanted to go Africa anyway." Strangely enough, I hadn't joined the Nation of Islam because of their views on how women should act, but I didn't draw the line with my husband when he issued that ultimatum. Fear can make a person do damaging things.

Once our family joined the group, I knew I would have no say in whether my husband selected another wife. I was acutely aware that in many cultures in Africa, Asia, and even in the United States, having multiple wives was an acceptable and rational practice and was not always driven by a man's desire to have multiple sexual partners. Nonetheless, my constant anxiety surrounding divine marriage, along with other stressors in my marriage, was the beginning of the crumbling of my relationship with my husband of ten years.

The Hebrews adhered to the very stringent laws laid out in the Old Testament and there were other rules that as in other religions were, in my opinion, more about control of the followers than the word of God. I personally struggled with the Law of Uncleanness, based on Leviticus 15:19-28, which, loosely interpreted, indicated that when a woman was on her menstrual cycle she was unclean for seven days. The effect of this for our community was that Hebrew sisters couldn't go into the kitchen for any reason, or sleep in the same bed with our husbands. We were obliged to carry a small handkerchief sized cloth that we placed upon chairs before we sat down. For a woman raised to keep the arrival and duration of my menstrual cycle private, I felt humiliated. A very paternalistic organization, not unlike the Amish or some groups of Muslims, or even fundamentalist Christians, women were very submissive to their husbands. Outspoken women like me were criticized for an assertiveness that came natural. Husbands that did not get their wives to obey were mocked as "squirrels."

Soon, I began to resent the fact that our deep desire to live in Africa seemed possible only though the safety and group cohesion we gained as members of the Hebrew Israelite Community. Because the more I adapted to the life of a Hebrew wife, the further I moved away from my true self.

My earliest memory of church was attending St. Ambrose Catholic Church, and later St. James Methodist Church, with a brief exposure to the Mennonite faith. You would think that the exposure to different forms of worship would affect me somehow, yet none of them made a significant impact on me. In fact, by adolescence, I flatly refused to attend any church. Rejecting the conformity of religion seemed to be part of my DNA and becoming a Hebrew did not change that.

As we began to prepare for our departure, we pondered the assets that we would bring with us to Africa. We did not just want to be in Africa, we wanted to contribute. The Hebrew Israelite Community in Liberia already had a construction company, a go-cart track at Cooper's Beach and a diamond mining operation in progress. Muasa and Kwesi were expert swimmers and had been trained as deep-sea divers in preparation to lead the Hebrews' diamond-mining project. Although it was all very exhilarating, I was still afraid to move forward. Nevertheless, when I finally made the commitment, I vowed to give one hundred percent. In retrospect, I can say that I always kept my end of the bargain, at least with my mind and body, if not with my heart.

Shortly after joining the growing ranks of the Hebrew Israelite Community, we embarked on a three-country tour through Israel, Ghana, and Liberia. The tour was to show newly recruited Hebrews that might have a desire to live outside the country that there were actual settlements prepared to receive them. This was very important to persons interested in leaving America as the terror that had followed in the aftermath of the " Jim Jones Massacre" in South America in November 1978, where thousands of cult members had committed or been forced into mass suicide had created an air of skepticism about the motives of groups suggesting that followers leave America.

During the 1970's, the Israeli government opposed the immigration of the Hebrew Israelite Community and took elaborate measures to deny them residency status. They actively "profiled" all Blacks seeking an entrance visa, and those matching the criteria of potential members of the Black Hebrew Community were denied entry. The criteria, in my estimation, entailed—people who were coming in groups like a family; had a great deal of luggage, small children in tow. They were looking for people who were "counter-culture," a man wearing African garments, a woman wrapped in traditional garb, hair in a natural state.

Upon landing at Tel Aviv airport, our exploratory group of thirteen men, women, and children immediately fell suspect to the Israelis. After interrogating several male members of our tour group, they stamped our visa 'entry denied' and rerouted us to Italy. To be honest, I had not wanted to visit Israel in the first place, and so, while I was outwardly indignant at being turned away from the Holy Land, internally, I was thrilled with the revised itinerary.

My dreams lay in Africa and if skipping Israel hastened my visit to Ghana and Liberia…hallelujah!

Binah at Cooper's Beach

COMING HOME TO MAMA

January 15, 1979

Several months after the tour, and before embarking on our trip to Africa, we abandoned our African names for Hebrew names. When reading the Bible, I noticed that some of the disciples' names changed as they grew in spiritual consciousness. The same applied to myself, and my family, on our journey forward. Walter, who had initially become Muasa, now became Elrahm. My name had gone from Susan to Sijui, and finally transformed to Ahnydah, which meant, 'I know God.' My children also received Hebrew names. My son Gyasi became Penemiel and my daughter, Tonya, became Binah. In the excitement of moving to Liberia and being introduced to new people who would only know them by their new names, my children embraced their new names as one who receives an affectionate nickname. They fit in, the other children had Hebrew names and so did they. The name-changing ritual seemed an important step to leaving behind our American personalities and affirming our new lives and spiritual growth that we wanted to embrace in Liberia.

In America, it was the proverbial "cold day in hell," when our plane departed Chicago and crossed the Atlantic Ocean toward Africa. Thirteen hours later, I stared out the window, awed at the lush sea of green and brown arching up to greet us. As we descended rapidly into Liberia's Roberts Field Airport, I knew that our lives had changed forever. We were leaving behind our apartments, jobs, friends, families, and predictable futures for an opportunity to do what most African Americans never even dreamed. This wasn't a two-week vacation or study abroad trip with our church or civic organization—we were coming home to our Motherland to live, work, and create a new life and future.

When we landed in Africa, we were officially Hebrew Israelites, and comfortable with our new names. My husband and children shared our first anxious moments as transplants in Africa with our friend, Ade and his children. Getting off the plane, it was obvious the trip had taken its toll on all of us, but especially me who had to appease a breastfeeding baby seated on my lap for thirteen hours.

Penemiel was nine months old and colicky when we made our journey to Africa. Suckling was the only way to calm him and my breasts were raw from being gnawed for most of the flight. When he was not breastfeeding, he was either screaming or passing gas. Often, his explosive bowel movements overran his diapers and ended up ruining my clothes, as was the unfortunate case during our flight. What a way to start a journey!

Binah resembled a bedraggled brown bunny rabbit with her thick ponytails on either side of her head—one standing straight up and the other straight down, molded in place during the flight from New York. And so we arrived in Liberia, West Africa, the land of our dreams—cranky, drained, disheveled, and exhausted.

Stepping off the plane, I inhaled and felt suffocated by the unnaturally high humidity and the scalding heat. It was a though someone had their mouth over mine, sucking out the air. I didn't want to mention it to anyone. Here it is, I finally arrive at the place I've always wanted to be—and a little heat and humidity was making me uncomfortable? Sweat pearls oozed from my skin as my body struggled to acclimate to the heat and I fought the urge for my last meal to make an untimely comeback. Holding my son with one arm, I remember freeing my colorful, and now organically yellow stained, cotton skirt from the crease of my sweaty buttocks. Wet feet slid around in my sandals and the center strap cut between my toes as we walked down the ramp toward the terminal. The sand, stirred by my footsteps, turned into mud in my shoes as I plowed my way through the heavy airport doors. Once inside the terminal, I noticed three specific things: the noise, the hustle, and the smell. Instantly, I became enthralled with the smells of Liberia and its people as I became acutely aware of human musk that was both appalling and enticing.

As we took in our new surroundings during the first moments of our arrival, a state of heightened sensory awareness enveloped us all. Against the backdrop of majestic palm trees and under the African sun, the people in the airport wore clothing more vibrant than anything I had ever seen. Everywhere I looked, everything seemed magnified to the tenth power. When we made it to the 'Arrivals' terminal, I was shocked at how different it looked compared to the airports in the United States. Instead of moving conveyor belts to hold our luggage, there were only scarred aluminum and wooden tables surrounded by people begging to carry our bags to the taxi in hopes of a tip. At the time I didn't reference the differences as poverty, I was caught up in the adventure.

Standing in the airport, fighting to get our luggage through Customs, everything was unfamiliar except for the faces of the people. My husband was the first to remark that he felt like he was looking at his relatives from Jackson, Mississippi. Soon, we were all finding similarities between us, and the Liberians who went about their business, without knowing that they were making cameo appearances in one of the most important days of our lives.

I was acutely aware that most of the people that I saw at the airport were darker than me, a rare occurrence in America but something common in Africa. I had always felt self-conscious of my light skin. The more aware I became of the history of slavery, the more I had longed for darker skin, skin the color of my mother's. Light skin was a reminder of children conceived through the rape of women by their slave masters.

Sitting in the airport, I smiled as I thought of the pie-faced, toothy grin of my Aunt Bertha, and the strong angular face of my Aunt Betty Jean—a small-breasted woman with a tiny waist, concave belly, and a really large butt! Watching the people pass, I knew I was where I belonged when I saw Aunt Betty Jean's big-butt twin stroll by, head erect and majestic as she balanced a huge basket of dried fish on her head. Despite the passing melancholy over having just left the life we had known, our possessions, and our extended families, the faces around us captivated me, and I felt fulfilled and finally connected to and validated by something beyond the shame of slavery. Relocating to Liberia was a bit like reconnecting a severed appendage. You desperately want to be whole again, but there is the ever-present fear of rejection.

We fell in love with Africa during our first three weeks in Ghana and Liberia. It was amazing and encouraging to see that Blacks from America could live and thrive outside of America where they had historically been abused and treated unfairly. The cheerfulness and warmth of the Ghanaian people overwhelmed us, but Liberia was the country to steal my heart.

Three lovely homes housed the Hebrew Israelite group of nearly sixty people, members of what was known as "the Pineapple Mission." It was named after one of Liberia's sweetest products; its lush, dark golden, syrupy sweet pineapples. Life in Liberia on the Pineapple was as sweet. We lived well, dressed well, and successfully operated a construction company, Nation Builders, that employed scores of indigenous Liberian workers. All fears I had of my family being unhappy or distressed in their new environment quickly faded and were replaced with elation and joy.

After returning to America from our African tour, it took a scant two months to put our affairs in order. We withdrew our meager retirements, sold our possessions, and prepared for permanent relocation to Africa. I remember the popular phrase that White Supremacists used to taunt civil rights advocates during the turbulent 60's and 70's—"America, love it, or leave it!"

We left it!

Elrahm &
Ahnydah

AWAKENED FROM MY SLEEP

I vividly recall the morning after the April 12, 1980 coup. Forty-six days earlier, aided by Sheryrah, our midwife; Rackemya, her sister-wife; and my husband, Elrahm, I delivered a beautiful daughter in the 98-degree heat of our bedroom. Sheryrah's and Rackemya's husband was in the States, leaving Elrahm as the male head of our household. Our families shared a large four-bedroom home in a rural enclave called Lakpazee Road that sat about a mile and a half off "Old Road, inside," as the taxi drivers called it. Inside, short for further away from the main road.

We named our daughter Zevah, which in Hebrew means, 'brightness and splendor of God.' She was born healthy and round, weighing close to nine pounds. As soon as I recovered from the labor, I regained my vanity and quickly replaced flowing maternity gowns for my favorite tie-dyed wraparound skirts and matching tapered tee-shirt tops. I was fortunate that breastfeeding helped my stomach quickly recollect its former flatness so that I felt not only comfortable in my old clothes, but beautiful and confident as well.

The Hebrew laws demand a resting period after the birth of a child, allowing the mother to accept and bond with her newborn. For a boy, a mother is required to rest for forty days, and for a girl, eighty days of rest is required. The thinking is that a woman's body is more complex and it takes more out of the mother to create a girl child, than a boy. When the coup took place, I was forty-six days into my into my eighty day rest, and six days earlier, I had quietly celebrated my twenty-seventh birthday.

It was close to 9:30 in the morning and I had finally settled into a cat nap with Zevah after being up and down all night nursing her. Suddenly, my husband burst through the front door breathless, wild-eyed, and disheveled. His swollen face told the story. He had been beaten, thrown to the ground, and pinned down at bayonet point by a group of Liberian soldiers he had encountered on the Old Road. Although he had a slim frame, his height, reaching 6'4", made for a menacing figure. His African print dashiki, vibrant against skin the color of unsweetened chocolate, combined with his full beard, resembled a member of the Mandingo ethnic group. He had been a city kid all his life, born and raised in Chicago, first living with his large family in the Henry Horner housing projects, and then street-polished on South 43rd Street. Raised around the almost casual violence of the city, he was not a man easily frightened, but I remember the fear distinctly etched on his face when he ran into the house that morning.

Other members of the household, having been roused from their sleep by the commotion, entered the main room to see what had happened. Elrahm continued to ramble on about a coup taking place and people being flogged. I scanned the living room, and despite the fear on all of our faces, my husband's presence comforted me. If he had not been there, we would have only been a room full of women and children, frightened and alarmed. Rackemya was eight months pregnant and Sheryrah was holding seven-month-old Yosheyah. Also present was NeEmah with her six-month-old baby boy, Amadiah. NeEmah had come in February to await the arrival of her husband. Lastly, there was me, Zevah, and Penemiel. My eldest daughter Binah, along with Rackemya's daughters, lived in the dorm for older girls, which was located about a mile away on Airfield Road.

My husband's expression was one I had never seen before. As he shared the details of his assault by the soldiers, I felt the gravity of the incident. A teacher by profession and a lover of discourse, Rackemya probed Elrahm for answers. Although I was sitting right next to her, it was as though I heard talking from a distance, as if through a very long tunnel. At that moment, all I wanted was to scream so that I could release the mounting tension that was making me queasy.

Somehow, I cut to the chase and said what we were all thinking rather than trying to beat around the bush. I managed to formulate a cognitive sentence, looking at my husband and saying, "Now that the Tolbert government has been overthrown, what is this going to mean for us. We went to sleep feeling safe and now we aren't." What I hadn't said, though, was, *does this mean we might have to go back to America?*

My husband read my thoughts, the flash of impatience in his dark brown eyes effectively told me to shut up.

"I just need some information. I don't see anybody going to the market at the end of the road," Sheryrah said, the silver bracelets clinking annoyingly on her sienna-colored arms.

"No one is going into the market, people are afraid. There isn't anything more to say."

NeEmah, a willowy, woman with coffee skin and wavy brown hair, had slipped into their bedroom, returning with a cassette radio combo which she placed on the small coffee table between the two sofas. We huddled around the radio, now the centerpiece of our sparsely decorated living room. All we could hear was static, while frantically searching for a clear signal. There was no programming.

Rackemya opened the market bag that contained the jumble of fresh vegetables and spilled the raw rice that Elrahm still had the presence of mind to pick up after the soldiers released him. After examining them, she sat them in the kitchen for later, and then rejoined the group around the radio.

"Well, at least we can eat today," she said in a light voice that belied the seriousness of the matter at hand.

I cared nothing about food. I was haunted by mother's voice on our

34

final call from O'Hare Airport moments before we departed for Liberia. My gut had ached at the contradiction between her words blessing me to do what I needed to do, and the trembling of her voice begging me to stay. I bore the weight of my promise to take care of her treasured grandchildren and myself no matter what. Unfortunately, "no matter what" had come sooner rather than later. In just a single night, the stability we had taken for granted, the life that was so promising to us had transformed into an uncertainty that made my heart slam against my chest, and sucked the very air from around us into a vortex of apprehension—no warning, no sudden signs.

As in typical rainy season, it had poured down earlier in the day, but it soon became sunny and bright—a stark comparison to how we were feeling in the house. Pensively, we watched as soldiers patrolled the road, followed by the infrequent occurrence of a jeep carrying jeering soldiers, ejaculating their rifles into the air and honking their horns. We had never put curtains up in the living room windows, which ran straight across the front of the house; because we had never felt, there was anything to hide. We never realized there might come a time when we would want to conceal ourselves from someone in our adopted homeland.

Inside, we were fixated on the radio, despite the fact that there was heavy static on the one channel with any reception. We tried to tune into the British Broadcast Corporation (BBC), but for some reason, only landed sound from ELBC, the Liberian station, which continued to play the Liberian National Anthem repeatedly. We hoped that the playing of the anthem signified that there would be some announcement, and so, we kept the radio on as its crackling sounds punctuated our conversation. Silently, I recited the Lord's Prayer in Hebrew, which I thought might make the prayer more powerful, *"avinu shebashamayim yitkadesh shimcha,"* and slowly, my stomach stopped churning.

Finally, the anthem faded and we heard an indistinct voice claiming to be Master Sergeant Doe. We strained to hear over the static, but it was twice as difficult with Doe's accent, which was one of the thickest I had heard.

Having worked upcountry diving for diamonds in the interior, Elrahm could understand the patois, and so, we looked to him for translation. He told us that essentially, Liberia was now in the hands of twelve men who called themselves the Peoples' Redemption Council, headed by Master Sergeant Samuel Kanyon Doe. Stupefied, we sat there wondering how people who could barely speak English would be able to run the affairs of the country. Repeatedly, we heard that the PRC was in charge of the country and that President William R. Tolbert, head of the True Whig Party, was dead. After listening to the same announcement again and again, we became numb to it and it essentially became nothing more than background noise.

Refocusing on the group, Rackemya turned and asked no one in particular, "How could this have happened?"

"I bet the CIA is behind this. I don't care what they say, those men aren't smart enough to penetrate Tolbert's elite Executive Mansion guard," Elrahm replied while peeling a ripe banana and polishing it off in two bites. Then he opened another and slid half to the waiting hands of Penemiel. "Sisters, let's be clear—nobody goes outside, not even on the front porch, until we know what our position is. We had relationships with people in the Tolbert government. We have to be careful."

"Do you think that the soldiers will harm American citizens?" Sheryrah asked, her normal Cheshire grin faded to an indignant pout.

"Do you really think those people on the radio even know how to determine who is or is not an American?"

Elrahm was right, and the fact that he was, made us even more vulnerable.

"Let's just grab our passports and sit tight. That's something concrete that we can all do," he said exiting the living room to change his muddy pants, "If anyone comes to the front door, call me. Don't go to the door by yourselves."

"America has to have a hand in this," Rackemya said, tying her head wrap for the second or third time in the past twenty minutes. I glanced at her soon to explode belly and knew she had to keep calm.

"Right now, we all need to focus on our safety," I said evenly.

The PRC announced a dusk to dawn curfew, 6 p.m. until 6 a.m. for everyone in Monrovia, Liberia. Meanwhile the PRC was looking for "par-ti-cular people." The list of specific people they said were wanted for questioning, sounded more like a death list than a simple request to come forward for "questioning" by the PRC's military tribunal. Accusations of the commission of, "crimes against the people of Liberia" abounded, and I quickly came into a deeper understanding of the importance of the presumption of innocence—something that Americans tend to expect.

From where we sat, we felt that President Tolbert's son, A.B. Tolbert, with whom the leadership of the Hebrew Israelite had a very cordial relationship, and C. Cecil Dennis, Minister of Foreign Affairs for the Republic of Liberia, along with other cabinet officials, would surely seek and receive asylum at foreign embassies. However, over the next ten days we learned that the cabinet members were all rounded up and had been taken to the Central Prison, which stood on Lynch Street on the grounds that housed the barracks for the Liberian army.

The international community as well as by the Organization of African Unity pled for clemency, but on April 22, 1980, thirteen high ranking cabinet members, including C. Cecil Dennis, Minister of Foreign Affairs and the Minister of Justice, were tied to telephone poles on Monrovia's beach and shot by a drunken firing squad in a televised execution. The BBC account of the execution depicted them as particularly cruel. Accounts said that there were only nine stakes dug into the sand, the last four cabinet ministers to be executed were forced to witness the gruesome murder of the first nine before meeting their own fate. A. B. Tolbert, took refuge at the French Embassy, but was reportedly dragged from the Embassy by soldiers and taken to prison. The facts are obscure but despite international pleas, A.B. Tolbert, son of President William R. Tolbert and the son-in-law of President Felix Houphouet-Boigny, of the Ivory Coast, was secretly removed from prison and killed.

Instantly, a few things became abundantly clear to us. First, we understood that in the aftermath of the April 12 coup, Liberian soldiers, who largely reflected the native or indigenous population of the country, were targeting the descendants of freed American slaves who had formed an upper class of people known as Americo-Liberians, for retribution. The term Americo referenced their sojourn as slaves in America, and their point of origin. They were Liberian because they had, in effect, colonized Liberia in 1821 and 1822 when they first began arriving, many through the efforts of the American Colonization Society, which saw the integration of freed slaves into American life as problematic. Instead the colonization society developed, supported and implemented a plan to return the freed slaves to Africa, specifically to Liberia and Sierra Leone. These freed slaves, ripped from many countries in Africa, displaced from their own ethnic roots, became Americanized during their years in captivity. These now freed "Americanized" slaves met an indigenous population in Liberia still rooted in their own cultural traditions.

We were supremely ignorant of the complex political reality of the country, and the festering hatred between the various ethnic groups of indigenous Liberians and returning settlers, and their relationships with an additional group with tremendous influence in Liberia. They were the so-called "Congo people" or migrants from Central Africa during the transatlantic slave trade. In fact, the term Congo is often interchanged and used to describe the entire group of Liberians who colonized Liberia in the 1800's, whether they came to Liberia by way of America or not.

The April 12 coup was just one in a long history of cultural wars and skirmishes that were part of the background of the Liberian people. Somehow, someone forgot to mention this little well-known fact to us before we arrived in Liberia in 1979.

Happy to be leaving behind the burden of American racism, we were oblivious to the brewing undercurrent of hatred felt by the tribal Liberians, who felt left out of the mainstream of their own country. Liberia is a country of vast natural and mineral resources, and because of long-standing political stability, she was host to thousands of foreign investors which extracted huge profits from the country while its country folk remained in the throes of poverty and illiteracy, deepening the seeds of hatred.

Although we dressed mainly in African cultural garments, we weren't fluent in the local English dialect. We kept to ourselves and the majority of our relationships outside of our Hebrew Israelite Community were with the Americo-Liberians that controlled the government and regulated outside investments. We were, in a word, vulnerable.

An indescribable fear gripped me while I peered through the windows with a view of the dirt road.

"Come quick! Look!" Sheryrah shouted.

We all rushed to the living room windows just in time to see soldiers dragging a woman and her husband, crying, screaming, and fighting to be let go, out of their house. We sat in helpless silence as soldiers, who only weeks ago had been loyal to the Tolbert government, dragged the couple into their Range Rover, leaving their house open for all the locals to loot their home.

I prayed while witnessing all of their possessions being taken away and their home trashed. The gossip on the road was that anyone who wanted revenge against their enemy simply said their name to someone in the new PRC government with the implication that they, or someone in their household, was a threat to the PRC's power.

Our saving grace was that everyone on Lakpazee Road knew we were Hebrews and American citizens. I can only assume that is the sole reason the drunken soldiers did not come and ransack our home—or worse.

The blessing of living communally is that you share the joys, tribulations, and responsibilities. Each night, the brothers rotated guard duty, in an attempt to protect our house from the dangers of outside. Grocery shopping was now handled by our men so that the Sisters would not have to face threats from the Liberian soldiers. For the most part, the days passed uneventfully, which we weren't complaining about. Little by little, we became more comfortable with the changes in the country, and we realized that we were finally seeing things the way they really were and always had been.

Between the coup and the restriction of my Biblically mandated eighty days of postpartum rest, everything seemed to move in slow motion. I was anxious to get on with life, but at the same time, alert to little nuances. I came to understand that sitting on the sidelines forces the average person to notice details that might otherwise be missed. I began to suspect that my husband was having a "special relationship" with NeEmah.

Sitting there and watching something clearly develop between Elrahm and another woman, I remembered how the Hebrews had presented me with an idolized version of divine marriage, which I had bought, and became bitter over what I felt was a double betrayal. I brooded and silently pined for May 14 when my eighty days of rest would officially end.

Elrahm was a quiet, studious man. His height, the smooth chocolate of his skin and the thick brows that emphasized a moon like quality of his face gave him a commanding presence. However, he was extremely self-conscious and emotionally fragile. That was our secret. The Hebrew brothers were expected to be strong and dominant in their relationships and that had not been our reality. We had been best friends and before becoming Hebrews we had discussed all doubts. I thought we would continue to do so. He, for instance, knew that I was struggling with the concept of being inactive in the community for eighty days. I had made up my mind to follow the rules, so that I was not viewed as a troublemaker and the other Hebrew brothers respected him, but I wanted to be able to openly discuss things with him. We had always talked about everything. Now whenever I wanted to discuss how I felt about this new life we had taken on, he shut me down.

"Ahnydah, you just need to sit on down and listen!" he roared. "The Brothers run this, *not* the women."

It was a verbal slap that I received over and over again.

With two weeks remaining, my housemates took it upon themselves to lift some of the restrictions and integrated me back into the household routine. Rackemya's belly was huge, she was not going to last until my eighty days were up. They needed the extra help, and she needed to rest. I managed my responsibilities, doing everything from hand washing cloth diapers to mopping the floors, everything except cooking on the coal pot. Although I was happy to be involved in the house routine again, I was still disappointed to see NeEmah go with Elrahm to help shop for food for the main house as well as the girls' dormitory. After all, NeEmah was Amadiel's wife.

One evening, shortly after my return to light duty, Rackemya, Sheryrah, and me celebrated by taking a walk down the dusty road for an orange Fanta and a paper cone of roasted ground peas. It was my first time off our front porch in several months. Finally, in the quiet of the evening, and with the muggy night air on our faces, Rackemya broke the spell.

"Ahnydah, you feeling anything strange in the house?"

This was my opening. For so long, I had been bottling up my thoughts and feelings, and I could finally open up and release everything. "You mean the fact that NeEmah and Elrahm seem to have some kind of *fascination* with each other?" I asked, without bothering to mask the venom in my voice.

Sheryrah released a long sigh of relief. "God, we noticed it too but we didn't want to bring it up."

"I've been doing nothing else *but* watching and fuming."

"I've been fuming for you! I'm so sick of Rahm. I thought he was better than that," Rackemya replied.

"Well, when I was at the other house last week, I heard that her husband is coming soon. Once he's here, he'll take NeEmah to Israel." Sheryrah shook her head. "Poor guy doesn't even know what's been happening. They have only been married for a year—something is definitely lacking in that marriage."

"Well, Elrahm and I have been together for over ten years and something is wrong with *our* marriage. There is nothing divine about what's going on."

"My God! I'm so sick of her finding excuses to get in that truck with him," Rackemya ranted. "It doesn't take Elrahm all day to buy the little bit of groceries we need in the houses. The only thing in the market is greens, bitter ball, rice, and palm oil. What's so hard about that?"

"Yeah, and the guilty *divine* snacks she keeps making me are working my nerves too."

"Girl, I'm surprised your breast milk hasn't turned to butter," Sheryrah replied quickly, making us all smile.

We drank our icy orange Fantas under the starry night sky and laughed the way you laugh when you hear the music playing and know that the dance isn't over.

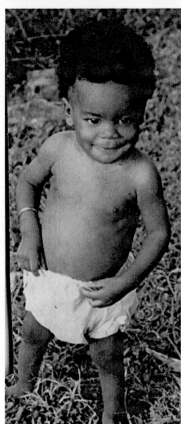

*Penemiel
after a bout
with
dysentary*

BEGINNER'S GRACE

In Liberia and Israel, Hebrew sisters deliver their own babies. When the Pineapple Mission was founded, there were trained nurses present, but over time, they retired and were replaced with midwives. The midwives were responsible for performing pelvic exams, leading childbirth education classes, training birthing coaches, as well as assisting in actual deliveries. Our vegan diet, youth, and the fact that our lifestyles provided us with plenty of exercise, made our Lamaze style deliveries as smooth as any expectant mother could hope for. However, easy deliveries weren't a guarantee. Rackemya's delivery reminded us of that by providing us with a few scary moments.

When Rackemya's water broke, the water was brown, a red flag that the infant had begun to pass mercromium, its first bowel movement, in utero. Sheryrah, and Kwesi, who had just returned to Liberia from the United States, made the decision, especially given the dawn to dusk curfew, to transport Rackemya to a hospital. Time was of the essence. Saint Joseph, the Catholic Hospital, the nearest and best hospital in Monrovia, was scarcely fifteen minutes away.

Rackemya lay down in the back seat of our white van while Sheryrah timed her contractions. Kwesi drove, unwilling to trust the trip to either of the two Liberian brothers who also rode in the van for backup. Normally a good driver, Kwesi drove like a lunatic, except at the three military checkpoints that lay between Lakpazee Road and the hospital. At each checkpoint, the soldiers demanded a bribe "cold water" to proceed. Having finally arrived at the hospital, Rackemya was transferred to a cold empty room, and lay on a surgical gurney. When Sheryrah communicated to the nurse about the brown tinged fluid, she ran into the room and began pounding her flat hands against Rackemya's stomach, pressing down forcefully until the baby, a beautiful little girl, was born. Kwesi, stunned, witnessed the delivery from the doorway while arguing at the staff because there was no doctor available. The hospital wanted to keep Rackemya and the baby over night, but Kwesi angrily refused.

"Hell, if I wanted to beat my daughter into this lifetime and damn near kill my wife, I could have avoided three checkpoints and done this at home!" He shouted after sucking his teeth in disgust.

A few years later, I heard of a Liberian friend's sister dying in the interior of the country during childbirth from a ruptured uterus. She was having a long delivery and a wooden mortar was placed on her belly to press the baby out.

I say we were lucky that night. Unfortunately, it would set the tone for a later time when I probably should have made a trip to the hospital and didn't.

During the 1980 coup, it was still an advantage to be an American living abroad. We reasoned that the new PRC government wanted to continue receiving America's generous foreign aid package while avoiding pissing off the American Embassy by manhandling its citizens. However, because we had no contact with our Embassy, there was no gauging whether we would be ousted from the country, harassed, or even worse.

In the days following the coup, we prayed a great deal, staying up many nights and discussing the future of Liberia. We questioned our decision to come to Liberia and debated if we should return to America.

Nevertheless, after much discussion, we would wait and see how things would work themselves out. We reasoned that we had left America to learn about Africa, and this was part of the learning experience. So we sat, night after night, listening to the Liberian radio and the BBC as the country's history unfolded.

In those days, American women were not primary targets for the retribution of soldiers, and by the end of May, we gradually resumed our normal activities while keeping a very low profile. Still, I was paranoid over my light skin and did not wish to be mistaken for being White from a distance. In an attempt to look more Black, I loosened my cornrow braids and picked my hair out into a huge afro. Unlike so many Black women who become frustrated with their hair, I was thrilled and felt blessed for my thick nappy hair. Looking back, I was exceptionally clueless and naive. I had left America in hopes of leaving behind major conflicts between black and white, yet I had entered a whole new world where there was another conflict, and I hadn't the faintest idea of what it meant for tribes of the same race to clash.

Between April and June of 1980 as conditions in the country slowly moved toward a semblance of normalcy, the days were long, hot, and boring. We had box fans, but the electricity, like everything else after the coup, was sporadic. The curfew brought serious shortages in food distribution, and some days we worried weather we would find food at the local market. We divided our time between praying, listening to the neighbors' gossip about who had been dragged from their homes for questioning or detention, and sitting around the radio listening to the news. Although we struggled to understand Liberian English, we found it becoming easier to listen to the broadcasts coming through the BBC and Voice of America.

The life we had come to lead was a stark contrast to the life and freedom our community had initially enjoyed in Liberia in 1978 and 1979. Then, people came and went freely throughout the country. No curfews and no checkpoints. The Hebrews lived and celebrated communally. On Sundays we would pack everyone into the van and spend the day at Cooper's Beach, a pristine place covered in soft, white sand and surrounded by magnificent palm trees of all varieties. The sun would sparkle against the warm ocean water, and the view was breathtaking. Cooper's Beach had a small lagoon that caught the ocean's overflow, an ideal place for non-swimmers, like me, and children. Locked in the house, I reflected on the first Sunday I had spent at the Beach and recalled staring in silence at the peace of the ocean and feeling closer to God than I had ever felt in church. The beach, any beach, was a sanctuary compared to the confining walls of the house.

Communal life was hectic, especially for me who had come from a small family. At times, I struggled with the strict regimentation and collaboration required to make our Hebrew community run properly and smoothly, but that was counterbalanced with times of lavish social events. Struggle circled, but fun and joy lived among us, and we flowed back and forth, enjoying the easy, friendly, pace of Liberian life as we knew it.

Post-1980 coup, confined to our homes at dusk, naturally, everyone was feeling a little stir crazy. Most of the remaining Americo Liberian leadership of the country, and thousands of Americo Liberian families, had fled the country. It became impolite to ask about friends who had departed.

People were just…silent.

When the diamond mining expedition, which had brought my husband and Kwesi to Liberia, failed, Kwesi returned to the States to work on the Hebrew's International Staff. Elrahm remained in Liberia and became an employee of the community's Nation Builders Construction Company, even though much of the construction in the country came to a halt. At one point, it became so volatile that the Liberian workers of Nation Builders staged protests outside of the main office for backdated wages still owed to them. I was grateful that Elrahm hadn't been sent to the States, Ghana, or Israel without us. Our men were shifted around from one place to another and sometimes were away from their families for extended periods. Kwesi would be gone for an indefinite amount of time. Our Mission Leader had a family in Israel that he only visited a couple of times a year. There was a great deal about the Hebrew Israelite Community that I was trying to understand. I continued to have lingering questions about my husband's relationship with NeEmah.

Concerned about the survival of our families, we became creative in finding ways to make money. One particular way was riding into town and selling our jewelry to the Mandingo goldsmiths who flourished in downtown Liberia.

Despite the political uncertainty, our indigenous Liberian friends assured us that once the newly established PRC government met with foreign governments and corporations with economic holdings in Liberia, business would resume as usual under the Peoples' Redemption Council. The PRC went to great lengths to convince foreign governments that its citizens were safe in the country, despite the fact that the coup and its actions—overthrowing President Tolbert, executing Tolbert's Ministers, and the rumored killings and thousands of detained Liberians—had been televised for all the world to see. Liberia's relationship with the United States appeared to normalize. After all, Liberia was in a strategic position to allow the U.S. the use of Liberia's sea and airports as a staging ground for swift response to security threats around the world. That alone could cause America to gloss over human rights issues that festered underneath the surface attempts to present a picture of a country returning to normalcy.

As we moved into the dry season, the rain tapered, we returned to a less turbulent version of life in Liberia. At least, as normal as we could expect after all that had happened. Decades later, it would be stated that the April 1980 coup was only the beginning to a slow downward spiral, from which Liberia would not recover.

Thankfully, the PRC lifted the curfew, and Nation Builders received several new construction contracts. We began to hope. The brothers returned to work, and the sisters resumed shopping for cloth to make garments in town. Although we regained our rhythm, the coup and the economic drain it had placed on the country and on the Hebrew Community had left me feeling helpless. Additionally, a growing sense of uncertainty about my relationship with Elrahm caused me to reflect upon my mother's advice: "Never go anywhere without your carfare home."

When I was in high school it was rumored that some guys would take a girl out and then tell her "Fuck or walk back!" My mother's girls were never to get into a situation of powerlessness. Her edict was clear. Hebrew doctrine or not, my mother's voice egged me forward. By attaching my fate to the Hebrew Community I had spun myself into a cocoon. Yet inside the tight, barely lit cocoon I was slowly gnawing my way out, something was about to be born in me. Love it or leave it. Fuck or walk back. Never go anywhere without your carfare home.

All lessons I would take to heart in the coming months.

Ahnydah Rahm

AN ENTREPRENEUR IS BORN

In Africa, everybody has a hustle. Liberians find something that people will pay for and provide it. Americans make excuses for being non-productive, but in Liberia, unless you are hopelessly insane or severely deformed, you have to find a way to make money if you want to live. My stepfather came from a family of career postal workers and my mother was a hairstylist. Yet in Liberia, I found myself drawing upon the legacy of my biological father and my grandfather, both entrepreneurs, and unearthing my own talents.

In 1980 and before the Chinese began to farm in Panesville, finding fresh vegetables, even in the Lebanese grocery stores, was difficult, particularly in the rainy season. Once a shopper found fresh vegetables, the challenge was then transferred to the cook to make creative dishes from the short, fat, discolored stalks of okra, dwarfed eggplants, and bitter ball, which for the sake of reference, is like a small version of bitter eggplant, that mimicked poison. Occasionally we found a few collard greens and were able to revel in a dish that tasted like 'home.' Rather than using herbs in their dishes, Liberians cook with copious amounts of red palm nut oil, and add flavor with an extremely hot habanero pepper, which I came to love. Yet, after more than a year in Liberia, I still found myself craving broccoli, cauliflower, cabbage, string beans, and mushrooms—all things I had never seen in Liberia.

I remember the day my hidden business skills revealed themselves. I stood in Abi Joudi supermarket, soaked from rain and shivering from the air-conditioning. Rainy season was always a struggle for me. In America, I was the person who took a sick day on rainy days, but during rainy season, it rained every day and all day long on occasion. No way could I sit around and do nothing. There was no running from the rain. Oftentimes, it would rain so hard that even an umbrella was not useful. Those times, I would wrap my braids in a turban, tie my lappa—the two yard piece of African cloth commonly worn either as a skirt, or baby sling to tie an infant on your back—and simply deal with it. It was mid-June and the rain that had soaked me was unexpected. Next month the rain would disappear until December, and then complaints about the heat and suffocating humidity could pour forth.

When I shopped, it was often in bulk for several houses. On this particular day, while the stock boys were retrieving cases of whole-wheat flour and split and black-eyed peas from the warehouse, I browsed while I waited. Still shivering from the rain, I hoped that the rain would abate before I had to hail a taxi back to the Old Road. Everything in the grocery store was imported from abroad and many of the packages were in languages I couldn't read. Portuguese, Danish, Arabic, French, Pakistani, Lebanese, Chinese, Italian, Spanish, British, and American products sat side by side. It was fascinating to see the products coexist whereas the people from the countries they derived from often did not. I became enthralled with trying to decipher what was in the packaging by looking at pictures or picking out familiar words on the packaging.

I continued browsing, taking note of the Danish milk in wax cartons and then stumbled upon a shelf of one-pound bags of dried beans and found mung beans. Mung beans, commonly used in Asian cooking, are delicious sprouted. I had regularly sprouted mung beans in the States, and wondered if there was enough life force in these small, green beans to sprout. It was more common than not to buy dried beans at the market and get them home, only to find them infested with weevils—protein eating bugs. However, these mung beans looked fresh, and there appeared to be a large supply on hand. I had a glimmer of hope. Happily, I purchased a package for a dollar and thirty cents.

Once home, I thoroughly washed and soaked the mung beans, carefully placing them in a Ball glass canning jar, covering the opening with a mesh baby diaper, and securing the top with a rubber band. I maintained a vigil, rinsing them at least twice a day, and after three days, my dedication was rewarded. Small spouts were developing into beautiful fresh bean sprouts! My lack of patience, an unnerving trait that I had prayed repeatedly to overcome, made it difficult to wait for the sprouts to peek their heads out of the shell of the beans. I would have to learn to the virtue of patience. My future success would depend on it.

Rice is the staple food in Liberia. While I craved Irish potatoes, macaroni and cheese, noodles, couscous, and millet, eventually I adjusted to the daily diet of parboiled rice. Besides rice, there was cassava root, which I was surprised to learn is the basis for tapioca pudding. On the rare occasions that I ate cassava root, it was either boiled or roasted like a potato, and slathered with butter. Yet I never felt satisfied after eating it. But, with my homegrown bean sprouts, sautéed with onions and pepper over rice, it was a little taste of home and something to look forward to.

In the aftermath of the coup, we were grateful to have food that was grown locally and sold fresh daily in the market, rather than waiting at the Free Port for a shipment of imported food to dock. We thrust ourselves into learning the preparation of indigenous cuisine, and mastered cooking the vegan's version of potato greens and rice, bitterball and rice, collard greens and rice, palm butter and rice, beans and rice, and now, thanks to my newfound venture, we had beans sprouts with rice! When we stumbled upon a Lebanese store that had dusty bottles of soy sauce, we thought we were in the Promised Land—pun intended. For get about the Wok, we could now prepare Chinese food in Africa using a skillet and a coal pot!

As it turned out, we were overly optimistic about how soon the country would return to pre-coup normalcy. The Americo-Liberians that had fled the country were invited back to their homes in Liberia by the PRC government. Some returned, while others learned from relatives that in many cases their homes had been taken over by soldiers, damaged or destroyed. We were very divorced from knowledge of what was really happening in Liberia. However, we did know that the construction industry did not rebound. We had no choice but to lay off all but a few of our Liberian workers. We had thought it was rough before, but now the money was even scarcer. When the company shut down, my daughter Binah was a gangly eleven-year-old, her brother, Penemiel, barely nineteen months, was just learning to walk in order to get out of the way of his three-month-old baby sister, Zevah. Obviously, caring and raising for three young children in a foreign country, away from the support of our biological family, made us seriously consider whether or not we should return to America.

No return trip ticket in hand, though. We had come here in hopes of generating money through the Nation Builders Construction Company, the diamond mining operation upcountry, and a farm, an idea we had created once living in Liberia. The plans were solid, yet they had all fallen through for reasons unforeseen by any of us. But I had an idea.

That week, I grew an extra batch of bean sprouts, packaged them in individual plastic sandwich bags, and took them into town on my next shopping trip. The manager and internal auditor at Abi Jodi's was Mr. Waddeah, a handsome Lebanese man with a unibrow and a full handlebar mustache. Abi Joudi supermarket courted the business of foreigners, attracting thousands of Lebanese, East Indian, and Asian families, not to mention those individuals affiliated with approximately fifteen foreign embassies. I asked to speak with Mr. Waddeah privately and was led to his small office near the loading dock. There, I sat and proposed my genius business plan—that he sell my bean sprouts on consignment. We agreed that I would supply Abi Joudi fresh bean sprouts on consignment at a dollar per bag. We would split the sales 75/25, my favor. Those that didn't sell, I would take back and as a loss. I would provide my own signage and Mr. Waddeah would give me refrigerated display space.

After several days, I returned to the store by taxi to check on the freshness of the sprouts and was elated to look in the case and see that they were gone. I collected my cash and continued bringing thirty bags of sprouts each Tuesday for the next five to six weeks. One afternoon, Waddeah pulled me aside and mentioned that all the bean sprouts were selling out before Tuesday afternoon and suggested that I bring more bags, even more frequently. My bean sprouts were a hit!

When I initially began selling thirty bags of sprouts per week, I received a profit of about eighty-five dollars monthly. That might not seem like a whole lot by today's standards, especially in the States, but in Liberia, between the years 1979 and 1990, it was possible to get someone to cook your meals six days a week and do some cleaning for as little as fifty to seventy dollars a month. Needless to say, I was profiting significantly, and my idea was a full-fledged success.

With the exception of the Hebrew brothers, the women and children stayed home and did not interact much with the general Liberian community. While this separation was comfortable for most of our group, for me, staying within our tightly knit community was a denial of my original impetus for coming to Africa. Heady from the increased responsibility of shopping for our household, and eventually for multiple houses as we became more adept at leveraging our collective resources, as well as maintaining my bean sprout business, I became inspired to make a larger contribution in Liberia.

Regardless of the coup, I still felt that Liberia had the talent, the resources, and an opportunity to become one of the most progressive countries in Africa, and I wanted to be a part of its ascension. After all, I hadn't come to Africa just to be a homemaker and sell bean sprouts. I craved a challenge and wanted more access to the culture and interaction with Liberia's people.

In early August of 1980, I was invited, along with leadership and other members of our Hebrew Community, to visit the Liberian National Red Cross, a branch of the International Red Cross Society. The International

Red Cross Society had been founded in 1863 by a Frenchmen, Henri Dunant, who after seeing the horrors of war in Europe, thought that civilized societies should, even in the midst of war, agree that the wounded and prisoners of war should have humane treatment. After first organizing the neutral body in Geneva, Switzerland, the Red Cross began organizing Red Cross Societies around the world. The Liberian National Red Cross had the distinction of being the first National Red Cross Society in Africa and was founded by an Americo Liberian, Mrs. Jeanette King Cooper, an 87-year-old powerhouse.

I was excited that Elrahm and I had been chosen, with a couple of other members, to join the entourage of the leader of the Hebrew Community, who was designated the title of Prince. This also felt strangely like a date. Dressed in our best cultural garments, we were finally together without our three children and I remember us holding hands on the ride to town. On the drive Prince and Khahil, his attaché, who also doubled as his personal driver, briefed us on the growing relationship between our community and Mrs. King.

We rolled up to the Red Cross Headquarters, a gated multi-building compound on Lynch Street, in our beige Mercedes Benz sedan. As we toured the buildings with Mrs. King and her staff, I was impressed with her vibrancy and clarity of purpose. Her pride in the Republic of Liberia being the first national society in Africa to me, symbolized her dedication to the progress of the people of Liberia. Instantly, I felt aligned with my unspoken desire to make a greater contribution. As we stood on the back balcony of the spacious building, I peered through the open door of the Red Cross Well-Baby Clinic, and felt it beckoning to me.

That sunny afternoon as we departed she spoke to each of us individually.

"My Dear, feel free to come back, this is your home."

Her words washed over me like a benediction and I was convinced that the Red Cross was my porthole to accessing the culture of Liberia. The very thought that I might have a chance to participate in a program, which would put me in constant and direct contact with everyday Liberian moms made my heart beat faster.

Ahnydah teaching at The Red Cross

WORK IS LOVE MADE VISIBLE

I craved every opportunity to learn and to understand Liberia. If we wanted to remain in Liberia, we needed a deeper knowledge of the people, the ethnic and tribal tensions, and the cultural practices that affected the way the people thought and behaved. Volunteering at the Red Cross offered me an opportunity to do just that.

Initially, we had arrogantly dismissed Liberian English as an ignorant bastardization of the English language. How "American" to want people to understand us from our language platform while not valuing theirs. However, after the coup, we quickly realized to truly integrate ourselves into the Liberian culture, we had better get busy learning to speak Liberian English. Not only did the vast majority of Liberians in Monrovia communicate with each other in Liberian English, but also, it was easier than learning the sixteen dialects spoken throughout the country.

It is an internationally recognized fact that people considered the most highly educated speak multiple languages. At some American universities, PhDs are not conferred in certain disciplines to anyone who is not fluent in another language. I have heard that a person is not truly well educated until that person can think, understand, and express themselves in linguistic symbols different from their own. In America, most of us confine ourselves to English, unless we are forced to do otherwise. In the interior, Liberians speak their own tribal dialect and the dialects of surrounding ethnic groups that they need to trade with. I quickly faced my linguistic limitations and began to value the lingua franca. Forgetting about my embarrassment, I tried my best to master Liberian English.

By mid-August, I was volunteering several times a week at the Red Cross Well-Baby Clinic. As a lactating mother, I wanted to share my experience and be an example for Liberian women who were being seduced to use Nestlé's canned milk, rather than their own breast milk for their children. While mothers in America or Europe are able to choose whether to breastfeed or use formula for reasons of convenience, in developing nations, where women do not consistently have the money to purchase formula or may not have clean conditions for mixing formula, canned milk makes a major contribution to the infant mortality rate. It was common for mothers to simply increase the amount of water required for the powdered milk when it began to run low and they had no money to replenish it, resulting in a sharp decrease in the nutritional value of the formula, which often led to nutritional diseases and starvation of infants.

When I started volunteering, Penemiel had just begun to walk and I was carrying my fat nursling, Zevah, along with me to the daycare center. Every Tuesday and Thursday, I woke the children extra early and had my husband walk us to the road so we could get a taxi into town. Zevah was my lactating infant model, and Penemiel went along so he would have an opportunity to socialize with Liberian children. I would also have an opportunity to face my linguistic deficit and to learn by doing how to communicate in my halting Liberian English. I had already begun to understand that 'O' at the ends of words kept the language fluid and affirmed the preceding noun. It also had a tonal quality to it. Such that 'O!' spoken abruptly by itself could express surprise, wonderment or anger.

On my first official day as a volunteer, the Secretary General of the Red Cross Society walked me across the breezeway to the Well-Baby Clinic and introduced me to the two Ministry of Health nurses stationed there. The room reserved for lectures held wooden pews allowing for a seating capacity of about twenty-five women. On this particular day, it was half-full of mothers with their babies. The women came to the clinic so that their children could receive the appropriate baby shots, as well as get their monthly weigh-in. The room appeared sterile with its clean white walls and floors, and the nurses in their starched white uniforms. In the reception area, a six-foot table held a multitude of posters, including one that depicted a woman, smiling and nursing her baby, while another showed a baby getting an immunization. There were also two rooms, with red doors, that I assumed were for exams.

The clinic served expectant mothers, as well as babies from birth until approximately three years of age. Watching the efficiency of the nurses, and the intimacy they had with the small group of women seated in the pews, made me feel like I was a part of something special. As I perused the clinic, I noticed that a couple of the indigenous mothers, probably in their early teens, had applied eyebrow pencil, red lipstick and even dangling earrings on their baby girls. There was even one little chocolate-skinned baby whose mother had dyed her hair reddish-brown. Mary, one of the nurses, reprimanded the mother, asked why she had colored the baby's hair, and then told her that the dye was too strong and could hurt her baby's head. I recall the woman looking sheepish as Mary pointed her finger and said, "You must not do it again 'O'!

At the time, I remember feeling judgmental and appalled that a mother would think a baby needed cosmetics in order to enhance her beauty, but the nurse just laughed and said, "If you get mad at everything these little girls do you will not sleep 'O'!

It was obvious for those of us who knew better that the baby's mother simply didn't understand the magnitude of putting a product designed for grown women on a baby. To unsophisticated Liberian mothers, the "civilized" products flooding the Liberian market were good simply because they came from somewhere else. Oddly, Zevah fit right in with the "made-up" baby girls with her thick, naturally rosy lips and brows and lashes so clearly defined, she looked like a little made-up woman. At the time, I wondered why even "small women," the affectionate term for baby girls, were thought to need assistance in enhancing their beauty.

That day, I stood nervously before my first group of mothers with my made-up looking little girl, that the women called "fat baby," and spoke while the nurse translated my Standard English into Liberian English. I hadn't made it past introducing myself when my daughter began to root around my top, the universal baby language for, "I want milk." Naturally, I went and sat on the table in front of me and pulled out my breast to nurse, and as I did, I noticed the women smiled approvingly while still appearing somewhat amused that I was nursing right before them. To them I was a "civilized," which meant that I had options that were more convenient. They were aspiring to be civilized, and thought in order to do so, they needed to give their babies Nestlé milk, yet there I was, pulling out a tittie for my baby to suck!

Almost immediately after I began feeding Zevah, the women in the group started talking quickly and animatedly amongst each other. I can only imagine the stricken look on my face, concerned that these women were laughing at me. The nurse in the Well-Baby Clinic had a face that was thin and fox-like, and she had a crooked smile, which while warm, belied a hint of conspiracy, which only made me more self-conscious.

"Mrs. Rahm, I will help you talk. You must not worry 'O'," she whispered as she turned the room over to me.

"Good morning sisters! My name is Ahnydah and this is my baby Zevah. I know that some people like canned milk, especially in America, but I came to tell you that breast milk is so much better for your baby than Nestlé's milk. Breast milk has all the nutrition your baby needs. See my fat baby?"

The women grinned at Zevah who had closed her eyes and was completely engrossed in suckling.

"Tha baby love tittie 'O!" one woman said in jilted English, and with that, a warm maternal knowing encircled us. They all laughed when Zevah, feeling all eyes on her, opened her saucer-like eyes, and turned toward the women, giving them a quizzical look while still maintaining a firm grasp on my breast.

Zevah was my icebreaker that day and gave me credibility before all those Liberian mothers. I talked a little longer about how happy nursing babies are.

Nurse Mary concluded the talk for me, "So the woman say, If you got money, If you don't got money 'O' you can feed you baby. We say, no Nestle 'O' my sistas."

Knowing it was critical that I build a relationship with these women from the start, I offered Zevah to a woman in exchange for her beautiful baby boy. I knew that handing her my baby in exchange for hers conveyed my trust and willingness to share motherly responsibilities.

I left the clinic feeling exhilarated to have volunteered, yet also slightly deflated by the language barrier. Going to the Clinic, I knew there would be one, but didn't realize how challenging it would be to deliver my first breastfeeding talk while relying so heavily on a translator. Even though I could understand the women pretty well, they could hardly understand me without my nurse translator. However, there is a universal language that I could understand, the copious smiles, which we all shared. I was encouraged by that. The taxi ride home felt like an eternity, as I was anxious to share my first day with my housemates.

Once I arrived home, I made a beeline for the kitchen where I knew someone would be working or cooking. Sure enough, Rackemya was sweating over the coal pot just outside our back door, cooking dinner. Sheryrah holding her baby son, Yoshiah, heard me enter and came from the bedroom out to the back porch where Rackemya and I stood, tending several dishes on the coal pot. I could tell they were as anxious to *hear* about my day, as I was to *tell* them about it.

"Well, how was it Miss Red Cross volunteer?" asked Sheryrah with a wide grin. She had an inviting smile that was a perfect complement to her round, brown-skinned face.

"I'm not going to lie—I was a little nervous and scared. Liberians have a way of always smiling at you that shows respect but does not necessarily mean understanding or agreement. There were moments when I felt as if they thought I was just a stupid American, know-it-all.

The women gazed at me, enthralled with what I had to say even though I thought I was only rambling. "Anyway, the Clinic was immaculate. I was able to put Zevah down on the floor to scoot around and the Clinic nurse was exceptionally helpful. Zevah stole the show, when she pulled up my top looking for her milk! They all thought she was the cutest thing. But get this—I picked up one of the baby girls and she had *make-up on*! A baby!"

"What?!" Rackemya exclaimed looking over her wire-framed glasses.

"You heard me right. I was initially drawn to her because unlike all the other baby girls with studs or tiny hoops in their ears, she had long dangling earrings. And when I held her close, I noticed that there was make-up covering her face!"

"How much make-up?" Sheryrah asked.

"I'm talking red lipstick, which had smeared on her fist because she was teething, and two heavy Betty Boop black eyebrows."

"You are joking, Ahnydah!" Rackemya said, appalled at what she was hearing.

"Ahnydah are you sure it wasn't Kool Aid? I have seen red lips on babies before and I thought it was from Kool Aid."

"No my sister, l-i-p-s-t-i-c-k! The nurse said the country women are so ignorant that they think that the little girls look better with makeup. Not only that, but she told me she's had to care for the scalps of babies that have allergic reactions from their mothers using Clairol to color their hair either red or jet black. In fact, the nurse warned the baby's mother about it but they disregard her because the native women see no harm in it."

None of us could imagine putting make-up on our little girls, let alone dying their hair. We sat in the kitchen for several more hours, discussing the corruption of Africa by a forced emphasis on a European standard of beauty. Rackemya suggested that during my next visit to the Clinic, I emphasize how sensitive a baby's skin is. I appreciated her suggestion and took it to heart, but I didn't tell her how difficult that simple statement would be to get across to the Liberian women who had barely understood when I was discussing something as natural as breastfeeding.

Not only was I fighting the language barrier, but most of the mothers were young, still in their teens—children themselves. And on top of all that, the Clinic nurses suggested I focus on demonstrations of breastfeeding rather than passing out flyers because the women were illiterate. I felt twice as frustrated once I realized how much we depend on the written word for communication. Here, I could hardly speak the language, and they could not read.

"There is just so much I want to do and I don't know where or how to start. Hair dye causes skin irritation, but baby starvation, dat sump-ting else a-gin." I found myself slipping awkwardly into Liberian English for emphasis.

"It's just criminal what these bandits are doing, handing out these advertisements of so called, 'civilized women' feeding their babies powered milk. They don't understand the culture, or even realize how many women don't have access to clean water on a consistent basis. All they care about is selling their product," Sheryrah said.

Before I could respond, Rackemya called out and I looked in the direction of the kitchen.

"Ahnydah, are you and Zevah ready to eat? Food's ready."

And with that, I transitioned from being a concerned Red Cross volunteer to being a Hebrew Israelite sister at home with my family.

"Let's sit on the porch. Can we bring the card table outside?"

"Good idea. It's so gorgeous out, we might as well enjoy it while we can," I said putting Zevah down on the living room floor. "Where's Elrahm?"

"Haven't seen him since this morning," Sheryrah replied.

I brought the card table and four folding chairs to the front porch. Penemiel woke from his nap, soaking wet. After changing him, I joined my housemates with our children for dinner. Our porch was semi-enclosed and once seated, we were barely visible from the road. From our vantage point, we could watch people walk north down to the market at the end of the road, or walk south toward the Old Road. Market women were going home with the remnants of their potato greens, palm oil, ground peas bobbing atop their heads in large aluminum pans.

The smell of cassava leaf, rice, and country peas cooked in palm oil filled the air as Rackemya brought our plates to the table.

"There's more if you want, but I just thought it would be easier for us to get started if I fixed the plates."

"And we thank you," Sheryrah said.

"Cold wata 'O," the voice of the cold-water man came from the base of our front steps. It was dinnertime, and when you eat food loaded with pepper, you want cold water to wash it down.

"My man, wait 'O'!" Sheryrah ran inside her bedroom. She returned as the seller was removing the cloth donut that cushioned his scalp, and placed the pan of frozen water on his knees for her selection. She gave him fifteen cents for three plastic sandwich bags of frozen water.

"I just had to have cold wa-ta today," Sheryrah said.

"Myself!" I responded in high-pitched Liberian English so that she would give me water as well.

"Ahnydah, I'm going to have to practice my Liberian English more," Rackemya said, taking a sip of the cool liquid before continuing. "You and Sheryrah are becoming comfortable with it and I still feel stupid."

"It's because I spend more time around Liberians, and the math teacher in you wants to dissect Liberian English rather than just let it come naturally. Just let yourself go."

"Are we talking about Rackemya loosening up?" Sheryrah asked with a big grin on her face. A collegial laughter filled the porch as we all acknowledged that Rackemya loosening up was near impossible since she liked to plan and organize for everything.

Gathering our children around us into small hand-woven chairs, we fed them from our plates. Penemiel and Yoshiah were older, and each sat on a piece of plastic with their small plates and spoons, attempting to feed themselves. Before we knew it, they were both covered in palm oil and rice grains.

Rackemya nursed Schlomeet on her right breast while eating left-handed. We laughed that becoming ambidextrous was the by-product of nursing.

As the sun set, and our toddlers sat happily 'feeding' themselves, we talked quietly, enjoying a faint breeze that had materialized and soaking in the local color as it floated past our porch.

A half hour later, the Nation Builder's van drove up bearing Elrahm in the driver's seat and NeEmah at his side. My lips were pursed in a thin line, but I grimaced inside.

Each time I volunteered at the Clinic, I brought my son, Penemial so that he could play with the Liberian children, while Zevah and I demonstrated breastfeeding to the mothers. After working in the Clinic for a couple of hours, I would return to the day care center to Penemial.

When entering the day care, a large room where the little children sat in wooden chairs carefully lined up in horizontal rows, I remember hearing the strains of:

> Hey diddle diddle,
> The cat and the fiddle,
> The cow jumped over the moon,
> The little dog laughed to see such sport,
> And the dish ran away with the spoon!

It seemed odd to me that children in Liberia would be singing *Hey Diddle Diddle* an English nursery rhyme. I remember asking about African songs and the caregivers smiled shyly, but no one responded.

I would later learn that the leadership of the Red Cross dictated the use of American and English songs that were considered a depiction of "civilized" songs.

The four caregivers that were in the singing room sat each with a small rattan switch, either in her hand or on the floor beside her. Rattans are very thin dowel like rods that are used "unofficially" for corporal punishment in the childcare centers and schools. As I watched one of the women change a baby's diaper, I glanced over at my son seated in a front row, looking disconnected and apprehensive.

What immediately caught my attention was the pandemonium that took place in the room down the hall. Following the noise to the back playroom, I observed that there were about twenty children, between the ages of two and four years old, playing with wooden blocks the size of bricks. Some of the larger children were tossing the blocks around the room like soccer balls. Another couple of kids were running and tackling each other to the ground. I was alarmed that these children were not in separate groups by ages, and even more unnerved by the fact that they were unsupervised. Returning to the front room where my son sat quietly, I tactfully asked one of the caregivers why the children were left alone. They gave me a bewildered look before responding with a slight chuckle, "Mistress Rahm, the children are just playing."

I remember watching horrified as a little girl screamed upon being cracked with a block and watching a bump rise on the child's forehead. The caregiver ran to the crying child to comfort her, then turned, rendering what in Liberia is called, "a helluva slap," to the face of the older child that had thrown the block. The lack of supervision shocked me and I was alarmed that the caregivers had not predicted that the children of various ages would not know how to play independently with the blocks. I gathered my son, and we left the day care center, but the images of the children I was leaving behind troubled me.

Thursday, I returned and tried to keep both of my children with me. However, in the midst of my working with the women, one of the nurses thought she was doing me a favor and took my son across the breezeway to the day care center. I did not press the issue but when I returned, I noticed that the children in the front were singing the same songs from Tuesday, and in the back room, the older children were going wild. This time I decided to ask to speak with the manager of the Center but unfortunately was told she was out.

At the time, Anna Cooper was the Secretary General of the Red Cross. Anna reminded me of a fashion model. It was obvious to me that her clothes were imported or bought in America. Her soft hair, worn in a neat bun, gave her an air of elegance and refinement. I mentioned my concerns about the conditions in the childcare center and thought that better supervision was needed. We spoke briefly, and during our conversation, she shared that the day care director had fled the country during the coup, leaving the position open to anyone who might like to fill it. She also expressed her personal concerns over the lack of supervision and safety and communicated that she had been checking on the Center more frequently. What she said next would change my life forever. Removing her glasses, she looked me straight in the eye and asked, "Mrs. Rahm, would you be interested in taking the position?"

I didn't respond immediately, still trying to comprehend what she had just asked me. Seeing the shock in my face, she continued, "The women that care for the children are uneducated, 'country women.' If you could take the job, even part time, *whatever* you could do would be better than what I know is happening right now in the Center."

Although I was shocked, I knew from the moment the words left her lips that I wanted the job, which was crazy since I didn't know the first thing about running a childcare center. Nevertheless, I couldn't ignore the little voice inside my head encouraging me and telling me that I could, in fact, do it and successfully.

Still, I had sense enough to ask her to give me some time to consider her offer. I had to figure out if I could run the childcare center and continue to sell bean sprouts. I also wanted to know how much time it would be taking away from my family. My heart thumped inside my chest the whole way home, but it wasn't fear I felt running through my veins, it was exhilaration.

For the first time in a very long time, I felt fully alive.

Teacher Kollie and the children

THE JOURNEY OF
A THOUSAND MILES BEGINS

Once home, I immediately confided in Rackemya. She was the obvious confidante as she had been a public school teacher in America and was now the Principal of the school the Hebrews were developing for our children in Liberia. I explained the situation and asked her for her advice. Her assessment, after our initial and several subsequent conversations, was to go for it. I think, for as excited as she was for me, she was just as excited that she would get to write a curriculum that I could use. She felt that my best option for success was a two-pronged approach. First, lead by example. She told me that I should demonstrate how the children should be managed, and then train the women to follow my example.

I submitted my curriculum vitae and cover letter to Anna Cooper, while continuing to volunteer in the Well Baby Clinic. It was the middle of August 1980, several weeks before the Board of Directors would convene and discuss my application for the position of Director of the Red Cross Day Care Center.

On September 1, 1980, I was invited to meet the Board Members. I was surprised to find that the President of the Board, Linnie Kessally, was an African-American woman, a graduate of the University of Chicago, and married to a prominent Liberian army officer. Although she was British-formal, there was warmth radiating from her when our eyes met. That simple gesture telegraphed her approval and made me feel at ease.

Late that afternoon, the Board voted to hire me at $400 a month— twice the average wage a government employee earned monthly. They described the position as part-time. That description was the delicate Liberian way of not offending me with a salary less than what I would consider reasonable in the U.S., but what lay ahead of me was not a part-time endeavor.

That afternoon, I was emotionally overwhelmed and felt extremely anxious to meet my new staff for the first time. I had left my nursling at home for the day so that I could be unencumbered during the interview. When a woman breastfeeds, the flow of milk is tied to her emotions. When excited, the milk just gushes. Emotions surrounding my new appointment caused letdown reflex to go haywire! I mashed both breasts with the heels of my hands, pressed, to slow down the milk, rushed home, anxious to nurse my daughter.

The coup had occurred April 12 and now, just six months later, not only did I have thriving bean sprout business, but a job that would allow me to earn a salary. I sat in the taxi, speeding toward Old Road, Lakpazee Way, and savored my independence and victory.

The next morning, the taxi pulled into the Red Cross compound at 8:00 a.m. I decided that it would be best, for my first day, to leave my children at home with my housemates. Aretha Kollie, a large, dark-skinned woman, welcomed me and then escorted me to my new office. She was a big-boned Kpelle woman with a hearty laugh that warmed up a room. She was black and fine, and to this day, I still smile when I remember her confiding that she sometimes used axel grease to make her raven hair shine.

My glass office allowed me to look out into the large playroom that was the home of those awful life-size wooden blocks. My first act as Director was to have them put in a storage room until I could figure out how to manage that dangerous activity. Other than removing the blocks, I decided it was best to observe and learn what exactly was going on in the Center so that I would know what, if anything, was benefiting the children, and what needed to be changed. One thing that stood out in my mind and unnerved me was that the caregivers, who were called baby nurses, while well intentioned, were overwhelmed by the amount of children. There simply weren't enough caregivers to give the proper attention to each child. Additionally, there weren't enough toys or activities to engage the children. Lacking the skills necessary to manage the children, they would strike them with the switch-like rattans for things that small children have no control over, like wetting themselves, losing their balance and falling on another child, or getting bored quickly and resorting to creating their own "fun."

During lunchtime, the caregivers continued smiling at me, all the while trying to figure me out. I was offered food and tried to explain, not very well, that I didn't eat meat. Aretha, who was very quick on the uptake, gave me a plate of hot rice, which she poured heated palm oil and pepper over. It was tasty, I was happy and noted her resourcefulness.

After I had finished my lunch, I watched quietly as the five women herded the sixty-five children into the back playroom for lunch. The caregivers reminded me of security guards in the way they stood over the children as they ate. Some were feeding smaller babies, but other children were left to their own devices. Liberia, at least in 1980, was a very religious, mostly Christian, country, yet the food went unblessed and there was no modeling of table manners. Small children, who obviously needed assistance, were instead allowed to dump their food on the table and eat with their hands, often the small aluminum spoons they had been provided went untouched.

I retreated to my office and peered out from behind the protection of the glass, wondering how in the hell I was going to implement a curriculum that would transform this childcare center into a place I would want my own children to attend, a place I would be proud of. Thus began the mission that would keep me occupied and enthralled for the next ten years.

The Red Cross Day Care Center was located on Lynch Street, in the center of town and three blocks from Abi Joudi Supermarket, allowing me to check my sprouts during lunch, and even chill sprouts in the refrigerator at the day care center for a later delivery. Eventually, a few curious staff members made a snack of sautéed packages of overgrown spouts with palm oil and pepper. There was no waste, just blue sky!

With the proximity to the Abi Joudi Supermarket, I added a second weekly delivery and targeted several additional Lebanese grocery stores. Because Abi Joudi was the largest of the Lebanese owned grocery stores in Liberia, it made it easier for me to pitch my sprouts to other storeowners who trusted and followed Abi Joudi's lead.

I approached several Chinese restaurants in downtown Liberia. The largest called The Mandarin had a red pagoda style edifice and an upscale, largely foreign clientele. They seemed a natural choice.

When I approached the restaurant's owner, an attractive light-skinned Americo Liberian woman, she called for Alfred, a slightly built, effeminate headwaiter who was very cordial. I thought I was doing well until I met with the Chinese chef. He joined us and as I discussed the quality of my bean sprouts then provided them with a sample to try, I noticed the chef's rude behavior. I was certain that I was not going to get The Mandarin's business.

I later learned from Alfred that the chef did not like me because the Chinese had a farm in Panesville but had been unable to strike a deal with the restaurant's owner. At the time I had approached the owner, the restaurant had been using canned sprouts. I suspect that I had unwittingly undercut the Chinese farm's price for the same fresh sprouts.

One week later, they had me stop in to place their order for the month. They ordered fifteen pounds of sprouts for every week, which they paid for upon delivery. My home-based business that started in one supermarket had expanded into three grocery stores and now a restaurant!

THE SILENT MONSTER

While following my dream to live in Africa, I made some very serious errors in judgment. The Hebrew Israelite Community in Liberia were vegans, which meant we gave up all animal products including eggs and cheese to promote optimal health. However, I occasionally "slipped" and had a grilled cheese sandwich or a cup of ice cream. We also didn't believe in inoculating our children with live bacteria for protection against disease, so when we decided to travel to Africa, we tugged at the grapevine and found a doctor who shared our beliefs. He discussed each vaccine with us in detail and outlined the toxins involved, but in the end, allowed us to choose which vaccines we would accept. Penemiel, my son, was six months old at the time. I thought that as a nursling, he would get his immunity to these diseases from me and so I fell into a false sense of comfort about having him inoculated for the trip. My daughter, Binah, ten at the time, received all but the cholera vaccine because we were not going into an area where cholera was prevalent. My husband and I both had a booster shot, but elected to skip the cholera shot.

I have had a lot of time to reflect on how the initial decision to exempt Penemiel from receiving vaccinations left him open to diseases that compromised his health. Like many memories that leave a bad taste in one's mouth, the full effect hits hard, but the initial cause slips into the seclusion of the subconscious mind. At the time, the decision to have Penemiel receive his immunity to Typhoid, Diphtheria, Whooping Cough, Cholera and Measles via my breast milk seemed entirely rational, at least for the tour of West Africa. However, after returning from our tour and deciding to make West Africa our home, that fateful decision was not revisited. The Board of Health shot card falsely stated that Penemiel had received the proper inoculations against infectious diseases. That was only the beginning of the problem.

Post-coup, we downsized to save money on housing. Our family moved from the semi-secluded house on Lakpazee Road to the Peace Villa. The Peace Villa was the seat of the majority of the social activity and housed the largest number of Hebrew Israelite families. It was a gorgeous home with spacious rooms. The house had six bedrooms, four bathrooms, and wrap-around granite balconies. The first floor boasted a large carport efficiently converted into an elementary school for grades K-6, and there was a large front yard for our children's play.

As our children seldom strayed beyond our gated compound, it was difficult to understand how measles found its way to us. I suspect the measles arrived on a plane with an unexpected group of teens from a Chicago high school, their choral instructor, the brother of one of our leaders, escorting them. It wasn't an ideal situation, having twenty teenagers living in our house with us, but without sufficient time to prepare for their trip, they had no choice but to ask to stay with us for the couple of weeks they would be visiting Liberia.

From my perspective, it was exciting that we were established enough to host a tour group from my hometown. I could show American teens that people just like them lived and thrived in Liberia. The visit proved a mixed blessing since we were already living in crowded conditions. Our houseguests arrived just as we were experiencing a shortage of beds and bedding. A few days after they arrived, one of the visiting children came down with a fever and rash that our paramedics diagnosed as measles. The overcrowded living situation provided for prime conditions for the measles to spread throughout the children's bedrooms.

My workday started early and I rushed home during the Center's naptime to complete my chores. I spent hours every evening washing clothes and diapers by hand in the bathtub of our bedroom suite. Later I would spend precious time with my children before bedtime. I wasn't involved with the touring choir from King School except that they had visited the Center one day. I didn't even know that my eldest daughter Binah was ill until her best friend Aylah said "Emah (Hebrew for mother) Ahnydah, Binah is burning up and she has this rash on her face and chest. She has been crying all day. She sent me to get you."

As soon as I entered the overcrowded room that served as a dorm for the older girls and the visiting girls from King High School, I could literally smell the strong musky odor of fever. Rushing to Binah's bedside, I noticed the red rash that she had scratched raw.

I began mopping her rash with calamine lotion soaked cotton balls, and tried feeding her soup and tea, but she remained miserable. The temperature hit 90+ degrees, and she had to stay inside wearing sunglasses to protect her eyes. As the measles spread, our house became an itching nightmare. In addition to caring for our own sick kids, we also had to tend lovingly to the visiting children who were homesick for their parents. A lot of whining and whaling ensued and the Emahs where stretched pretty thin.

While I continued to go to town and work at the Center, the stay-at-home Emahs took care of all the children. We kept them on nutritious diets and painted them with calamine, and in short order, everyone got better. The kids from Martin Luther King High School returned to America having had a very rich experience in Africa, measles notwithstanding!

We breathed a sigh of relief, and things went back to normal, until we noticed that Penemiel, who was almost two, seemed to be cutting another tooth. He was feverish and inconsolable, and after a week of restlessness and irritability, he spiraled into diarrhea and a relentless fever, despite dosing him with chloroquine—the medicine we used for malaria. When he lost his appetite, I really began to worry. *Nothing* before that time kept Penemiel from his food. When I tried to spoon-feed him, I noticed that the inside of his mouth was inflamed, making it very painful for him to eat. He would clamor for food but when it reached his mouth, he would clinch his teeth and jerk his head away, even rejecting his favorite mashed banana and butter pear (we know it as avocado). After a week of trying numerous tactics to get my son to eat, I mentioned his symptoms to a member with a medical background and a veteran of Liberia. He took one look at Penemiel and diagnosed him. Measles.

The possibility of Penemiel having measles hadn't even occurred to me because his symptoms didn't look like those of the other children. He'd had a small fever but no rash. It wasn't until a friend of mine asked if I was sure that I'd had him inoculated for measles before coming to Africa that I remembered I hadn't! Now my small son with his beautiful coal black eyes was suffering because of my ignorance.

When we think of ignorance, we typically think of someone uneducated and illiterate, but oftentimes, even thoughtful, intelligent parents can make mistakes because they think they're making the right decision at the moment based on beliefs they believe to be correct. So in that moment, sitting in my wicker chair in my clean bedroom, walking barefoot on floors I scrubbed nightly with bleach and water, I could not have felt more ignorant than if I were illiterate and wallowing in filth.

My poor baby had already weathered a bout of dysentery and a couple of cases of malaria, in addition to the normal teething and colds that children suffer through, and he hadn't reached at even two yet. His tongue was swollen, mouth was raw, his stools became constant, slimy, frothy foul smelling diarrhea, and he was wizened like a shrunken, listless old man. Binah recovered from measles, and between her, Rahm, and me, we kept an around the clock vigil, trying to get Penemiel to take an ounce or two of electrolyte fluid. We regularly bathed him in cool water to try and drive the fever down, but nothing made a difference. Although I tried not to show it on my face, in my heart, I felt he was slipping away.

I managed to forget my fear for a few hours at work, but on my ride home, the dread would creep back and dig a hole in my chest. If someone asked me today why I didn't just take my child in my arms and go to the nearest hospital, I'd have to admit that although the thought crossed my mind several times, I was in a foreign country among people that I didn't know or trust. Sadly, I only trusted the people that I had come to Africa with.

One night, as I sat in our bedroom breastfeeding Zevah, I noticed that she would take a sip and then turn her head toward her brother as he lay watching from the bed. Zevah was a very sensitive little girl, and it seemed, at least to me, that that she was keeping a watchful eye on her little brother. I remember his feeble cry and the feeling of helplessness as my healthy child greedily drank my milk while my sick baby lay starving.

"God, did you have me bring my beautiful black-eyed son to Africa to die?" I cried aloud. "Yeah, though I walk through the valley of the shadow of death, I will fear no evil, yeah though I walk through the valley of the shadow of death, I will fear no evil."

I remember sitting there, repeatedly chanting the only portion of the twenty-third psalm I could recall. I knew that I had to move beyond the fear that had me paralyzed and do something! I was sure my son was dying, my son whose coming had been told to me by the garb draped woman so long ago, the black-eyed boy whose spirit reminded me of my murdered brother, now lay dying.

Meanwhile, Zevah drank her belly full and dropped off to sleep. I laid her down and lifted my son, holding him close. Shortly, I noticed him rooting, the reflex that nursing children have to locate the breast. Instinctively, I uncovered my breast and allowed him to nurse. He was so weak I could barely feel his suckling, but I knew I was comforting him and held him and rocked and prayed until we drifted off to sleep in my rocker, holding on to each other.

Miraculously, when I laid him down, he slept through the night for the first time in many days. The next morning, I noticed he had only slightly soiled his diaper. It seemed wrong to nurse a sick child and a healthy child from the same breasts, but my motherly instinct kicked in. I knew, somehow, that what I was doing was helping. I told no one, continuing to nurse Penemiel regularly in the privacy of our bedroom.

Several days later, my husband walked in on me nursing Penemiel. I was initially afraid of what he would say—Penemial had stopped nursing long ago, and I thought my husband might feel that I was jeopardizing the health of both children, one of them in radiant health, by sharing my breast milk between them. I wondered whether he would want to consult with our paramedics. When I told him that I saw improvement in our son's health after I began nursing him again, Rahm encouraged me to continue and to keep giving him the bitter teas that our paramedic staff had been boiling from local herbs. I read from the tender look in his eyes when he held Penemiel that while he had never said anything to me, he had also been afraid our son would die.

After a week of continuous breastfeeding, Penemiel's tongue was no longer inflamed, and the light had returned to his eyes. Soon, he could hold down solid food, and it only took another couple of weeks for Penemiel to regain his playful ways and hefty appetite.

Around the time when he was regaining his strength and health, I realized that his curly black hair was now thin and reddish. Of concern were two things—he had a distended belly and everything he ate came out looking the same as when he had eaten without an attack by any intestinal bacteria.

I showed my husband a photo of an emaciated child about our son's age that I had found in a World Health Organization booklet. Our son looked like the child. We had almost lost our son once, and we weren't going to take our chances at losing him again. We took matters into our own hands. Up until now, the Hebrews had taken care of our medical situations internally and I had been satisfied with their results. We used natural healing methods and had no relationship with medical doctors. Penemiel's sickness illustrated to me that we were taking undue risks with our childrens' health. I asked one of the nurses at the Well-Baby Clinic for a referral, and they suggested Dr. Rosita Marshall, a well-respected Liberian pediatrician.

My earnings from the Red Cross went primarily into the communal financial pool. Those of us that worked outside the community received an allowance to take care of lunch money and taxi fare. Whenever our grocery money was short, rather then keep the sprout money, we integrated it into the daily grocery money. However, we realized that we needed money to take care of our son. When our children need things that were not part of the immediate budget, we had to make a request to the leadership. Sometimes we were given what we wanted, other times the request was held in the queue. This was one of the main reasons that members had to be resourceful and come up with ways to bring in money on their on. My husband took one of the thick gold chains that he wore around his neck into town and sold it to one of the Mandingo gold dealers to pay for our son's medical care. I remember dressing "Neemie," a nickname coined by his father, to go into town and see Dr. Marshall. I wanted him to look his best. He was naturally a handsome boy, but bouts of dysentery, malaria and measles had disseminated his little frame, and he looked like a cheerful old man. Guilt washed over me, followed by the shame of how I had allowed illness to ravage him.

Dr. Marshall had a comfortable office and a genial manner, but when she saw my son naked, I instantly felt her unspoken condemnation of me as a mother.

"Mrs. Rahm, you work for the Red Cross. Does your baby go to the clinic there?"

"No, not regularly. He mostly stays at home. Dr. Marshall, I just can't seem to keep him well."

She went about documenting his previous illnesses like the trained clinician she was.

"So, he has had multiple bouts of malaria and dysentery and is recovering from measles. You've been here since 1979?"

"Yes, and he is always putting things into his mouth, I thought he had gotten a hold of something when he had diarrhea or that the fever was from teething."

"I see. Surely he was vaccinated in America before he came to Liberia? You have to have the shot card filled out to get a travel visa."

"I know, but my husband and I didn't believe in vaccinations."

"*Both* of you didn't believe in vaccinations?" she inquired.

"I thought he was going to get immunity through my breast milk."

"And so you took the chance, Mrs. Rahm?"

I decided it was best to be honest and just say yes without any further explanation. Here I sat, a so-called "civilized" woman, responsible for the well-being of children whose parents entrusted them to my care, and I felt like a negligent mother to my own child.

Dr. Marshall agreed to work with Penemiel, but only if I would bring him to her office every day for two weeks while she monitored his condition.

"I'm going to put baby Rahm on a re-feeding program. His body has forgotten how to metabolize food while he's been sick."

I was relieved that she never used words like starvation and malnutrition, but it was clear to me that's what we were talking about. I shared the restrictions of our vegan diet, and while she was skeptical of the diet, she respected our food restrictions. She made sure I named our protein substitutes for meat, fish, eggs, and cheese.

"You will need to create a schedule and prepare snacks ahead of time. Your baby needs to eat something every two hours."

"A whole meal?"

"No, small snacks, a cracker with peanut butter, a piece of banana, he should have milk, at least twenty-four ounces a day."

"We don't use cow's milk, but I can make milk from bene seeds and ground peas with our blender."

"Okay, we'll see how that works. The idea is that he needs lots of protein in small amounts and lots of carbohydrates. See what you can do, and we'll see him daily for awhile." Without looking up she asked, "Does this time of day seem a good time for you?" I was relieved that she didn't lecture me and ashamed when I heard my voice crack.

"I'll manage it Dr. Marshall, I will."

"Don't worry too much Mrs. Rahm. Your son will be just fine, but you have to follow my instructions."

I cleared my throat. "Dr. Marshall, will his stomach ever go down?" I had to know if I he would be permanently disfigured.

"Yes, in time…in time," she responded in a tone that was reassuring. I stepped from her office feeling that my son had received a second chance.

Over the next four weeks, I followed Dr. Marshall's directions perfectly. I made enough whole-wheat crackers on Sunday for the entire week, then I spread them with freshly ground peanut butter from the market, or sometimes sesame tahini from the Lebanese grocery store. We had an electric blender and I made milk from raw peanuts, called ground peas, and crushed B12 tablets, adding a bit of white sugar for sweetening. I alternated mashed fresh butter pear, and bananas, or fed Penemiel oatmeal for breakfast. The re-feeding plan required that I give my son a couple of ounces of peanut milk every hour, and a wholesome snack every two hours after breakfast. Besides the food, I supplemented his diet with a daily dose of iron and a multivitamin. He got malaria medication weekly. Measles had nearly taken my little boy. Dr. Marshall had been clear that Penemiel needed an uninterrupted stretch of wellness to fully regain his health. I would see that he got it.

Because of the way that Dr. Marshall had worked with me to take care of Penemiel, I recommended her to our leadership on several occasions when we had pediatric problems beyond our paramedics. She became the first Liberian doctor that the Hebrew Israelite community entrusted to care for our children.

This experience was one of many awakenings I had in Liberia. I loved my children more than my own life, and the realization that I hadn't zeroed in on how quickly a baby can become gravely ill gave me an understanding, on a very personal level, of how Liberian women who work so damn hard to eke out a living, can unwittingly sacrifice the lives of their children.

When I first arrived in Liberia, I was judgmental, but this personal experience peeled away a thick layer of judgment.

Penemiel had a long road to full recovery. His distended belly haunted me until he was nearly five years old. Every time I reflect on the night when my spirit directed me to nurse my son as he lay near death, my eyes fill with tears. There is a saying that *God takes care of fools and children.*

On that night, I believe I hit a double.

PART II

LOVE AND PAIN IS LIKE
SUNSHINE AND RAIN
- FRANKIE BEVERLY

*Zefron in front of Sweet Africa, a
Hebrew business*

THE REAL WORK BEGINS

Only after I said yes to the dream of bettering the level of care at the Red Cross Day Care Center did I began to see how monumental the task was. In hindsight, I also realized that my very presence in Liberia, and the lessons that I would learn over the next decade, seemed to be a karmic debt foreshadowed by that reader in Hyde Park.

The day care center I inherited operated like other childcare centers in Monrovia. The Directress' role was to provide all instruction while the nursemaids fed the children and kept them clean. When the Directress was not working with a particular group of children, they were expected to sit in neatly arranged rows of wooden or hand-woven chairs and repetitively sing English nursery rhymes, songs that neither reflected nor affirmed the culture of the children that sang them. Of course, singing songs is a short-lived activity for small children who want to be moving. After ten minutes, the nursemaids were popping children with rattans. Change comes slowly. Even though I was working to make changes, I was working a half day and assumed that corporal punishment resumed as soon as my taxi pulled off Lynch Street.

Behind the kitchen was a musty storeroom, infested with cockroaches and boxes of brightly colored, imported, mostly broken toys. There were colorful Playschool trucks with no wheels; Fisher Price toys with no moving parts; Quaker oatmeal cans full of broken sets of Legos; and a full set of those "killer blocks." There were also haggard white dolls that truly baffled me.

I approached the situation delicately. "Aretha, why do we have all of these white dolls?"

"They chilren luff those dolls, Mistress Rahm."

"I hate them! Aretha, don't you know that doll makers have dolls that look like you and me? I cannot believe I am in Africa and all the dolls are white. I just can't believe this!" Speaking with such vehemence, I thought of R&B giant, James Brown's song, "Say It Loud, I'm Black and I'm Proud!"

Aretha smiled and said in her throaty voice, "Mistress Rahm, some of the parents brought those dolls. They will feel hurt if they don't see them or if the chilren say they have no dolls, it will not be good 'O!'"

The white dolls won a momentary victory, but I fully intended to integrate the doll collection so that little Liberian girls could see themselves as mothers of children that looked like them, and not as nursemaids for the children of foreigners. Fruitlessly, I scoured the Lebanese and Indian shops that sold toys at inflated prices, but I never found black dolls. I seethed with disdain for the white, ravaged dolls housed in the musty toy room. To me, they represented self-hatred, but at the same time, I knew that I had to respect the feelings of my students and their parents.

The culture of Liberia had been shaped by practices transported across the Atlantic Ocean by the Americo-Liberians, the freed men and returning ex-slaves. As they emerged from slavery and attempted to govern themselves and the native peoples of Liberia, they did so against the backdrop of mimicking social practices developed during their servitude in America. The unintended consequence was a culture that relegated native Liberians to second-class roles. However, with the coup, change was in the air and inclusion of the native peoples was going to be an ever-increasing reality.

I had a vision that the day care center was an opportunity for me to use some of those nationalist dreams I had brought with me from

America to encourage my native staff. I yearned to train them to work more effectively with the children, as well as how to repeat my pre-planned lesson plans in the childcare center with their own children and communities. No matter where we are, women tend to lift and support one another. We share knowledge, which, regardless of our culture seems to be what we were put on this earth to do. Equally, it might be why we are the culture bearers in the first place.

Having researched and published a brief essay in *Essence Magazine* in the early 70's, I was passionate about the importance of early childhood education. Training the nursemaids to become real caregivers, and to take responsibility for providing learning activities as co-teachers, was going to be a real task, but also very empowering for the women.

Every time I closed my eyes at night in the quiet, before I drifted off to sleep, I wondered whether I was enough for the task that I had chosen; wondered if I could create an atmosphere where the caregivers, the children's parents, and I could work together to provide learning opportunities for their children. Our resources were very limited, but I knew that the way to move the Center and the women forward was to tap into their national pride.

Most of the families that brought their children to the Red Cross Day Care Center were native people who had fought their way through a system that had discriminated against them to become Liberian civil servants. There was an atmosphere of hope in Liberia, and a sense of pride in being a Liberian, and I planned to use that fierce pride to carry us the distance.

About two months after I took over the childcare center, I met with my staff. My Liberian English was still mediocre, so Aretha stood by as my interpreter.

"I know that y'all are used to the Directress doing all the teaching, but I want to try something new. I want to train y'all to do the teaching."

I was met with nervous eyes that quickly looked down. I wasn't getting the response I wanted, and didn't know how to proceed.

Thankfully, Aretha saved me, excitedly saying, "Ain you hear da big ma? She say ourselves will be teaching the chilren?"

The blank looks changed to ones of disbelief, looks of *'Is she crazy?'*

"These are *your* children. It is important for them to have more attention, and currently I am the only one who can teach them. But I can make the plans and train *you* to teach these children, and then you can go home and teach the same things to your own children and to your friends' children."

"Mistress Rahm, we don't have education, we cannot be teachers," said Rebecca, the Ghanaian woman who was politely definitive in her logic.

"I hear it, but I will show you what to do. It will be hard, but not too hard, if you will just try, Rebecca."

Everyone smiled a broad smile, except Ma Mae. I knew she was the only one showing what she actually felt. *Thank God for her* I thought.

"Ma Mae, why are you twisting your face so, are you mad?" I asked.

"No, I'm not mad Mistress Rahm, but I *am not* a teacher, I will *not* be teaching 'O. They don't pay me for dat. If we had a lots of toys, the children would have more things to play with to keep them busy, but I myself, will not do it, I will not do it 'O!"

"Ma Mae, we can make toys from other things we have at home and can find in the market. I will talk to the Secretary General about getting new toys, but NOT everything can be imported. People are not traveling abroad freely yet." I felt my ship sinking. "Look, we can't base what we do in Liberia on toys coming from London or America; it will never work 'O!'" I took the opportunity to show the staff that I was truly trying to pick up Liberian English. "Children who are stupid cannot build this country," I said.

I hit a wall. Mae was the rose protected by thorns. I circled for reentry. "Ma Mae, I would not lie to you. YOU can teach these children. I am not lazy to teach the children!" I said, my frustration rising.

"But our money be the same 'O'?" Rebecca said, her voice rising at the end to let me know she thought my notion of working more for the same money was stupid.

"Yes, the money will be the same, but you will feel better about the time you spend here."

Aretha jumped in, attempting to help me persuade the women. "Myself, I get tired of chasing the children all day, and I don't have the heart to use the rattan. When I get home, I'm too tired to talk to my own l'il sweetie. I just want her to be quiet, have her tea and bread, take bath, and sleep."

Aretha's heavy voice carried from the front to the back of the daycare center.

I sensed that having Aretha on my side had been powerful. She was their leader, they trusted her. Except Mae, I saw their faces open up to possibility. I knew if Rebecca agreed her Ghanian friend Vivian would also agree. Aretha would lead the others and the fact that I had forbidden the use of rattans would either frustrate them further or make them hungry for tools to help control their young charges.

"Wouldn't it be good if one day I open my own school and Aretha takes Red Cross over as Directress?" I said.

I had planted a seed that I thought no one noticed or if they did, they didn't feel it was possible for them. I stood there indignant waiting for someone to respond. There was only silence.

I returned to my office. I heard the children waking from naptime, closed my office door, and stood looking outside to the yard below. I was angry, frustrated. I knew that I could teach the women skills they didn't have, if only they gave me a chance. I distracted myself by watching a group of men sitting in the yard next door eating their lunch and laughing.

"Mistress Rahm." Startled by Aretha's voice I spun around.

"Yes."

"They will do it 'O'.

She smiled and quietly walked away.

The women that worked for me were all intelligent, most spoke *at least* three dialects, and all were decent workers, some better than others. I had already defied logic by selecting Ma Mae Printer, the eldest and most intractable, to care for my daughter. Mae was a tiny woman. Soaking wet, she didn't weigh 100 pounds. When she wasn't scowling, she had a huge grin and perfect white teeth. Her skin was taut and leathery, and I guessed she was between fifty and fifty-five years old. Mae had infinite patience with babies, was meticulous in keeping her tiny charges clean, and boasted that the children she cared for never, ever developed diaper rashes. On the flip side, she displayed marked impatience with the older children. She liked control, but the problem is toddlers can't be controlled. Ma Mae's biggest shortcoming was that she liked the status quo. She was argumentative and stubborn and resisted learning her new duties. She had developed the habit of smiling in my face while I was talking to her, but when I would glance back over my shoulder as I walked away, I could hear her cuss me under her breath. Two-faced. I reflected upon the mentality bred by a lifetime of feeling like a second-class citizen in one's own country, and understood why she resented me, and realized that I had to bear and overcome it.

I observed that every day during the children's naptime, when the nursemaids ate together and regrouped, Mae always left the Center in a rush. When I asked why she always left, the other women gave me the run around, but when I persisted, Aretha said that Mae left to feed her grandson. I probed more deeply into the matter and learned that Christian, nicknamed CeCe, was nearly two years old and was left home alone in Mae's room. At lunch, Mae walked half a mile to check on him and feed him. It broke my heart to learn that all day Mae was taking care of other women's children while her own grandchild was alone in a locked room with things that could harm him.

When I asked why Mae just didn't bring the boy to work with her, my staff told me it was against the Liberian Red Cross policy. The Secretary General felt that if the nurses brought their own babies, they wouldn't take proper care of the children left in their care. Again, I drew a parallel between slaves in America leaving their babies alone to work in the fields or go to the big house to nurse and care for Massa's children.

I brooded over the situation for a while, trying to balance whether I should address it or leave it be. I wrestled with how Mae, who was paid $100 a month, could possibly afford to pay for childcare. Frankly, Mae wasn't my favorite person and I knew that even though I would be sticking my neck out to help her, she would still be mean and hard to deal with. When I finally called her in to discuss her grandson's situation, she confided that her daughter, Cece's mother, couldn't care for him. Mae told me that when CeCe was just a baby, she'd gone to visit her daughter who lived with her boyfriend, and she found the baby burning up with fever, covered in sores, and sickly. She had begged the girl to let her take CeCe, and she nursed him back to health. I remembered meeting her daughter once when she had come to the Center looking for Mae. She only spoke Gbassa, but when I looked in her face and watched her move, it seemed that she had a developmental delay, which accounted for CeCe's neglect. CeCe made Mae smile, and that alone meant he had special powers. In her life, there was CeCe, church, and work, in that order.

I respected Mae's lunchtime departure. The other staff members were a bit peeved about my wanting to help Mae. She gave everybody a hard time, and she was the only one who still refused to cooperate with the program I created for them to assist in presenting lesson plans. Mae's situation was unique, and while I understood that making a change would set a precedent, a change needed to be made.

Aretha and I discussed and agreed that Mae should bring CeCe to work, but that she couldn't be the one to take care of him. Rebecca reluctantly agreed to help.

"Mistress Rahm, I am doing this for you, not for Mae."

"I understand and thank you 'O,' Rebecca."

It didn't take long for the Secretary General to notice Mae arriving with CeCe and called me into her office to discuss it. She was very displeased that I had allowed Mae to break the rules, and candidly told me that I had placed my employment on the line. I swallowed her scalding criticism and told her we had worked it out between ourselves, and that as the Director, I had a right to use my discretion in matters involving my staff. Unaccustomed to having her authority questioned, she puffed up like a blowfish but didn't say anything more about the arrangement.

Slowly, I began to feel that I was making a dent in the wall that stood between my Liberian workers and me. Each weekday morning, I hopped into a taxi with my baby, baby bag and lesson plan books in hand. I would work all day, and then at night, after the kids went to sleep, I would sit up creating more lesson plans. In the very early days when I could barely communicate with my workers, my only incentive to keep going was a promise that if I could get through the morning, I would give myself permission to put my head on my desk and cry when the children were put down for nap. In the beginning, I did this almost every day, but eventually, I earned Aretha's loyalty and then surprisingly, Ma Mae's.

Aretha and Mae were powerful, each in her own way. Whenever I wanted to try something new I'd run it past Aretha. Whenever I wanted to know what was wrong with anything, I would ask Mae.

When I could get them both to agree on anything, I knew we were golden.

Getting the bathrooms cleaned properly was yet another mountain. The Center had a modern ceramic tiled bathroom that housed four stalls and two face bowls. The problem was simple but unanticipated. The staff didn't have indoor toilets in their own living quarters, so there wasn't much sensitivity or skill around sanitizing a bathroom. Because I was part-time, I rarely used the bathroom in the Center, but on one particular day, I did. I happened to see brown streaks on the wall, and upon closer examination, found that the streaks were feces. I sent for Boima, the newly hired janitor, who immediately cleaned the streaks with a rag and Pine Sol. As I began to question him, I lifted a toilet seat, discovered dried urine, and splashed feces.

I gave strict instructions to Boima to clean under the toilet seat, and he said he understood. However, the next day when I checked to see if Boima had cleaned the bathroom, I lifted the toilet seat, and it was as disgusting as ever. I knew that he had understood what I wanted and took my case to Aretha.

"Aretha," I said gestured to the unsightliness, "Look under this toilet seat. Boima has not cleaned under it, even after I spoke to him about it."

"I will talk to him, Mistress Rahm. He will clean it."

Aretha went to find Boima, and a few minutes later, I knew she had talked to him when I heard him talking non-stop and slamming doors. Out of the corner of my eye, I could see Aretha following him and saying something that I couldn't make out.

"Hey yah, the big ma said…" and I realized she was trying to convince Boima to do the work he had been directed to do.

The conversation went on for quite awhile, and as I sat there, I became angry. Walking briskly to the front of the Center, the voices lowered when the caregivers saw me approaching. Everybody resumed their activities with the children.

"What's happening?"

With a sheepish smile, Aretha said, "Mistress Rahm, I was just telling Boima what you said about the toilet, but he is vexed 'O'."

Turning to Boima, I pointedly asked, "Vexed for what, Boima? Come to my office. You too, Aretha."

Once inside the office, I sat behind my small desk looking up at Boima and Aretha standing shoulder-to-shoulder in front of me.

"Sit down please. Boima, you are the janitor and you get paid to keep the *whole* Center clean. What is the problem with you cleaning the bathroom?"

"I can't clean poo poo 'O.' I can mop the floors and clean the walls and the sinks, and I wipe down the seats, but you don't pay me to clean poo poo."

I wondered why Aretha had a smirk on her face, but I would soon learn.

"Aretha, you told Boima to clean the bathroom? Did you show him exactly what I wanted him to do?

"Yes, Mistress Rahm."

"Boima, explain to me why you can't clean under the toilet seats. It doesn't make sense to have the top of the seat clean, while under the seat is still dirty. You are a man. You know that a man lifts the seat to go to the bathroom. The girls sit on the seat, but the little boys will touch that filthy seat with their hands."

"Mistress Rahm, I man, but *I'm not used to it. I don't clean other people's toilet.*"

"Boima, you are not changing diapers, but if a child gets sick in the bathroom, and you are here, I expect you to clean up the toilet. I pay you to keep the toilets clean, on top, under the seat, and inside the bowl. I'm not asking you to put your hand in the toilet. We have rubber gloves."

"Mistress Rahm," Aretha began. "I gave him the gloves and he threw them on the floor, I gave him the brush for the toilet and he said he not doing it!"

I remembered an old saying, "You can't teach what you don't know and you can't lead where you won't go." I knew what I had to do.

Several days later, I showed up for work wearing baggie orange dance pants and a loose tunic top instead of the fitted African lappa suits I typically wore. I brought a market bag holding new containers of cleansers, a scrub brush, a brand new toilet brush, sponges, and a couple of pairs of yellow rubber gloves. I was also armed with a serious attitude.

On the way into the bathroom, I told Aretha, "Let the nurses in the Well-Baby Clinic know that we'll need to use their bathroom for a few hours while ours is being cleaned."

Then, I closed the bathroom door with instructions that no one was to enter. Throwing open the bathroom window, I let the sunlight bounce off the ceramic tiled walls and let the breeze flow through. I hummed to myself as I cleaned every reachable square inch. When I was satisfied that I had cleaned the bathroom beyond my personal standards, I christened the clean space by freshening up in the sink and changing into my business attire.

When I exited, Aretha was waiting, trying to read my face.

The next day, Aretha cleaned the bathroom. The day after, she informed me that Boima had taken over cleaning the bathroom, even under the toilet seats and inside the toilet bowls. He finally understood that if he didn't clean the bathroom the way we wanted him to, I was going to fire him. I was glad that he heard that from Aretha, and not me.

That was a good day; a day when I sat near my office window, looked into the sunshine on Lynch Street and was glad to be in Liberia.

Ahnydah with Red Cross visitors

BRICKS WITHOUT STRAW

My workday slowly began to get longer and longer. After complaints reached the Secretary General about the behavior of the caregivers when I wasn't around, she began making afternoon spot checks and reported seeing the caregivers laughing and talking among themselves instead of being attentive to the children. In response, I began to stagger my schedule, coming early on some days and late on others, but I finally realized that in order to manage effectively, I needed to be there at least six hours each day.

I began putting in more time at the daycare, while trying to balance caring for my own four kids, a husband, as well as my responsibilities on the Hebrew compound. I rose at 5:00 a.m. to wash diapers or get my ironing done. By 6:00 a.m., I was in our communal kitchen preparing breakfast for all the children in the house. If it was my day to prepare dinner, I was also prepping the evening meal. I was awake twenty hours a day, running on fumes.

My first few years in Liberia I found I often felt bruised by the feeling of being an outsider, something I had not intended to feel in Africa. Yet my dreams for the day care center kept me excitedly coming to work every day. The challenge of making an impact on the women I worked with and having them make an impact on the children in the Center became so important to me. It satisfied a need to earn my space on this earth. Our community was developing a number of business and farming enterprises in Liberia and I felt my work with the Red Cross was my contribution to that work.

I always felt that Anna Cooper, the Red Cross' Secretary General at the time, and I had a complex relationship. When we met, I had not only liked her, but also secretly admired her. In my eyes, she was a classy woman with a friendly face and polished manners. As an Americo-Liberian, Anna was a member of a social class that accorded her an elevated status. As an African-American, I was fleeing a system that devalued my self-worth. From her vantage point, I was a foreigner, unfamiliar with the ways of Liberia, and I felt that I was "coming home." With respect to my optimism that I could train my staff to provide instruction to their young charges, she felt I had inflated notions of the capacity of my staff. There was an undercurrent of unspoken friction between us.

At the same time I can admit that during those initial years I was tactless and driven to the point of seeming ruthless. Once I had set my mind on a goal, I steamrollered ahead, a trait that sometimes proved to be my undoing.

For as much progress as I had made, there was still a long way to go if I was going to be successful in getting my staff to do more than just babysit. My long-term goal was working myself out of a job, but the success of my plans depended upon my staff being able to replicate the lessons. Clearly, we were nowhere near attaining that goal any time soon. We didn't have a typewriter most of the time, so I carefully hand printed lesson books. Each book listed the materials needed, the concept to be taught, and a step-by-step description of how to proceed. I carefully choreographed every step, down to the minute detail that I wanted the teacher to smile at the children, regardless to the answer given when a lesson was underway so that the children would always feel encouraged to try. I planned two structured learning times per day, once in the morning between 10:00 and 11:30 a.m., and again in the afternoon after naptime.

In the age of computers, it's hard to imagine handwritten lesson sheets, yet that's exactly what I did. I wrote in a carbon notebook so that I could keep a record of each lesson as well as be able to tear the sheets out for each caregiver to use without having to have the entire book. The popular lessons I rewrote many times. I created scores of lessons for counting, teaching colors, shapes, and sorting skills, citizenship, art, and table manners. We created our own book of Liberian songs we enjoyed, and we made up songs for the children. I created the lesson plans, and Aretha and I each tested them. If a lesson seemed too hard for either the caregiver or the children, I modified it. All the lesson plans were filed in my office on a bookcase.

Whenever I found time in the afternoon to shop, I'd visit one of the Lebanese stores that sold imported coloring books, and after buying several, I'd spend the remainder of the afternoon carefully tracing the figures, as many as ten or fifteen at a time. It was actually easier to do that than to find a working mimeograph or copy machine. Occasionally, one of our parents would take coloring sheets to work and sneak photocopies for us. Art had always been my worst subject, but in order give the children coloring book pages, I spent considerable time improving my sketching skills.

Toys imported by the Lebanese merchants were marked up as much as six times what they cost in America. In 1982, a small Fisher Price truck that might have cost between seven and eight dollars in Chicago, would cost forty dollars in Liberia. To keep the Center's tuition low, it was impractical to purchase imported toys. Then, we received a Godsend. The Hebrews Israelites were holding a Sisterhood conference in Atlanta, and a Sister and I received airline tickets to represent the Sisterhood in Liberia. I arranged for the Red Cross to give me two hundred U.S dollars to purchase toys for the Center, and made lists of toys that I wanted to purchase. The trip was just what I needed. I had left America abruptly, and was elated to be with my family again, and thrilled to show Zevah off and share photos of my other children and our home. I thought it was important to share my life in Africa with my family still in America. That trip served so many purposes, among them, I truly believe it made my mother feel that we were safe and appeased some of her fears. It was the perfect trip.

However, our re-entry into Liberia made the plot thicken once again.

After our thirteen-hour return flight, our plane finally landed at Roberts Field and it was only then that I realized I should have requested someone from the Red Cross to meet me. After getting someone to handle my bags we got in line to go through Customs. I handed the man our passports, my Visa, and the letter I carried from the Red Cross saying that I was bringing toys for the Red Cross Child Care Center.

"Ma, open the big bag yah." I opened the bag filled with Fisher Price, Romper Room Toys, brown dolls, tea sets, and Lego toys. It was a carefully chosen assortment that I hoped would help make our child care center a much more interesting place to play. Slowly, customs officials encircled me and I knew something wasn't right. With fear quickly overwhelming me, I tried to explain the toys to the officer. "These toys are for children in the day care. Please don't take any of them."

I realized in my preoccupation with selecting and transporting the toys I had not addressed the practice of workers at the airport or seaport extracting a bribe of money or merchandise to admit products into the country. It's called 'cold water' or a 'dash.' Now I was in trouble. I had no official escort and I had no extra money.

"Hey yah, leave the Big Ma my people, you got cold water, go now and close the woman's bag!"

I was relieved that someone had the authority to end the toy assault. My bags cleared, and shortly thereafter, they were loaded inside a taxi.

When I reported to work on Monday, I presented the receipts totaling a little over $200 but after inventory, I had lost about a third of my toys in "cold water."

I focused my attention on staff training, as well as building a relationship with each of my employees. I needed to earn their loyalty, and in order to do that, I needed to find out who they where and what they wanted.

Mae wanted to raise CeCe and live to see him finish college. Viv, who like Rebecca came from Ghana, was quiet, almost withdrawn, except when it came to children. She wanted to get married and remain in Liberia. Markel was Gbassa and had a quiet affable exterior, making it seem as though nothing ever rattled her. She was the kind of person who would take and take and take, and when she got angry, she would slap her ample hips and strut. With a high school diploma, she was the most educated of all of my caregivers. Marta was our Gio 'mommie pepper,'—pepper, because she had a temper hot as African pepper. She was quick to anger and slow to cool. Marta was raising her sister's children and would do anything for them. They attended a government school, and instead of going home to wait for her, they came to the day care center after school and waited. We always kept lunch for them, and I often looked over their homework.

Aretha was the most ambitious and my communication gateway. She was smart, resourceful and generous, as well as exceptionally raw and opinionated. I recognized that she was a natural leader with her high self-esteem and standards. She always wanted the very best of everything, and her vision for herself and her family was large—she hoped her daughter, 'Sweetie,' would be educated in America, and I knew she would do everything in her power to make that happen.

In time, I sensed that my staff had been discussing my approach to running the Center amongst themselves, and had finally started to see value in their new roles as teachers. From time to time, someone would remark, "Mistress Ahnydah, the children behaving better now," or express delight in feeling that their contact with the children was positive and less stressful. Aretha had begun to brag about their training to her friends.

I noticed that the market women and parents visiting the Well-Baby Clinic watched my staff in action, teaching children to learn to distinguish between same and different pairs of buttons, or to count with broken chess set pieces. They would roll around in cartons filled with packing peanuts and learn to dress themselves by putting paper clothes on large brown paper dolls created by the staff in a Paper Doll-Making Contest.

Things were going well, and one thing I know about myself is that as soon as things start becoming easy, I seek another challenge. I thought that if I could be successful training my nursemaids to become teachers in the Red Cross Day Care Center in Liberia, I could become instrumental in bringing our concept to other Centers in Monrovia. It didn't make sense to waste women's skills, who were creative and smart, and relegate them to roles of diaper changers and nose wipers in a country that needed to move forward and educate its population.

I began meeting with other day care center directors to become familiar with their programs, and finally collaborated with another daycare director in Sinkor to co-train our employees. Deb ran an upscale center where the parents paid twenty-five dollars more in tuition than at the Red Cross center. When I met with her, she was very excited about the learning exchange, and we decided to collaborate our knowledge and effort in order to provide a training session for our respective staffs.

Initially we convened the workshop at the Red Cross Day Care Center, and to ensure that both our centers had staff, I sent my staff to her center to cover for her staff that morning. It was an 'out of the box idea' that I don't think anyone had ever tried before. After receiving our students from their parents in the morning, my staff took taxi's over to Debbie's Day Care Center, while Deb's staff arrived at our center.

The workshop was from 8:00 a.m. to noon, and the staffers returned to their own daycare centers during the children's naptime so that the parents were not wise to the staff swap.

My staff returned very excited, and upon comparison, said they liked several aspects of Deb's program and were excited about the fact that Deb's staff earned more money and had more toys imported from America. However, when it came to comparing the work that they were doing, they expressed pride in their critical role in teaching.

As a result of the increased training, my enrollment quickly rose to a record 100 kids with only five caregivers. Aretha was forced to wear multiple hats as supervisor, caregiver and cook. Despite the fact that our administration wanted us to take all children who applied, they refused to hire additional caregivers or even replace our janitor, who had quit. My staff was mopping the floors, pulling the garbage, and cleaning the bathrooms. Aretha, always the quick thinker, found Andrew, a Krahn boy, who was willing to work as our janitor in exchange for food.

Andrew was a likeable boy who always wore a smile on his face, and even better, he actually knew *how* to clean! Every day after he left high school, he came straight to us and scrubbed the Center floors and bathrooms until they were spotless. In addition to helping in the day care center, he served everyone in headquarters. Whenever he saw the van carrying the Secretary General or the President of the Red Cross pull into our driveway, he raced downstairs and grabbed their briefcase and packages. When the drivers with supplies entered the gates, he was there to help unload. Soon, everyone knew and liked Drew. After he was with us for about ninety days, the Secretary General allowed us to pay Drew fifty dollars a month.

He was wonderful with children, and when our overworked staff redressed the children after naptime, he helped by changing the little boys' clothing. Even with Andrew's help as cleaner and assistant caregiver, the child to caregiver ratio was much too large. From the staff's perspective, they had additional children and the added burden of me requiring that they continue to follow the daily lesson plans. I was desperate for a solution.

I have come to believe that the spawn of desperation is genius! I woke up one morning with an idea of where I could look for volunteer teachers. I took a taxi over to the University of Liberia and visited the social science department to see if I could get students to come into the Center and offer their services and help. I met with a professor who suggested that he send students to help me each semester, Monday through Friday, if I could plan a student teaching module for them, and give them an assessment that would be a component of their final grade. His idea was a Godsend. I was ready for the first group of five student interns in two weeks.

My orientation for the University of Liberia interns incorporated my vision of providing the native caregivers with skills they could use in the childcare centers, as well as within their own families, resulting in raising the level of education and childcare in the country. I explained my training methods for my staff and showed them my handwritten lesson books. I hoped I could capture them with their own idealism, and I won! The students became my enthusiastic partners. We staggered their arrival times so that some arrived in the morning, and some in the early afternoon to work along with the staff and children.

In addition to helping decrease the student to caregiver ratio, the University of Liberia interns were tasked to create a group project that would benefit our childcare center. At the end of each semester, each intern was to write a short reflective paper designed to capture their experiences and offer us ideas for improvement. Because their end of the semester project was their last chance to positively affect their grades, they competed to outdo one another. Our university interns were creative and spared no expense in time or money to make a valuable contribution.

Just recently, a colleague introduced me to the concept of Asset Based Community Development. The term wasn't familiar to me, and when I requested a definition, I was told that it meant, "Looking at the community as being full of assets and engaging work in that community by leveraging its assets rather than looking at deficiencies."

I could only smile.

Ahnydah and visitors to the Liberian Red Cross

SEE THE WOMAN BORNING 'O!'

Borning is the Liberian local term for giving birth."

My youngest son, Zefron, was delivered on the balcony of the Peace Villa in the enclave called "Old Road." My labor with him was by far the most peaceful and spirit-driven of my five deliveries, even though at the very end, his birthday became somewhat of a spectacle.

By 1981, there were a little more than 100 Hebrew Israelite men, women and children. We were posed with the problem of setting up a school that would educate not only our children, but also Liberian children. We leased a space in Kakata that had once been a rubber plantation. There were at least ten acres of land on which to build a school and a compound for our Community, and offered the opportunity to educate Liberian children who had no school in the area. My children, along with the other school-aged children, were sent to live in Kakata on what we called the kifar, a Hebrew word for village, while about thirty-five of us lived in a huge two-story, seven-bedroom home we named the Peace Villa.

The children who lived in Kakata on our kifar visited their parents in Monrovia from the Sabbath on Friday evening until Sunday afternoon. Other times, the parents traveled from Monrovia to Kakata. My husband was in Ghana working on the mission we had there, but ordinarily he was responsible for transportation and shopping for the Kakata group. In Kakata, the sisters cared for our children and made sure they boarded the truck to visit Monrovia. Even so, the closer I got to my delivery date, the more I sulked over the feeling of isolation from my family. Now that I had taken my two-month maternity leave, and entrusted the day care center to Aretha hands I was bored and testy.

Several weeks earlier, two of the Hebrew sisters, returning from shopping, had busted into the Villa, bubbling over with the news that Margaret, our washman's wife, had delivered her child by herself! They had passed her pregnant en route to town, and returned to find her preparing dinner with a baby in the crook of her arm.

May 16, 1982 had been a bright morning, six months into rainy season. It had rained earlier, but by 10:00 a.m., when I rose to eat my breakfast of parboiled rice, pepper, and palm oil, the sun was blazing hot and the road was drying up leaving behind small puddles in the gullies where the rain had not fully drained back into the red earth. I showered and dressed in my favorite red-white-and-blue cotton African gown. It was loose, comfortable, and despite my forty-pound weight gain, I felt attractive in the outfit. Throughout my pregnancy, I had worn my hair parted down the middle and braided in two thick cornrow braids, anchored in back with an elastic band. I remember plucking a red hibiscus flower from the bush in the front yard and securing its stem in the braid above my left ear. For the past few days, I had awakened with that burst of energy that always made me feel "light" and ready for childbirth. Our clothes were clean, the bedroom and bathroom floors had been "on hands-and-knees" scrubbed, curtains washed and re-hung, and all the new baby's possessions arranged neatly in a special wicker basket.

By mid-afternoon, I had the inkling of early labor, and yet I managed to go about my daily routine without anyone detecting my discomfort. I knew, though, that my time of being unconfined was running out. When I finally acknowledged the harder contractions, I quietly escaped into my bedroom and reclined on my wicker chaise, breathing through contractions for another forty-five minutes.

As dusk settled over the Old Road, I looked out from my bedroom window locking a gaze on the Fan trees and the clotheslines in our backyard. I wondered how my husband was. He had always been with me for our children's' deliveries, and I had come to rely on the comforting sound of his voice to pull me through the hard contractions. I remembered the pressure of his hands massaging my lower back and I began to cry. I hoped his spirit was with our soon-to-be-born child and me. Even though we had drifted apart, I knew that he still cared for me. I felt he was disappointed in me. I didn't feel that I fit into the Hebrew way of life, and I probably never would, but I did my best at giving the appearance of conformity. My dream was always about Africa, never Israel.

The bulb in my reading lamp had blown, so I decided to take one last stroll down the dusty road to the small shop for an icy cold orange Fanta and light bulb so that I could read during the coming nights when I knew I would be up with a crying baby. My contractions were now twenty to twenty-five minutes apart. Walking would increase pressure on my cervix, helping it to open and causing a speedier labor. This being my fourth child, I felt that I could gauge how much time I had to "walk about."

Thirsty and craving a sugary Fanta, I made my way down the back steps of the Villa, and down the dark winding road. Stopping at intervals, I breathed through several contractions and was alternately feverish and chilly. A couple of times, after an especially robust contraction, I looked wistfully back at the Villa. I could have turned back, but I was enticed to keep walking by a slight breeze that caressed my face like a feather. Long and preferably solitary walks have always been my way of finding my center, and had become an evening ritual.

When I reached the small shop, a zinc shack with a wide service opening, two Liberians that I knew from the area sat there. One smirked and commented to his friend, "That belly will soon come 'O'." I smiled and secretly rode a couple of contractions with the skill of a rodeo buckaroo while paying for my order at the service window. Slowly, I lowered my body onto a small, metal, kitchen-style chair with worn green padding at about the same time the owner brought my Fanta and laid the light bulb beside it. I thirstily took several swigs from the icy bottle before realizing that it was nauseatingly sweet. I clutched my light bulb and began to make what now seemed an impossible trek home. My contractions came faster, and I had a transitory fear that I *could* actually deliver my baby on the road in the dark.

The pressure on my cervix was incredible, and I was sure all my organs were fighting to burst through my vagina. I leaned against the wrought iron fence of a house, gasping on the side of the road, still about three city blocks from my destination. Mercifully, the pressure subsided as I coached myself to breathe in through the nose, one-two-three- four, out through the mouth, one-two-three and moved forward. It took me nearly twenty minutes to go a distance that normally was a five-minute walk. The nearer I got to the Peace Villa, the more I worked to maintain a nice even gait. As I finally entered the house, I nearly bumped into my friend Ben who was obviously getting ready to leave.

He must have discerned something out of the ordinary because he looked at me and asked, "Are you *alright,* Sis?"

I wanted to shout, *"Hell no!"* but instead, I said I was fine, and held my belly up as I climbed the stairs. Quickly opening my bedroom door, I scurried to release my last meal in the face bowl. In my experience, when it gets to this point, I know it is my body's signal that, "It's about to be on!"

I rinsed the sink with cold water and sat on the throne. It was then that I noticed the sensation of passing a reddish pink clot of blood and mucous, called the mucous plug, another signal that my cervical opening had further widened. Getting up, I removed the lampshade and screwed my light bulb into its socket.

I'd said nothing to my midwife, Sheryrah, who was in our kitchen with four other women cooking happily for a beach party the following day. As I approached, I could easily distinguish her from the others because of the sterling silver bracelets that clinked at the slightest movement of her arms. I managed to smile and wave at them before moving on. I sensed that they were probably talking about me and saying how heavy I looked.

Opening the sliding glass doors, I sat in one of four comfortable leatherette chairs. The large balcony overlooked a valley of one and two room zinc shacks, a few outhouses, and several brick homes of modest structure. The Peace Villa, rented from a wealthy Liberian executive, was the biggest and grandest home on our road. I loved sitting on its balcony and gazing at life from this vantage point. There I sat, in hard labor, on a warm night, enjoying a magnificent evening breeze while peering up at a thick black sky populated with twinkling stars. I was a co-creator!

Determined to have my space *and* a peaceful delivery, I closed the glass doors between the balcony and the dining area where several of our brothers sat, enjoying their evening meal after their return from selling incense, our specially formulated hair dressing, and other items in town. Reveling in the seclusion, I was safe and ready to fulfill my cosmic duty. It was now the responsibility of the Universe to take care of us. My contractions were now less than five minutes apart.

Labor is an inexplicable sensation. While focused on the rhythmic contractions, I became aware of the gentle roar of the ocean less than a mile away, and realized that my contractions were controlled by the ebb and flow of the waves splashing against the shore. I relaxed now, confident that my labor was in God's hands. I went limp in the low tide, knowing that the crest of each wave would accelerate the progress of my labor. With contractions about four minutes apart, I was aware of intensifying discomfort, yet during and after each contraction, I was at peace. The wind caressed my face and the stars winked in approval.

A Liberian sister that had recently joined our group walked onto the balcony, and because of an irritating urge, I requested a bucket into which I immediately threw up the rest of lunch. She went into the kitchen and shared her suspicions, and my midwife pounced immediately. She insisted that I retire to my room, but I held my ground, protesting that I was fine. Yes, I was in light labor, but it was nothing serious. After three natural childbirths, wouldn't I know?

Despite my discomfort, an incredible feeling of 'oneness with God,' came over me. I didn't want to exchange that for the confinement of our tiny bedroom and the uproar that my delivery would cause in our household. Ironically, Sheryrah was also pregnant. Her husband, Kwesi, was in the U.S. and she harbored many of the same anguished feelings that plagued me. The last thing I wanted was another out-of-sync woman delivering my baby. I had wanted our close friend Khahil, a registered nurse, to deliver me, but he was happy on our mission's administrative staff and adamant about his retirement from midwifery. In hindsight, I know I equated his presence with having my husband's support. Khahil and I were buds. He could always get me past my dark moods. However, since he didn't want to deliver me, I *was* capable of delivering my baby alone!

When the contractions were two minutes apart, I was struggling to keep inhaling through my nose and exhaling through my mouth, while making a valiant effort to keep my lower jaw loose. Midwives caution that during labor, when you clinch your jaw, you actually tighten your uterus, and are fighting the contractions. Whether it was truth or myth, I didn't want to thwart the process now.

I looked out over the balcony and below me. Zinc houses hold heat like ovens. The house directly across the road held a porch full of Gbassa women and men. Folks congregated outside to catch the evening breeze. The air was full of the pleasant murmur of Liberian English punctuated with native phrases. For a moment, I was concerned that the sound of their banter would distract me. However, I found that the steady hum of their voices anchored me somewhere between the earth and the stars, a reminder that I was still of this world.

One contraction ended and another immediately began! I found myself scooting down in the chair. I couldn't sit. I couldn't stand. It was just breathing and riding, no resting. Oblivious to being watched from inside the house, the glass door slid open, and at that instant, I felt the excruciating pressure accompanied by an uncontrollable urge to push. In split-second, dual images flashed across my mind. One was of the washman's wife delivering her baby in the dirt—something I had no intention of doing. The floors of our porch were granite, and newborns, with their accompanying fluids, are slippery. *What if my baby's head struck the floor?* My second concern was that I still had my panties on!

The incredible stretching between my legs signaled that my baby's head was close to crowning. It was going to be born on the Peace Villa balcony under the stars! The roar of the ocean's next wave brought it forth, and my midwife, up to her arms in whole-wheat flour, was caught off guard. She quickly sized up the situation and hollered over the balcony to Khahil who fortunately had just pulled the Benz into the driveway.

He bolted up the stairs, just in time to help me recline in the chair and deliver my son to the wild cheers of my very perceptive Gbassa neighbors.

"She borning 'O,' see the woman borning 'O'!"

I felt comfort from the deafening roar of the ocean, and the sound of Khahil's voice, who exasperatedly asked, "Ahnydah, didn't I tell you I was *not* going to deliver this baby?"

Yes, he had said that.

I gave him a grateful smile.

Zevah and Penemiel

WELL WATER AND PRAYERS

Not long after Zefron's birth, I moved with the rest of my family and joined the majority of the membership of the Hebrew Israelite Community in the kifar in Kakata. The scenery was majestic—I loved the cascading colors of green, the smell of the fresh air, and walking through the bush. Kakata held all the physical romance and beauty of Africa and the very concrete challenges of caring for our families without modern conveniences, while struggling to be economically and intellectually productive. I understood that my struggles placed me on par with women in developing countries around the globe. Living on the kifar gave me an opportunity to understand Liberia from a rural perspective. It is easy to judge mothers in the interior that lose their children to illness and chalk it up to ignorance but the burden of the lack of resources helped me understand the parable "she who feels it, knows it."

Now I sat on the floor with a large zinc bucket between my thighs, my arms embracing its nearly seven gallons of water. Inside the bucket rested the body of my twenty-month-old son. The moon's light streamed in through open wooden shutters, landing on the wet straw matting cushioning the gritty concrete floor. He was asleep now but his skin was clammy. I placed my hand upon his heart. Was it still beating? The water rose several inches above his waist. The fever seemed under control now, finally allowing his small body to rest and grow stronger while it continued to abate. And so, I sat guarding my baby, I dozed off and jerked myself awake at intervals to baste him with cool water and to stroke his soft wooly hair, while I waited for his father's return with the chloroquine.

My baby had convulsed today! Remembering the image of his tiny body jerking, as if electrified, and the terror I saw in the liquid brown eyes, caused my guts to tighten again. I had been so damn busy working around the compound, trying to cram a week's worth of chores into a weekend, that I hadn't noticed him dragging, but Zefron, the youngest of my four children, was chubby and lazy and always needed a good reason to move about. Quick to smile and curious to boot, I was intrigued at how he quietly observed insects before attempting to pick them up as if he was weighing whether their secrets were worthy of his interest.

Zefron had been such an easy baby. His delivery, while controversial, had been uncomplicated and beautiful. He cried and became a handful only when he wanted to nurse, and afterward, he was usually content. My practice was to nurse my children past their first birthday and then allow them to wean themselves. The first few times Zefron had refused my breast milk, I remember feeling rejected, which instantly turned to betrayal upon learning that his father had been slipping him ground pea milk laced with brown sugar between nursings. Nursing my son had been a welcome comfort at the end of the day, and yet I realized it was time to wean him because I woke up every morning exhausted from nursing-on-demand during the night. Still, he was my baby—I hoped my last baby—especially since breastfeeding and Rhythm, the idea of having sex only if when I wasn't ovulating were my only methods of birth control.

Early on a Sunday morning I had awakened before sunrise, dressed, and began to clean up the room around my sleeping husband and son. The kitchen was about three city blocks away on the opposite side of a large grassy field across the compound. It was my cook day. When I entered the open-air kitchen, there were already other sisters helping to prepare the childrens' breakfast. Once breakfast was served, we would begin prepping the rice, greens, and beans for dinner.

As soon as breakfast was finished, I rushed back to my room to pick up my washing supplies. Afterwards, I walked down the hill with my large bucket, wooden scrub board, washtubs, and three cakes of wash soap before returning to separate and carry my first loads of clothes to the stream to draw wash water. I had clothes for a family of six to wash and was relieved not to have Zefron underfoot. I hoped he would sleep for a while and then Binah, his big sister, would dress him and take him to play with his siblings until I finished. My spirits were lifted as I anticipated having time to play with Zefron later. I loved the way he looked up at me with those enormous brown eyes.

By late Sunday afternoon, I had almost finished my wash. When I entered my room, Zefron was drenched in sweat. I bent over to touch him and his skin was burning. He was completely listless and probably couldn't have cried out for me even if he'd wanted to. I cradled him tenderly, reaching for a cup to draw water from the covered water bucket in our room. When the cool cup touched his lips, he flinched and then drained the cup thirstily.

Damn it! Malaria managed to sneak up on me again! I thought bitterly.

I refilled the cup and he drained it again. When he twitched a little, I dismissed it as the chills that typically accompany malaria.

I sat with him on the cloth-covered mattress, pulled back the curtains, and called outside to Vonnie, one of my friend's daughters. She was about thirteen years old, and was in a mixed group of Hebrew and Liberian girls playing NaFo, the clapping game popular at the time with Liberian children. NaFo reminded me of the game of 'hambone' I had played as a young girl. I sent her for Maya, our paramedic. When Vonnie dallied saying goodbye to her friends, I shouted at her to go straight away. She took off running down the hill. Maya sensed urgency and came immediately, leaving her own washing at the base of the hill. Because she only had one daughter, she could afford to help the women with larger families wash their clothing and bedding occasionally.

When she felt Zefron and saw his listless condition, she turned to me and told me to gather a bucket of cold water to immerse him in. Before I left the room, I looked back to see him twitch once more and begin to cry like a weakened cat. I ran down the hill saying a prayer with every step of the steep decline. Once I had reached the well that we used for drinking water, I pumped cold water furiously. With the help of another woman, I positioned the heavy metal bucket atop my head, feeling my neck muscles bristle under the strain. I didn't have time to feel pain— this was the quickest way and I had to get to my son.

Up the steep hill, I alternately wobbled and steadied myself. Liberian women routinely carried buckets of water on their heads elegantly, and I had learned from them that the trick was not to hold the head and neck rigid, but to allow the head and neck to shift a little to accommodate the movement of the load. It was more about rhythm than balance. Water occasionally sloshed over the sides of the overfull bucket, spilling thin streams of cold water down my face and back. Suddenly, I heard Vonnie scream. My first instinct was to drop the bucket and run, but I knew that all of the cold water was critical to my son's well being. I continued forward, a mixture of tears and water streaming down my face, as I tried, once again, to balance the bucket on my head while cautiously moving towards the scream.

As I cleared the hill, Vonnie ran to help me lower the bucket and rush it to my room. Maya held my jerking son in her arms, and if it had not been for her strong grip pinning him, I know he would have hit the concrete floor with incredible force. Her colorful head-tie was forced in his mouth in between his little tongue and picket fence teeth. We held him while she inserted the rectal thermometer, which read 104 degrees! It was obvious that his nervous system was struggling to fight a losing battle against malaria, and his body was reacting with a convulsion. The fever had to be reduced and held at bay if he had a chance at recovering. We also knew he needed medication, and so Vonnie went door to door on the compound, but was unlucky in finding any malaria medication.

Back in my room, Zefron had soiled himself so now a putrid smell hung in the air. Once bathed, I lowered him slowly into the water. He shivered and moaned calling, "Emah, Emah," while touching his head.

"I know your head hurts little man, but not for long. Hold on little man," I said to him, while my own teeth chattered from fear.

Meanwhile, someone had called our fifteen-year-old Binah, who now clung to the doorway, frightened and weeping for her little brother. Her best friends, Heema and Aylah, comforted her while Maya assured everyone that Zefron would recover and asked for prayers.

Soon after Binah arrived, Elrahm returned from the vegetable farm where he and the other Brothers had begun to grow some of the food for our community. He hadn't witnessed the convulsion, but he saw the fear in my eyes and knew how serious the situation was.

I was relieved to see him because I knew he would find our little boy some medicine, whatever it took.

"Didn't anybody see this boy getting sick?" His tone and angry glare accused me. I was mute, knowing that no answer would make the situation any better or the struggle to hold our ailing marriage together any easier.

There was a time when Elrahm had been not only my husband, and sexual partner, but also my best friend. The shift took place over several years and lately, we seldom talked to each other. He looked down at

Zefron and affectionately touched his face.

"Hey man, Abba's here 'O'."

Our son lifted his head to look up at his father, and grasped his extended fingers, responding softly "Abba."

My husband turned, glancing vacantly in my direction and left the room. I followed him outside and asked softly, "Are you going into town?

"I don't know, I'm going wherever I have to go to get some chloroquine." Then he looked down at me, placing his hands on my shoulders. "Are you alright?"

"No, but I will be when Zefron is better." He bent to hold me briefly and I remembered how close we had once been, then he raised his guard. "Take care of the baby; I'll be back when I find some chloroquine. The truck has enough petrol to make it to town," he said.

For now, all we had was cool well water, bitter leaf tea, and our collective prayers.

For the next several hours, Zefron was in and out of consciousness. His normally light brown face was pale, his rosy lips drained of color. Sometimes he'd look at me and we'd share a glimmer of understanding, while other times he was consumed with his own fight and seemed to barely recognize me. Binah and I maintained the vigil until I asked her to put her younger brother and sister to bed, promising that if Zefron became sicker, I would send for her. I knew she would cry herself to sleep in the girl's dorm, and even if she didn't know it, a part of my heart left the room with her.

As I sat with my son, I pondered why, with the lack of modern conveniences and the sickness we didn't just pack up and go back to America. I knew the answer was because we didn't really consider America home. While at a Red Cross banquet in 1983, I had learned of the election of Harold Washington as the first African American Mayor of Chicago. I had been ecstatic, proud, and yet strangely detached. Liberia was my home now. I took what was monumental news to Black people in America in stride, it was like hearing foreign news, and had nothing to do with my life.

I did miss my family in America, but in spite of the physical struggles that living in Africa imposed, I quickly forgot all discomfort after a shower, a good meal, and good company. America and the stinging pain of racism was an unrelenting ache that I was happy to escape.

As I sat holding my feverish son, I reflected on how I had dreamed of visiting Africa as a small girl, and recalled my first impressions from my visit to Ghana in 1978. I had relished walking along the white sandy beaches of Accra, splashing in the Atlantic Ocean, and visiting Black Star Square. A Ghanaian market woman had tied my eldest son, then Penemiel who was barely six-months, on my back with a lappa so that I'd have my hands free to explore Makola market.

Unaccustomed to carrying the weight of a child on my back, my lower back ached, but I ignored the nagging pain while my eyes and hands ravaged everything in the market. I defied all the travel warnings recommending that travelers not eat or drink from street vendors, and fell in love with the taste of Kinke, wrapped in corn shucks with green pepper sauce, and golden fried ripe plantain cooked with ginger and the succulent deep fried black-eyed pea balls. The thick stench of raw open sewage mixed with the smell of palm oil had nearly made me heave, but the thing I remembered most from my very first day in Ghana was how insulted I had felt over being called O Brunee,' which in Fanti loosely translates to 'White person.'

A friend traveling with us had overheard and saw my hurt look. Trying to make me understand and ease my feelings, he shared, "Ghanaians look at people by their culture, not their skin color. Identifying people by skin color is how they do it in America because of slavery, but other cultures don't see color the same way. In their eyes, you behave like White people, so you are O Brunee."

Who would have thought that we would still face barriers, even in Africa, our motherland?

I pondered whether trying to live our dream of living in Africa was the reason my baby was immersed in a zinc bucket fighting malaria, the scourge of West Africa. In Chicago, I would simply have driven my son to the emergency room of the closest children's hospital and sat anxiously in the waiting room while trained nurses and doctors ministered to him. Hell, he wouldn't even *have* malaria if we still lived in Chicago. But here, *I* was the doctor, nurse, *and* the mother with only cool water, herb tea, the promise of malaria syrup and my prayers.

As I sat on the floor watching my son, I settled into the comforting sounds of nocturnal monkeys, owls, toads, and insects in the surrounding rubber forest. A Mandingo friend had told me that between 4:00 and 5:00 a.m., the animals "pray God." I have often been awake in the early morning and witnessed this phenomenon—all noise abruptly stops as if the Divine conductor signals the end of the nocturnal selection. It was in this same silence that I sent my prayers for my son's recovery and asked for a sign that moving to Africa had been the right decision. Finally, in the stillness, a sense of peace washed over me.

Before I realized it, the sun had risen and tangled itself between the branches of the rubber trees, and the dew was melting on the grassy field outside our bedroom window. Zefron was cool now. His father had made the four-hour round trip and returned with the critical malaria medicine. The medicine and the cool water, as well as hearty prayers, had finally taken effect. I lifted my baby from the water, dried his shriveled skin tenderly, and lay down next to him on our bed for a few precious moments.

Palm wine tapper

LOFA WAS HEAVEN

It took about a month for Zefron to recover from malaria. I gave him iron drops and a multivitamin to build him up. By twenty months he was totally weaned from the breast. We continued our lives in Kakata. Mornings, I boarded the Nation Builders truck for town, returning home in the evenings to a dark rubber plantation and my family. Exhaustion was beginning to give way to bitterness. Nevertheless, I loved my work and felt no sacrifice was too great. I was good at what I was doing and felt myself growing in ways the Hebrews encouraged and supported. Finally the time for my one month annual vacation rolled around and I was happy to take it and be free of the long daily commute to Monrovia on the truck.

I secretly envied Don, one of our Hebrew brothers, because he was free from the rules of the Community. As an engineer with LCADP (Lofa County Agricultural Development Project), his official residence was north, in Lofa County. His job was bridge building. He also owned the Good and Plenty, a small snack shop in Voinjama, Lofa County.

On one particular trip, he came to Kakata to recruit Sisters to travel to upcountry to work at the snack shop. Lofa was the hub of many development projects, and was the home to the indigenous population, as well as many expatriates, foreign contract workers, and Peace Corp volunteers. Don had wisely realized that after the initial fascination of conquering the local cuisine wore off, foreign workers craved food prepared without palm nut oil and hot peppers. The Good and Plenty Snack Shop offered an Americanized menu, and business was 'plenty' good!

When he initially invited me, I was reluctant to go. I felt duty bound to spend my time off in Kakata with my family. Truth be told, I was dragging my body around, fighting the realization that just maybe I wasn't fit for the Hebrew mold. A dear friend had once told me, "Everything that is faced cannot be changed, but everything must be faced." But I was stuck. I knew I was unhappy, yet I kept telling myself everything would somehow straighten itself out

My heart ached over the ever-encroaching barrier between Rahm and me. Our son was weaned and I didn't want to become pregnant again, so there was not much happening on the sexual front. No matter what either of us did, we just couldn't seem to get through to one another. I kept hearing people call us 'unevenly yoked," and every time I heard that comment, I flinched. I worried if it was possible to hold our family together.

Rahm encouraged me to take Don up on his invitation to Lofa.

"Ahnydah, you are so tired you don't know whether you are coming or going."

"I don't want to leave the children," I replied, surprised that he had noticed. "I don't get to spend much time with them as it is, and at least they would see me during the daylight hours."

"Well, it's not like you would be on vacation here. You know you'll be on the compound work schedule, the cook schedule, and the bathroom cleaning."

"Well, I guess sometimes being away from your main j-o-b and doing something different is a kind of vacation," I said making a case that would allow me to go to Lofa without the guilt of leaving my children behind. I would still be working and I would be taking care of myself.

"Exactly, so go to Lofa and take your baby. I will look after the other children. You need a change, you are t-i-r-e-d," he said in a mocking tone that was meant to be friendly.

"I know." I felt exposed.

"Listen, if you go, I'll see if I can get up there for at least one of those weeks to spend with you and Zefron," he said, tugging at the full black beard that covered his cheeks and obscured the roundness of his face.

My spirits lifted.

"You promise?"

"Promise."

I allowed myself the excitement of the idea that Elrahm, baby Zefron, and I would have some time as a family together. It made the eight hour ride over rough terrain with no appreciable rest stops an exciting adventure.

Before I left, I talked frankly with my eldest daughter Binah and asked her to take care of her siblings in my absence. It was the Hebrew practice to have one of the other Sisters act as guardians during the absence of family, but I wanted Binah to reassure me that she would take special care of her younger siblings.

When I contemplate how Binah's life has evolved, I am struck by the fact that she has always, and still has, a special interest in the welfare of her siblings, which has not always worked in her best interest. Back then, her vigilance was a soothing balm for me.

Lofa was heaven to me with its picture perfect beautiful, mountainous country wedged between Sierra Leone on the west and Guinea on the east. In 1983, Lofa was flourishing and vital, one of the busiest agricultural and commercial centers in Liberia. Traders from Guinea and Sierra Leone routinely crossed into Lofa County with market to sell trade or buy. Not only was Lofa the seat of agriculture, producing rice, tobacco, cocoa, and timber, but it was also rich in deposits of gold and the infamous blood diamonds.

Although the primary ethnic groups are Lorma and the Mandingo, a diverse mixture of ethnicities, such as the Gbandi, Kpelle, Kissi, and Mendi also live in Lofa County. Voinjama, my destination, was its largest boarder town. Liberia was growing as the wounds of the 1980 coup seemed to have healed.

Much of Don's earnings supported our Community, and his work with LCADP was a source of great pride for us. In dry season, Lofa County's streams, lakes, and rivers were crossed on foot or in makeshift rafts. However, during the six-month rainy season, roughly May through October, when rains caused the waters to swell and overflow their banks, scores of desperate farmers and traders drowned every year. The rains severed ties between villages and markets in remote villages. During this time of year, for many, there was no access to Voinjama's Telewoyan Hospital due to the impassable roads and the lack of bridges.

Don rested between projects in a rented three-bedroom brick house perched atop a mountain. Mamai, a Lorma woman, kept house for Don. When we finally arrived in Lofa, I found the large brick house simply furnished and clean. It sat in the middle of a huge lot and had a spacious attached garage. There was a large kitchen, living and dining area, two bathrooms, and four bedrooms. The baby and I shared Mamai's large bedroom. Mamai was stunning at six feet tall, a long, slender neck, and a sparkling white smile. She greeted me warmly and fell in love instantly with Zefron. Her mother, Ma Jennie, taught me the only indigenous greeting that I would learn while in Voinjama. I remember clearly, phonetically, the greeting which meant, *hello how are you,* was, "unGA, daye hal ou see!"

Don, along with his long-time friend Ben, and Arnie, a college professor from Denver, shared management of The Good and Plenty Snack Shop. Their best selling sandwich was made of ground, seasoned, and pan-fried lentil patties on fresh sliced bread. The menu also featured fried plantain, a local favorite, "potato" pancakes, fried, grated cassava root patty, a recipe I developed, and a vegetarian steak sandwich product made from wheat gluten that amazed Liberians with its meaty texture.

The beverages on our menu were a tangy limeade sweetened with brown sugar and a delicious blended "milk" shake made from roasted and freshly ground peanuts, ripe bananas, and brown sugar. We also served a Liberian, and similarly an American favorite—Lipton tea.

He and I were kindred spirits in that we both had a real passion to make a mark in Liberia. His tales of cultural practices he had encountered in the bush, the gifts, including wives he had managed to refuse without offending the local chiefs, always enthralled me. Don understood, and let me vent about the challenges I faced at the daycare center. He was full of wisdom and helped me learn how to get things done by working through the Liberian system.

The weather in Voinjama was inconsistent. It would be hot as hell at midday, then would cool off to a pleasant 75 degrees in the evening. The real shocker was that at 5:00 a.m., it was barely 50 degrees before the sun had a chance to reach the sky. Normally 50 degrees is not cold, especially by Chicago standards, but having adapted to the hot and humid weather, I was happy that it was Mamai's job to rise first and build the fire in the coal pots so that I could dress quickly. Once dressed, I would sit by the crackling, coal pot fire to warm myself while frying the day's quota of burgers and steaks for the shop.

Elrahm had been right—it didn't feel like work flipping lentil burgers while soaking in this view. I could literally look out from my place on the mountain into the valley below. The crisp air, the clean smell of the foliage, the morning sounds all combined to infuse me with renewed vigor, and although I worked six days a week, I was unhurried by any external schedule. After the first few days, I was homesick and wondered why my husband hadn't joined us, but the peace and camaraderie of Voinjama had a settling effect on me.

While the sandwich fillings were being pre-cooked, one of us would stroll across the road to purchase freshly baked unsliced sandwich loaves and sugar cookies from our neighbor, Mr. Johnson's cooling racks. Afterward, we'd pack up and head down the mountain trail for the thirty minute walk to the shop. Mr. Johnson had two wives, and the thing I most remember about them was the perpetual smell of fresh baked goods, and the atmosphere in their home which was filled with genuine joyfulness that made me happy to be in their presence.

Once we arrived at The Good and Plenty, we bought our breakfast from one of the lanky Mandingo women who strode through town balancing hot pots of creamy cereal atop their heads while calling customers to eat in thinly shrill voices. "Morning Ka-la-mah!"

After breakfast, we organized our sandwich counter for the day's business and were ready to rock and roll between 9:00 and 9:30 a.m.

Ben had a daily ritual, which thankfully he shared with me. Each afternoon, he made a trek into the Voinjama market a few minutes away from our shop with a plastic quart pitcher, and returned with it brimming with fresh palm wine. Palm wine is naturally fermented, slightly alcoholic, and tapped directly from the flower of the palm tree. When fresh, it tastes like nectar of 7-Up with a kick. This ritual made for a happy and speedy afternoon.

Zefron adapted quickly to Voinjama. Mamai adored him and from day one spoiled him. She knew that Don and I were very close friends and she went out of her way to keep my little boy happy, well fed and entertained. It was like having a personal nanny and in that sense, it was a vacation.

After the first weekend came and went, I stopped hoping for Rahm to walk into the store.

Red Cross Kindergarten children line up for recess

UNWINDING

During my month at The Good and Plenty, I was surprised at the number of indigenous men that had begun to order sandwiches. Demonstrating the proper alignment of the two pieces of bread, I would bite into the sandwich on numerous occasions. It seemed absurd that the sandwich was not a universal concept. Funny, the things we just take for granted.

Because of its location in the center of town, The Good and Plenty became a meeting place for the clan and tribal chiefs. We even had a visit from one of the paramount chiefs, who was the highest tribal chief! It is a hierarchy, that in Chicago, ranked similar to precinct captain, Alderman, and Mayor.

Peace Corps volunteers and other foreign workers frequented the shop and brought with them recent copies of *Time* and *Newsweek* to share with us. There was always lively conversation over current international affairs and the BBC and Voice of America broadcasts. I felt lucky to have the best of both worlds—local conversation and news from around the globe. The Good and Plenty had become a unique cultural incubator, and for one seemingly quirky man, it was entirely something else.

Early one morning as I used a spatula to transfer warm lentil patties from the fire to the strainer basket, Ben nudged me when a pickup truck stopped in front of the shop.

"I thought it was about time for this guy to reach town," he said.

"Who are you talking about?"

"Here comes the Bird Man," Ben announced, while chopping the seasonings for us to use.

"The what?"

"Andy, the Bird Man. He goes into the bush and catalogues the birds languages. He's got beautiful photos and can mimic the sounds of exotic birds."

"So that's what the Peace Corps feels is important?"

"I doubt that. I heard that he's CIA and the bird thing is his cover."

"What would interest the CIA in Voinjama?"

"What did the CIA have to do with killing Tolbert?" Ben responded. It had been a commonly articulated suspicion of many Liberians that the overthrow of the Tolbert, the head of the Organization of African Unity government, was a CIA hit.

"Anyway, Andy comes in here every couple of weeks and eats. He brings in *The New York Times Book of Trivia* and *Times* and *Newsweek* magazines.

Just then, the door opened. Looking up, I saw a scrawny man, over six feet tall with jet-black hair and sparkling blue eyes, standing before me. The nickname fit—he looked like a lanky crane. After introductions and a little prodding, Andy shared that he was an ornithologist and his assignment was to travel the bush and photograph and catalogue birds and their unique languages.

While I was staring at this odd looking man I was introduced. "This is my sister, Ahnydah. She works for the Red Cross in Monrovia."

In the span of our two-minute interaction, Andy seemed more

focused on collecting information than relating to me or finding food.

"Really, how long have you been there?" was followed quickly by "What part of the U.S. are you from, Chicago like most of Ben's friends? What brings you to Lofa?"

When people ask too many questions too fast I get suspicious. I had nothing to hide but he was too nosey for my liking.

I was already moving away from our birdlike customer when Ben asked, "Andy, what you want today 'O'?"

"Give me a lentil burger and a banana shake."

"So it's A–nie-dah? Am I saying your name right?" Andy had resumed his line of inquiry.

"Yep."

"You like it here?"

"Well, I like working with the children and the women, but sometimes I get irritated with the way things get done, but hey, it's Liberia!"

"No lie."

Eventually he was satisfied and wound down his rapid-fire questioning.

Ben quickly mixed several spoonfuls of freshly ground peanut butter, ice water, sugar, vanilla and a fresh banana with a sprinkle of cinnamon in the blender. He poured it into a tall soda glass and sat it before Andy. I was sautéing onions on the portable griddle for the lentil burger. "Ummm, this is good. Hey Ben, you seen the latest *Newsweek*?"

"Naw, you got it?"

"Yeah," he said, pulling it from his backpack and laying it on the counter,

"Keep it until I come back if you want."

Life in Voinjama was rudimentary. People worked hard, and when they had free time, they commiserated over the tough times and laughed over their victories. Although Voinjama couldn't boast of having night clubs like Monrovia, it did have small shops that sold soft drinks, Super Malt, Club and Guinness Stout beer, local palm wine, and commonly used sundry items. They tended to have a table or two and a few chairs where friends sat and socialized.

I had been to the Market, a couple of small shops, and the local high school, and I had thought I had seen all there was, until Ben and Arnie took me to the movies one Saturday afternoon. A Lebanese trader owned the theater, which showed old films at a discounted rate. There were movies from India, Lebanon, and even the occasional American movie.

As we sat in the darkened building on long wooden benches, I noticed the theater quickly overflowing with moviegoers. Men and women came dressed in cultural attire, some in flowing robes, women in three-piece lappa suits, while others wore work clothes. Almost all the women wore head ties knotted on one side, or full two-yard head wrap. We had to move around to find spaces between them in order to see the screen. The room filled with the quiet murmur of the different dialects spoken by the audience. The featured movie was "Three the Hard Way," a 1970's Blaxploitation movie with former football heroes, Jim Brown and Fred Williamson, and marshal artist, Jim Kelly, three of my favorite chocolate-dipped hunks. Admittedly homesick, I sat anxious to see the action-packed film even though I had seen it in the States at least twice.

"I can't believe I'm in the mountains of Voinjama about to see a Black movie," I said as we had entered the darkened room.

Finding a seat, Ben turned to me and said, "Well, this is gonna be a little different, but Arnie and I've been here a couple of times and it's okay. I mostly get a kick out of watching the people enjoy it."

When the movie began, it only took a few brain-scrambling seconds for me to realize what he meant. All the dialogue was in Chinese, without English subtitles! Instinctively, I turned to Arnie, fixing my mouth to ask why the theater owner didn't have English subtitles. I stopped myself mid-sentence realizing that it really wouldn't have mattered since there were only a precious few people in Voinjama that spoke English.

"What's so funny?" Ben inquired.

Arnie grinned at me. "Oh you know you almost asked me why there are no English subtitles didn't you!"

The three of us busted out into raucous laughter and when the people around us gave us the *shut up* look, it only added to the hilarity. The quality of the picture was grainy but one could still interpret what was happening. Just as I had remembered, the three heroes where outmanned and outgunned, yet in the next hour and thirty minutes, they still managed to overcome the villainous White Supremacists group that had developed a toxin destined to contaminate the water supplies of Washington D.C, Los Angeles, and Detroit with a poison that would harm only Blacks, leaving whites unharmed. As the movie spooled, the titillated crowd cheered the heroics of the three African-American hunks, hammering home that there is so much more to communication than language.

Later that evening, the movie provided a stimulating segue way into a discussion of a futuristic novel called *The Tomorrow File,* published by Lawrence Sanders in 1975 that Ben had told us about. The book warned about the development of new chemical and biological weapons that would allow countries to fight wars that would eliminate the human collateral while leaving natural resources and infrastructure intact.

Ironically, that was just a few years before AIDS would hit Africa in full effect!

VIEW FROM THE PINNACLE

Going mountain climbing in a wraparound skirt and rubber flip-flops is among my sweetest memories of Voinjama. It all started spontaneously, as most good times do. It was a Sunday and a CLOSED sign hung on the door of The Good and Plenty. On Sundays, we typically rested during the day and ate an evening meal. I was sunning in the front yard when Ben suggested showing me the mountain while Zefron slept. I figured Zefron would be knocked out for a couple of hours, and remembering all the times Ben had bragged during his visits to Kakata that there were places in Voinjama, "where you felt you had been sucked right into the middle of a National Geographic photo," I knew I had to go. My curiosity had been aroused long before this afternoon. Peeking into the bedroom at my sleeping baby, I saw he napped peacefully and asked Mamai, returning from the market, to check on him for me. She happily agreed and we were off to see Ben's mountain.

It was a day of living by impulse and adventurous hearts. It took about twenty minutes to walk leisurely to the base of the mountain, and then we began to scale it. At every level there was another flower or bird egging me further up the mountain trail. There was more beauty than I had ever seen before and Ben, not a very talkative person, came alive in nature. Having spent hours watching the insects, flowers, and birds, he recounted his observations about the creatures we encountered.

Ben was wearing beat up gym shoes that provided him good traction. However, my sweaty feet slipped around in my rubber flip-flops and quickly became filthy. I guess it might have made good sense to go back and change shoes, but any mother knows that when your baby is asleep, you have to make your move. I was not about to miss this opportunity! Sweaty feet notwithstanding, I held my own on the climb. Occasionally Ben reached back and pulled me up onto a particularly steep ledge as we climbed higher. He was an agile climber and I followed effortlessly. His only instructions were *Just keep your eyes on the trail ahead, don't look down.* We climbed progressively for nearly forty-five minutes, pausing only to look at odd rock formations and the occasional beautiful wildflower asserting its divine right to thrive on a ragged ledge. It was pointless to ask how much longer we were going to climb since the top was our destination.

Finally, he announced, "Here we are."

There, at the mountain's pinnacle, was a small tabletop. Ben sat down, and I scrambled to sit alongside him. In seconds, just as he had promised, we were magically swept inside the "National Geographic photo."

The sun blazed, the sky a luminous blue and billowing white. Below us stretched a valley where indigenous women tended swamp rice. Despite the heat, an intermittent breeze cooled us, and I sat in awe while Ben pointed out tiny brown rice birds that lived from the bits of rice they picked from the plants and plucked from the ground. I was transfixed by the gorgeous panorama as we watched the color green present itself in infinite hues.

"See what I mean? This is cool, this is where I come when I want to see clearly."

I could hardly respond coherently without weeping.

Atop that mountain, wrapped in silence, I felt the presence of an unlimited power. The interconnection of everything in the universe suddenly made sense. I felt the relevance of dominion and recollected a passage in Genesis:

"Let us make man in our image, in our likeness, and let them rule over the fish of the sea and the birds of the air, over the livestock, over all the earth, and over all the creatures that move along the ground."

--Genesis 1:26

I have no idea how long we sat quietly, melting into the peace that embraced us. As the sun began its graceful descent, my maternal instincts resurfaced, and I intuitively felt my son stirring. It was time to leave this hallowed ground and its serenity to return to the world of motherhood and dinner-to-be prepared.

Nevertheless, my spirit was full—exhilarated in a way it had never been before.

One thing I would learn shortly thereafter—the difference between climbing up the mountain, and then down the mountain, is that on the ascent, Ben was in front and I could follow his footsteps. Even if he stumbled or kicked rocks loose, I still had a sense of what was going on ahead of me. I had a perspective of forward progression. However, on the way down, with Ben going first meant that he was actually *below* me and the only way to make eye contact was to look down. As we turned to make the descent, I glanced at Ben for direction. That glance led my eyes down the mountainside, and brought with it the reality of exactly how high above ground we actually were. My stomach somersaulted and I dizzied, clinging to the mountain terrified.

"Oh God, Ben! I'm going to fall! I didn't know we were going up this high, I can't go down!"

Panic defies logic. I wanted off that mountain immediately and was battling hysteria, trying to calm myself enough so that I could make it down the mountain alive. I reminded myself that I had come to Liberia to live, not to die by falling off a mountain. At this point, I had no idea how I had even made the climb up, but a part of me, the rational part, realized that staying on the mountain was not an option. I had a baby boy sleeping at the house and three other children in Kakata that needed a mother. I inhaled deeply to collect myself, trying to rationalize with myself that Ben had scaled the mountains dozens of times safely.

Through my mental fog, I heard Ben say, "Ahnydah, I wouldn't have brought you here unless I knew you could climb down!"

I desperately clung to that thought. He had affirmed that it was possible for me to climb down!

"Okay," I replied, squeezing my eyes shut while fighting to stop the queasy feeling. I had never known that I was afraid of heights, perhaps because, besides airplane rides and the occasional rollercoaster, I'd never voluntarily been this high above ground.

Ben must have quickly surmised that if he failed to manage my fear I really would lose it and probably fall. There was no Voinjama Fire Department, no mountain rescue workers with pick axes, ropes and pulleys, and no cell phones. Only Ben and me. He realized that he had to get his panic-stricken friend down his mountain, and I realized that in order to get down the mountain, I had to trust Ben with my life.

"Just listen to me and take your time. We can stop whenever you want. Just remember, you can't look down, okay?"

Anyone who *really* knows me will tell you that although I have mellowed over the years, following other folks' directives blindly and going slow, are not my strong suits. I was operating strictly on grace now.

I broke the "don't look down" rule a few more times. There were moments that I just needed to see Ben's face and know that he was still down there, leading me to the safety of the ground. I tried to look more out than down so that I was never looking all the way down. Sometimes I got it right, sometimes I didn't, but each time I breeched the rule, Ben would patiently stop and wait while I fought to control my panic. I remember him telling me these weird little jokes along the way to keep my mind off the climb. I laughed through chattering teeth. I was scared but determined to make it down for my baby.

To complicate the current drama, I had to pee. I was happy for the blessing of a very strong bladder; otherwise, Ben would have received a golden shower. He tested the trail, and somehow, I managed to follow. We continued our descent very, very slowly while he repeatedly coaxed me along the way.

"Let's just go to that ledge below," or, "Just a little bit further," and, "Yes, you are almost there; plant your foot down hard," and finally, "It's almost over. You can look down."

My feet, sweaty under normal conditions, seemed to pour water and slid in my rubber flip-flops. At one point, I asked Ben if I should just kick them off. He vetoed, saying the slippers were protecting my feet and without them, it would be worse, so whenever possible, I dried my feet on my lappa skirt. But even with slippers I scraped my ankles and cut my toe on the jagged rocks. It was excruciating, but finally, thankfully, we reached the base of the mountain.

Leaning against it, I regrouped and thanked God.

As we made our way back to the house, I happily anticipated the sound of my crying baby. Dinner was definitely going to be late, and obviously, we were both ravenous, but my first order of business was to pee. In the past hours or so, I had come to respect Ben, and oddly, myself, in a new way. Ben continued to refer to that mountain as "his mountain," but on that day, I claimed Ben's mountain as my mountain too!

Four weeks later, my husband had not kept his promise. My vacation was ending and it was time to leave Voinjama. The night before we drove back to Kakata, I hurried home from The Good and Plenty Snack Shop to wash my son's diapers. While I was busy washing a final bucket of diapers, Don, who had just driven up in his dusty pickup truck, burst into the house and excitedly insisted that I come outside. I grabbed my son, who had been sitting on the floor outside the bathroom, and swung him onto my hip. Following him as he walked around the side of the house and pointed, I stopped in my tracks.

"Check that out!" he shouted as though unveiling his personal creation.

The full moon had risen and was a glimmering perfect gold sphere nestled atop the adjacent mountain—our mountain—putting us at eye-level with the moon!

I was transfixed by the magical spectacle. As we stood there silently, drinking in the moon's majesty, tears fell from my eyes and slid down my cheeks. Zefron's eyes widened and blinked at the sight of the moon shimmering directly into his face. Its ambiance and beauty embraced us. The coolness of the evening breeze whipped through our loose garments, causing them to flap against our bodies. We were joined in a spiritual intimacy, so close that chills razored through my body. My wondrous month in Voinjama was over. I was full again and ready to return to my family.

Baby EliTikvah

HER NAME MEANS HOPE

Her name was EliTikvah, or, "my God is my Hope," in Hebrew. She was a surprise pregnancy born into a dying marriage. A midwife who understood my struggle, told me to consider my baby's name an affirmation so that each time I spoke her name into the Universe, I was making a positive statement, one of hope. I was thirty-four, and way 'back in the day,' there was a stigma of women over thirty having children. You were considered, by conventional medical wisdom, to be "over the hill," as far as procreation was concerned, and you were the object of criticism by friends and acquaintances, considered inconsiderate for taking not only a personal health risk, but also taking the risk of giving birth to an imperfect infant. Times have certainly changed since then! At any rate, I already had four children; my eldest was ten years older than her closest sibling. *So why was I pregnant?*

Hebrews didn't believe in artificial methods of birth control, and my husband had insisted I comply. I hadn't subscribed to surrendering control over my fertility, and in fact, had arrived in Africa with a diaphragm, which Elrahm discovered and pressured me to throw away. I quickly become pregnant with Zevah, and in attempt to delay having another pregnancy, I breastfed her for as long as I could as a method of natural birth control. However, after my return visit from America, she had begun to wean, and I had became pregnant with Zefron. Exhausted from the continual cycle of pregnancy, breastfeeding, and pregnancy again, I went to a Catholic organization in Liberia for training in tracking my ovulation through daily temperature taking and the Rhythm method. Since it did not involve birth control by an artificial method, Elrahm reluctantly agreed, but still made me feel as if I was disobeying the rules of our faith.

My heart told me I had no more mothering in me, so when I found out I was pregnant *again*, I felt guilty, as if I had betrayed my inner voice. Here I was, a so-called "civilized" woman, and I had managed to fail at mastering the Rhythm method. Catholic Church or no Catholic Church, I didn't see how this technique even had a chance at being successful in a culture where women did not even have the right to deny their men sex. I pondered how women could develop, and how countries could develop if women weren't allowed to control their own fertility.

Zefron was no longer nursing-on-demand which suppressed my ovulation. I was pregnant because one evening, rather than fight the urge to be close to Elrahm, I rolled the dice.

That night, I conceived.

Because I desperately wanted the facts to prove otherwise, I attempted a stint at self-deception, which lasted until my period was late. In my personal experience, a late period always meant pregnancy—always. With the absence of blood, I *knew* I was pregnant. Silently, I dealt with the fear of how I would manage to bear another child, until my veneer cracked, and I shared my secret with my two dearest friends. They empathized *with* and *for* me. Both knew me well enough to know that my energy couldn't be contained on the abandoned rubber plantation we lived on in Kakata. We commiserated and discussed alternatives. Having an abortion was not a financial option, or at that time, a moral option. Since I was only a couple of weeks late, I decided to take a massive overdose of birth control pills. We had heard through the grapevine that it was possible to start your period with a massive hormonal overload from the pill, and so I shakily followed that course of action.

I left the Red Cross Day Care Center at naptime and found a pharmacy on Broadstreet that sold birth control pills. I purchased two packs and returned home that evening. It was a Friday and I wanted to suffer any adverse affects over the weekend so that I could be back to normal for work on Monday morning.

Friday night, after the beginning of the Hebrew Sabbath, I took ten birth control pills. Saturday, I carried on with my normal duties of cleaning the communal bathrooms and preparing breakfast for the children while choking down pills every few hours. First came the dizziness followed by the nausea. Fighting the urge to vomit, I lay in my room visualizing my period bursting through the walls of my uterus, leaving only the reminder of a bad scare.

The nausea continued, but there was no blood.

Saturday night was tortuous. I tossed and turned from dusk to dawn. Was I making the wrong decision? Should I have the baby? I slept fitfully while my subconscious released all my suppressed and haunting guilt. My husband lay sleeping next to me, unaware of the battle I was fighting. I longed to reach out, but I withered at the thought of his condemnation over my doubts of having another child. I awakened Sunday, still fighting my internal war. I knew I didn't want to have another baby, but I also knew that I could not choke down any more pills.

Sunday morning, I wept in my heart as I had, what so many describe as, an out-of-body experience. I watched myself dress Zefron for the day, then begin to clean the bedroom, and suddenly, chills and sweats shot through my body. As the perspiration ran down my scalp, I removed my head wrap for air. Burning, I flung open the shuttered windows of my room and screamed outside, where children were playing, for someone to bring me a bucket of water. Finally a knock came at my door, and with it, the very thing I had requested.

I grabbed a drinking cup and literally poured the water all over myself. I felt like I was on fire!

My husband and friends thought that I was suffering with malaria and put me to bed, but I knew that I was in the crosshairs of fear and guilt. The other sisters brought me cold water, wiped me down with cool towels, and dosed me with malaria medicine, and still, I felt as if I was afire. I knew the only way to appease the pain was to make my decision.

That night, as I lay quietly beside my sleeping husband and youngest son, I prayed. I vowed that if God would allow my unborn baby, whose health I had threatened with a massive hormone overdose, to be born without defect, I would somehow find the strength to raise yet another child. In the morning, my fever broke, as did something in my spirit. I recovered from the fever, but it would be a very long time before my broken spirit healed.

In the next weeks, instead of gaining weight, I lost it. Weight loss is common in malaria, so no one was alarmed. As I neared three months without a period, I told my husband I was pregnant and he seemed content. A big fan of *The Temptations,* he always used to say that he wanted enough children to sing five-part harmony. We never discussed how I felt about the pregnancy, but he knew me well enough to know I was despondent. What he didn't know was how to reach out and help me. He had a way of avoiding things that were difficult. I, on the other hand, knew that if I was to survive, I had to preserve my outer crust and that meant not reaching out to him for fear of sustaining further damage. The distance between us widened.

The last thing I wanted was for our leadership to learn that I had tried to stop the pregnancy. There had been a time when I could have told my husband what I had done and as my best friend, he would have kept my confidence. That trust had been recently shattered.

Several months earlier, Sheryrah, who was a midwife, and a paramedic in our community, had shared her misgivings about the judgment and skills of a new midwife. The new midwife, a recent arrival from the States, had been placed over the other paramedics simply because she was a friend of the most senior leader. Pure politics. But she was arrogant and often challenged treatments we had proven were successful in Liberia. Sheryrah felt her egotism, unchecked, one day she would put a life in jeopardy. I just wanted Elrahm to know, but not to share this information. I considered it pillow talk between a husband and wife.

For reasons that I never understood, he betrayed my trust and instead, shared my information as though Sheryrah was spreading hurtful gossip. She was summoned into a meeting with the leadership and while she sat on one side of the room, as the accused, they read a judgment against her that decreed she be separated from her family for 30 days, during which time she would leave Kakata and live at the house we maintained in Monrovia. She was devastated by the judgment and furious with me. However, most importantly, I realized that the bond between Elrahm and me, the level of trust that we had was gone. I would never again share anything with him that I didn't want every Hebrew in Liberia to know.

Pregnancy was difficult from the start. I wanted with all my heart and soul not to be pregnant—again. The never ending grind of washing clothes and diapers for six persons by hand; of cleaning and cooking while doing a job that I was passionate about, put me on par with what all working women in developing nations face. Now, I chuckle when American women talk about work life balance. For women in Africa and many other parts of the world, there is no such option. On top of all my responsibilities, my husband was often out of the country, or just had too little time for his family. I relied heavily on Binah, and while I began to feel guilty over giving her so much responsibility for the care of her siblings, I felt I had no other choice.

Now I felt a soul kinship with Liberian woman, market women, women who grew rice and other crops, women who work hard without childcare for their own precious children. What I was experiencing was actually *normal* in developing nations, and I tried hard to manage my life and not complain.

In Liberia, as in other developing countries, oftentimes the older children become "little mothers," in some cases embracing the role and loving their younger siblings, and in other cases, silently resenting the burden of being thrust from their childhood and conflicted because the person forcing them into that position is someone they love. I saw myself unable to spend the quality time with my eldest daughter that she needed, and sadly, our mother-daughter relationship has never completely recovered from that painful dilemma.

A few sympathetic friends, who had experienced aspects of what I was suffering, proposed that I simply quit my job and stay home and narrow my focus to only caring for my own children. However, beside the fact that we needed my salary, my work at the daycare center, doing outreach with Liberian women, was what gave me self-worth and happiness. No matter what, I refused to give that up. I had already surrendered my voice in my relationship with my husband and in the Hebrew Community. If I ever succumbed to pressures to stop working, I believed I would surrender myself, forever.

On the surface, my life appeared to be continuing normally. I fulfilled all of my responsibilities, both at home and at work, and no one even sensed that I was clinically depressed for almost the entire pregnancy. No one knew, except my unborn baby and me.

I didn't want to poison my baby, but all I had were toxic thoughts. From my dark abyss, I reasoned that if I had words of inspiration that I could sing, I could give my child hope that there was love to look forward to in the world outside of my angry womb.

I prayed.

One afternoon, while sitting in my office, praying for a sign that I could survive my pregnancy with a healthy baby and intact psyche, I heard "the song." It was almost as if my unborn child was chanting the song to me and it became my waking mantra. All day, every day, if I was not actively talking with someone, I was silently chanting the words to myself. At intervals during the day, when I was alone with my unborn child, I sang aloud: "I love the Lord, Oh I love the Lord, He eases me when the days are hard, He soothes my soul and He makes it still, inspiring me to fulfill His will."

I masked my depression by being extremely organized and by paring down my physical possessions. I chose three African gowns that would fit me for the duration of the pregnancy and packed everything else away. I selected one change of bedding and succumbed to a monk's lifestyle. Through grace, my husband was given an assignment that kept him in Ghana most of the time. I used bean sprout profits to hire a washman to help with laundry. He was a lifesaver because around this time I developed a complex about water!

Whenever I bathed or if water dripped on my body, it hurt me. I tried to work through it because I was rational enough to know having pain because of water was unusual, but in the end, the reality was every time water dripped on me, I actually felt pain. I had a donut shaped appliance that I dropped into the water and plugged into an electrical outlet to heat my bathwater. Nonetheless, it still hurt. From the time I was four months pregnant, until just before my delivery, I'd wet my wash towel, wring it out, and then wash up, trying very hard to avoid any water trickling down my skin.

My children remained in Kakata. Their care divided between several Sisters and their father, when he was in town. I now lived in a bedroom in the house the Hebrew Community maintained in Monrovia. This allowed me to avoid the daily, long bumpy truck ride to town and to get more rest after work. My children visited me on the weekends, and the fact that I wasn't responsible for their day-to-day care, along with the assistance of the washman, helped me get through those months.

Around this time, there were many well-meaning comments made to me by my Hebrew Brothers and Sisters, proposing that if my husband had another wife, our lives would be easier. I understood that having another woman who loved your husband and cared for your children made sense, but if no birth control was going to be used by either woman, it just didn't seem to be a good long-term solution. Not to mention my emotions surrounding losing any illusion of monogamy. At any rate, whether he found another woman or not, I didn't want more children.

In addition to my fixation about water, I also arranged and rearranged my few possessions. I became a germaphobe, constantly cleaning and sanitizing everything in my work and home environment. The bottles of bleach and DETTOL disinfectant soap became my new best friends. A few drops of bleach went into my nightly bath water, and I washed the floor of my bedroom every evening with a bleach water solution. My life had succumbed to a dull routine, wearing my hair parted down the middle in two thick cornrow braids and wearing one of three outfits to work.

One morning, Don, who had come from Voinjama to file a report at LCADP Monrovia, shared a taxi with me. I thought we were having a pleasant conversation until he said, "Ahnydah, you are depressed, and you need to talk about it with someone instead of hiding behind the pretext of being strong, because you're not."

His statement ripped through me like a switchblade. I became enraged. How dare he say that to me! Yet, instead of snapping back at him in anger, I burst into tears, and for the first time in a very long time, in the back of that taxi, I wept. Don had seen straight through my mask. This was the beginning of him becoming my closest confident.

I had known it for a while, but now someone had called me on it. I could no longer try to hide or deny my feelings of sadness and worthlessness—both signs of depression. I was happiest at work, the place where I felt like I could grow. The Red Cross Day Care Center was the only arena in my life where I had the opportunity to make decisions instead of having someone else make them for me. I felt useful and needed because there were people benefiting from my presence.

While at home I felt constrained. There were things about being a Hebrew that I didn't like, believe or agree with, and I didn't have a choice to just leave and find another church. This was my home. I held my tongue when I wanted to speak and followed customs that didn't make sense to me, and sometimes, that I didn't even agree with.

Despite having very deep relationships with many of the members of the Hebrew Community, I was always trying to find exceptions to the rules. Try as I might, I was a rebel and did not fit the mold of the Hebrew culture. There were two types of members of our community. Religious Hebrews that wanted to live in Israel and practice Hebrew Israelite culture in the Holy Land and Black Nationalists who joined the Hebrew Israelites and who viewed the affiliation as a way to accomplish a deep desire to reconnect with Africa. I was the latter.

The day that my youngest child was born was a bright, sunny day. I awoke feeling lighter and knew that it was the day. I was mentally ready and emotionally calm. My labor was a short four hours. As soon as I began to feel the contractions, I took a taxi ride to buy my favorite imported scented soap, and before I became nauseous from the rapidly advancing labor, I indulged myself in a plate of crispy, golden French fries from the Lebanese restaurant next to the Sinkor Supermarket. Ray, the pain-in-the butt Peace Corps guy assigned to the Red Cross and I both had a "thing" for French fries and shared our favorite haunts. We concurred that the only fries better than the restaurant next to the Sinkor Supermarket were the fries at the joint under the Palm Hotel. On my return trip home, I stopped the taxi a half mile from the house so I could walk the rest of the way home. I knew walking would help progress my labor and I was ready to see my baby!

I delivered a perfect, beautiful baby girl around 3:00 that afternoon. When they put her to my breast, I could see that she wasn't just beautiful, she was 'take-your-breath away' gorgeous, with her thick rosy lips, perfect skin and clear, bright eyes.

I silently sang our song, *"I love the Lord, Oh I love the Lord He eases me when the days are hard, He soothes my soul and He makes it still, inspiring me to fulfill His will."*

Waterside Market

CULTURAL DEEP DIVING

In the months following EliTikvah's birth, I began to understand that my struggles as a woman, along with those of my fellow Hebrew Sisters, were a mere blip on the radar compared to the extremely challenging lives of our Liberian sisters.

Anna Cooper remarried and moved to America in the early months of 1983. Despite some friction that had passed between us, I felt we had moved beyond that and while I was happy that she had remarried, I felt her departure was a loss for the Red Cross. Anna was a steady hand at the helm. She asked her trusted friend, Zaria Wright Titus, a former registered nurse to serve as the interim Secretary General of the Red Cross Society.

Zaria, despite her quiet and gentile demeanor, had the most captivating dark flashing eyes. I knew that there was a soul of great substance behind those eyes. Approval from the Secretary General was required

143

for purchases beyond the monthly food allowance for the Center and our basic cleaning supplies. Whenever I presented a reasonable request, she trusted my judgment. We began to talk a little about my family and she seemed genuinely interested in my life. We got along well.

Several months after her arrival, as I was signing in for the day, Zaria asked coyly, "Mrs. Rahm, have you ever heard of female circumcision?"

I had enough sensitivity to know that I was talking to a woman of Liberian origin, and that I was no expert on things Liberian, the least of which was circumcision—caution was a must.

"Yes, years ago I heard it mentioned, but I don't know much. It's when they remove the woman's clitoris, isn't it?"

"Well," she sighed, "Yes, that's part of it," she said, almost timidly. "It can be very dangerous and affect a woman's life long after the procedure. The Red Cross has been asked to become involved because some girls have had some problems while attending Bush Schools here in Liberia. I'd like you to attend a meeting of health professionals that I'm hosting at headquarters. Can you make time to attend?"

"Yes, I'll come. It sounds interesting."

Thus began a very enriching experience and opportunity to access the culture of Liberia in a unique way.

Female circumcision is a taboo subject in African culture. Years ago, I recall reading a poetic passage referencing circumcision in *Facing Mount Kenya,* by Jomo Kenyatta, the first Prime Minister and President of Kenya. However, during my time in Liberia, I would peel back a layer or two from the surface of this very complex and controversial cultural practice through my work with the Red Cross.

The inaugural group of seven met in the Red Cross' second floor conference room. There was Ms. Bandele Bicase, a businessperson from Sierra Leone; Rachel Marshall, a feisty retired nurse whose pediatrician daughter, Rosita, had saved my eldest son's life. Also present was Elisabeth Mulbah, a registered nurse that I knew from my work with the Christian Health Association in Liberia (CHAL), and Dr Coles, a male physician. Elisabeth and Dr. Coles had come from Phebe Hospital in Gbarnga. Lastly, there was Dr. Patricia Divine, a gynecologist practicing at John F. Kennedy Hospital.

Mrs. Marshall, the group's facilitator, shared her plan to have us conduct meetings and interviews with Liberian women. Our intention was to understand the scope of a number of cultural practices, including female circumcision. We would also focus on gathering data from Phebe Hospital in Gbarnga, and at JFK Hospital in Monrovia, since those hospitals saw a large number of tribal Liberians and could be convinced to share their data on the cases stemming from traditional practices in and around their geographic locations. Finally, we selected the Health Action Group (HAG) as a working name for our funding application being sent to international donor organizations. I was unimpressed with our progress.

Early the next morning, peeved, I cornered Zaria in her office. "Mrs. Titus, why did we have that meeting yesterday? Did I fall asleep or something? I never heard us discuss female circumcision."

She smiled with a twinkle in her eye.

"Ahnydah, the topic of female circumcision is taboo in Liberia. The fact that Dr. Coles stayed through the entire meeting bodes well for our future success. You must be patient."

She then went on to share information she had received from Mrs. Mulbah that Zoes, the traditional healers of her Kpelle tribe, often summoned her to Bush School when circumcisions went badly. Liz was an initiated member of her tribe and traveled into the Bush Schools to treat girls in secrecy. Zaria knew that Dr. Coles also routinely made his services available to Zoes to help when circumcisions resulted in serious infections or other complications, like excessive bleeding. He dared not jeopardize his status with the operators of the Bush Schools, but we had earned his trust at our first meeting through our sincerity and promise of discretion. Building that foundation was critical, and had resulted in Dr. Coles committing to attend another meeting.

Zaria encouraged patience and asked that I remain open so that I could learn from this experience. As the meetings continued, I practiced the art of keeping my mouth shut and asking infrequent and moderate questions. It took Africa to teach me what my mother had tried for years to teach me—"Every word that comes into your throat does not have to come out of your mouth!"

Our application for funding was accepted by the Inter-African Committee, (IAC), an international donor agency with a liaison office in Switzerland and regional offices sprinkled across Africa. The mission of the IAC was the eventual eradication of female circumcision and other traditional practices deemed harmful to women and children.

In addition to monetary support to carry out our work, the Inter-African Committee shipped us books, booklets, and videos to support our research on female circumcision. Our group's official name was changed from Health Action Group to, The Committee to Study the Effects of Traditional Practices that Affect the Health of Women and Children.

In October 1983, we held our first large meeting at John Fitzgerald Kennedy Hospital, bringing women practitioners from all over Liberia together. We invited an international guest speaker to discuss numerous traditional practices.

I remember it being a horribly hot day in the auditorium of JFK Hospital. No air-conditioning, but the windows were open. I sat in the balcony, which gave me an overview of the proceedings. The IAC had flown in a speaker to talk about traditional practices that they knew were common in Liberia. Among them were child marriage, the practice of marrying off girls as young as twelve-and-thirteen years old and the psychological and physical complications they face as they are thrust into motherhood much too early for their young bodies. One such complication is the obstetric fistula that are formed when women, usually very young women, with very small pelvis' are attempting to deliver a child vaginally in a rural environment. These girls can have many days of labor, resulting in trauma that causes a hole to form between the vaginal opening and the rectum. The result is damage in the vaginal wall that results in the continual leaking of urine and feces. The girl is shunned due to the constant stench she carries.

Another shock was learning that while in most cultures pregnant women are intentionally very well fed, there are cultures that enforce food taboos for pregnant and nursing women. Food restrictions that deny them sources of protein such as eggs, and milk where there are no available substitutes, and primitive birthing practices that include sitting on a woman's stomach or "jumping the belly" out. When the lecture turned to the birthing practice of forcing the baby out of the mother, the hair rose on my neck as I recalled the way the birthing attendant at St. Joseph's Hospital had used to hasten the delivery of my Hebrew Sister Rackemya's daughter. Her uterus could have ruptured and she might have bled to death as many women do. The final topic addressed was, of course, female circumcision. The idea was to talk more intimately about circumcision in small group breakout sessions.

In talking with my staff and other Liberian women about my work on the Committee, I learned that when girls experienced serious complications, or worse, died because of female circumcision, people would say "Da witch," using witchcraft to explain away occurrences they did not comprehend. As I read the materials, I understood why the myths abounded and why the shroud of secrecy around the practice of female circumcision was thick.

Consumed by the subject of female circumcision I discreetly asked my staff if they knew anything about this sensitive subject. In the afternoons, while the children were napping we took our lunch break, I occasionally shared what I was learning about traditional practices with my staff and although no one responded directly or admitted to being circumcised, they expressed mixed opinions about whether their daughters would be circumcised. I remember Rebecca, a shy Ghanaian, smiled and with downcast eyes asked "Mistress Rahm, why do you want to know about that?"

Growing up Black in America I was well aware that in our community, there are certain subjects you just don't share with persons of another ethnic group and I respected that. As far as they were concerned whether they were circumcised or not was none of my damn business, and it wasn't. In reality, many of the indigenous women belonging to all of the tribes except the Kru, who do not circumcise, and the Americo-Liberians and Congo groups, were circumcised.

One never really knows who is listening or affected by what I said or the way it is said. This fact became abundantly clear as I sat in my office one particular day while the children and caregivers sang in the large front playroom. It was the morning lull, just before the children burst into the back area where I set up the different tables for a variety of learning activities, and lasted until lunchtime.

I looked up from my desk into the round face of a young Kpelle woman who volunteered at our daycare center so that her little girl, an only child, could socialize with the so-called "civilized" children. She always seemed to be at her daughter's side, and I was surprised to see her without the child.

She approached cautiously. "Can I talk with you ma?"

I nodded and she sat in the chair in front of my desk. She was silent for a moment, perhaps trying to gather her thoughts and muster her courage. Moments later, she went on to share her personal account of her circumcision. She recounted that her grandma had led her home to the interior, or hinterland away from the costal portion of Liberia, during school vacation. Lowering her eyes, she remembered the sadness she felt when she left her mother, but also the excitement she experienced at the thought of spending time with her grandma and the opportunity to meet her other relatives who lived in the forest of Gbarnga, three counties north of Monrovia. After her first day, her grandmother gave her over to a Zoe who walked her, and other anxious girls, miles into the Sande Bush or Bush School, the site for training young girls about the ways of their tribe and concluding with the secret rite of circumcision.

Once in the Bush, the girls were taught many practical things and tribal secrets that an initiate can never discuss with anyone uninitiated, meaning uncircumcised. However, Jartu was able to share with me that the pain was horrible and unexpected, and that the procedure was, as I already knew, performed without anesthetic. Most heart wrenching was the fact that she realized that her mother had been party to the deception. Tears welled in her eyes as she spoke of the betrayal and the wedge it had driven between their relationship.

The caregivers and children flooding into our area suddenly interrupted her disclosure. This was actually the first of two conversations that we would have regarding her circumcision. In our second talk, she shared that she had delivered her daughter in London where she had accompanied her husband for college. She was terrified to get prenatal care because she didn't want a pelvic exam that would expose her to foreign scrutiny. However during delivery her vagina had ripped badly because of scar tissue developed during her circumcision. She had required significant vaginal repair. She delivered in a teaching hospital, and her doctor had paraded youthful residents into her room to look at her vagina, as though there was not a person connected to it. The trauma of her delivery and the resulting disregard for her humanity had left physical and emotional scars that for her had resulted in a broken marriage and low self-esteem.

About a year after the first Traditional Practices meetings began, we learned that Mrs. Titus' husband was seriously ill and that she was leaving the group to focus on him. Knowing her discrete nature, I believed that she had known of his sickness when she first set me on this path, and that it had been her intention all along to have me serve as her proxy. Her strategy had worked. I was happy to represent the Liberian Red Cross Society on this committee and more importantly, emotionally, and intellectually was now invested in its success.

At the time I was living in our Peace Villa on the Old Road and after every meeting of the Traditional Practices group, as soon as I scrambled out of the taxi, I headed for my midwife friends to debrief. I realized what I was learning was important. It was only a matter of time until we'd have a Liberian sister join the Hebrew Israelites and we wanted to be sensitive and prepared if she had been circumcised.

By February of 1986, I also wrote articles for the *Observer* on daycare and attended a workshop on HIV/AIDS in Nairobi, Kenya. I had amassed a library of books and pamphlets from The World Health Organization, the IAC, and other international organizations with information and, of course, diagrams of circumcised vaginas. Essentially three types of circumcision are performed. There is the clitordectomy, the removal of all or part of the clitoris. A more extensive procedure, where in addition to the clitoris, the small lips of the vagina are also removed. And finally, there is the most extensive type of circumcision, is called infibulation where *all* external genitalia are removed, the vagina is then sewn together and is propped open with a reed or straw while healing, to permit the release of urine and menstrual blood. The 'finished' vagina looks like a smooth neat seam. Most of the major complications are a direct result of infibulation. I was relieved to learn from our sources that the less radical form of circumcision is most commonly performed in Liberia.

Cutting away the flesh with unsterile implements resulted in more trauma, more risk of infection and more scar tissue. As a woman, I couldn't imagine that a vagina that had been subjected to so much pain could ever be seen as a component of sexual pleasure

When I first saw the diagrams of circumcised vaginas, looking so different from anything I had ever imagined, *I just had to talk about it.* I carefully shared my beliefs and feelings in our Traditional Practices meetings, everything was discussed in a very collaborative and respectful manner, so my gasps and 'Oh my Gods' would have been misplaced. However, once at home among my sisters I was free to relax, let my filters down, and really express my opinions.

"Girl, look at this picture. My stuff does *not* look like that," I said opening the booklet from the Inter-African Committee exposing various views of circumcised vaginas.

"Get out of here!" Sheryrah shrieked when she saw the three types of circumcision and I walked her through the grim details. A couple of other sisters on the midwifery staff joined us and led the discussion and shared page by page illustration of each and every point, ending with, "Then there is an even crueler, form of circumcision called infibulation or the Pharaonic circumcision." I turned the page.

"That doesn't even look like she has a vagina, it's a seam!" Sheryrah shrieked. "How in the hell can you even piss?"

"Well, before they sew you up, they insert a reed or straw in there so that urine and blood can escape. I understand that in some Muslim groups the wife's vagina is opened on the wedding night so that her virginity is absolutely assured."

Ahavah, a thick southern woman from Georgia, who often assisted in child birthing had a disgusted look on her face, "Pass me that dang book; I can't even imagine going through something like that and living."

"Well, the girls are really young when they are circumcised," I replied, "You have seen little girls in Kakata and Mount Barclay walking around behind a woman. They are painted or chalked white, I think that means they are in Bush School and the white means they are 'invisible' and no one should see or talk to them."

"Yeah'O', they are little girls with no tits,"

"Uh huh."

"Ahnydah, that is just barbaric," Sheryrah said, whose bracelets clinked as she folded the laundry she had hastily jerked from the clothesline.

Everyone agreed.

Rackemya said, "If I'd had all that done to my vagina, I can see why the Mandingo women seem alright with their men having other wives. Who would even want to have sex when every time was painful.

"Why would you ever want a man inside you?" said Ahavah.

"I know that's how we think but when I'm in those meetings people seem pretty damn calm about it. I can't imagine dealing with being circumcised or worse yet having my daughters have to endure that."

Conversations with Mrs. Titus replayed in my mind. I realized she had done me a favor by advising me to listen a lot and not interject my personal opinions. At those early meetings, were several circumcised females who were trying to make an impact on their own cultural practice by breaking the code of silence. I could never fathom the conflict between their deeply held cultural values and their personal awareness of the harmful ramifications of female circumcision.

One afternoon, while living in the house we called the Peace Villa; we heard shouting and frantic knocking at our front door.

"Ma, de baby coming 'O'!"

Our Gbassa neighbor came to call us, her sister was in hard labor and needed help. Because our neighbors had witnessed the very public birthing of Zefron on our balcony, they knew that we delivered our own babies. Sheryrah sprang into action taking Ahavah with her.

Several hours later, they returned exhausted but exhilarated. They had delivered a beautiful baby girl to a circumcised Gbassa woman. Sheryrah had been prepared and wasn't frightened by a vagina that looked different from her own. She had massaged the woman's perineum with warm palm oil and supported it with her hands during the delivery to prevent major tearing.

The information I had shared with our midwives had helped them gain the respect of our tribal neighbors.

Interesting enough, under my not so watchful eye, information about the practice had been staring me in the face and I wasn't tuned in—at least not at the time. While I lived at the Peace Villa, Fatu, a Mandingo girl of about thirteen came to 'spend time' as the guest of Val, an elder sister. Her home was Alhaji Sherif's Compound on Benson Street. Alhaji Sherif was a powerful Muslim leader in Liberia and most times Muslims would live together with their leader in multiple houses surrounded by a wall, called a compound. Fatu had a mother-daughter bond with Val. The single sisters in that house shared the double sized bedroom on the second level of the home. There was a girl's dorm atmosphere behind the closed doors of the bedroom and the shared bathroom. The running joke was that Fatu never removed her panties, even in the shower. One morning, I remember rushing from my occupied bathroom, into the sister's bathroom to brush my teeth for work. I knocked and entered, Fatu was standing in the tub taking a bucket shower and she was wearing panties that were soaked.

"Fatu, you take bath with your panties on 'O'? I asked. Fatu was a tall, lanky girl and she just had lathered from head to toe, yet she was wearing pale yellow, silky panties. She just smiled. At the time, I had a teenage daughter of my own and thought, "They are all crazy." In hindsight, I believe Fatu was concealing a circumcised vagina.

Once our children were down for the night and there was some space to talk, quietly we would look over the diagrams and just try to imagine having other women hold you down with all their might while you screamed in pain from being cut without anesthesia. I could only imagine that during infibulations a person could go into shock or simply pass into unconsciousness. In fact, I've heard that in cases of assault where the victim is stabbed or shot multiple times, the brain blocks the pain and they lose sensation. Muslim families of financial means, desiring the more extensive circumcision, tended to send their daughters, back to Guinea or Ivory Coast for Bush School. However, I was sure that somewhere in the Lofa or Nimba County, near the boarders of Guinea and the Ivory Coast, where there was a high concentration of Muslims, girls were being infibulated.

When I examine my personal feelings about female circumcision, I understand it as a practice that is physically and psychologically harmful to women. These practices reflect the fact that all paternalist cultures lay the burden of control of male sexuality at the feet of women. While I can condemn the practice, I can also deeply relate to the dilemma. What parent can't honestly confess that when their daughter reaches puberty, they begin to fear their budding sexuality? We wish there was some way, any way, to put their sexuality on lock-down. Yet it seems as if neither religion, nor reason, nor cruelty is able to succeed at this.

In 1986, Liberian women decided for themselves that while they understood the harmful effects of female circumcision, they were unwilling to sacrifice the spiritual significance of the initiation to their culture and age-old wisdom of their tribal history. They wanted their daughters and granddaughters to grow up good Gbassa girls, good Kpelle girls, or good Krahn girls, not just good Liberian girls. Ethnic identity and the passing of the sacred wisdom of their tribe was most important to these women. Liberian women favored bringing and keeping Zoes into the discussion of female circumcision. This way, there was the flow of education about harmful health consequences and the Zoes received lifesaving information on the importance of the sterilization of tools used in the rite.

Again, as a woman from another culture, my struggle was to remain objective and accept the fact that only Liberian women could be the decision makers on this issue. However, over the years, I have to admit to a curiosity about whether the practice of female circumcision was affected by the Liberian Civil War. I hope that the unintended consequence of war was the drastic reduction in this cultural practice.

Tikvah and children playing at day care

ONE FOOT ON A BANANA PEEL

'One foot on a banana peel, the other foot out the door,' a saying most often used when a person is in imminent danger of being fired from their j-o-b.

After EliTikvah's birth, I worked not only with the Traditional Practices group on female circumcision, but also with the Christian Health Association of Liberia. I can't really explain how I managed to balance my family, my job, and find time for development activities, except that I rarely slept more than four hours a night. When I wasn't working, I was constantly washing diapers or clothes, sewing my children's garments by hand, braiding hair, writing lesson plans, or attending meeting upon meeting. Alternately, supported and conflicted by the fact that ours was a communal lifestyle, I moved, often mindlessly, from one task to the next. The extracurricular activities allowed me to surrender my attention to my personal life, but burying my head in the sand was only a temporary measure and far from a solution.

Experiencing frequent separations from my children helped me empathize with the struggles of indigenous Liberian families who lived in the hinterland, who often went without sources of clean water, schools, and where the nearest medical care could be days away. Many routinely sent their children from the interior to live with distant relatives, and sometimes even strangers, Americo-Liberians who would keep their child in exchange for service in the home or companionship for another child. If the children worked diligently for the families who were caring for them, there was the promise of some level of education, or the opportunity for betterment that might someday enable them to help their siblings or aged parents. I also heard of situations where small children were sent from the interior to live in cities like Monrovia where they were little more than slaves. Some were abused and beaten until they ran away to become homeless "grunna," or grown children fending for themselves in the world.

The more I studied and observed traditional practices in Liberia, the more I critiqued the cultural practices of Hebrew Israelites that I had had agreed to accept as well as other cultural practices in general. Appalled, I watched indigenous Liberian women work themselves into premature old age and knew that my Hebrew sisters, at least in Liberia, felt as though the men were doing the decision making while the women bore the consequences of any action, or inaction they took. Liberian women had child after child, and like their Hebrew sisters were unable to ask a husband to simply use a condom to space our pregnancies. I also observed Lebanese merchants imprison their women and children, with lock and key, in apartments behind wrought iron gates, metaphorically locking them inside the Middle Eastern culture. I began to have an out-of-culture experience, spiritually looking beyond all the cultures that formed the ethnic tapestry of Liberia. One thing was for sure—I understood that being a woman, with its limited options, was infinitely more difficult than being a man in every culture I knew.

I was at a dangerous impasse, dangling between two worlds, rapidly approaching the reality that I was nearing the day when I must decide.

Was I really committed to being a Hebrew? Should I try to use my waning influence with Elrahm to convince him to leave and, failing at that, leave without him?

At home I was under a lot of pressure that I escaped in town. The sisters who lived in Kakata and in Panesville, those that didn't work or live in town were sheltered. I had been told by a the wife of one of the Red Cross Board Members that our most senior leader was gambling—and losing—a lot of money in the casino of Hotel Africa. This would account for why, despite the fact that our enterprises were bringing enough money to support us, we were always in some kind of financial crisis. I had witnessed the arrival and departure of three other heads of our Liberian Mission. The current leader was the only one I never liked. I had tried to befriend him in the spirit of the adage, "keep your friends close, and your enemies closer," but while my husband was in Ghana, he was in the habit of having our security to awaken me in the middle of the night for discussions in his room. It finally dawned on me that he was trying to seduce me! I stopped answering the knocks on my door and he began summoning someone else into his room for "discussions." I buried these thoughts in my work. I was doing something valuable at the Red Cross, something that made me proud.

I embraced and often reflected upon the psychic readers' foreshadowing that my Karma was "to learn to serve and serve willingly." Communal life had continuously provided me opportunities to observe myself in comparison to women in a parallel culture. The impact of those experiences on me was that I understood the parity of our lives, and that regardless of how it appeared to others, in the end, we are all just living the life we have and learning as we grow. I learned tremendous lessons about selflessness from living communally, but the path to that realization was complicated. Regardless to my personal struggles, I was committed to continue to serve…willingly. Well, as willingly as I could.

On a daily basis, EliTikvah and I moved between our work at the Red Cross Day Care Center and meetings for numerous non-governmental organizations (NGOs) in Monrovia. My little girl was always in my arms or tied to my back in a lappa. One evening, after our Traditional Practices group, Mrs. Marshall, a woman of incredible directness, approached me, taking me off guard.

"Ahnydah, why is this baby so miserable?"

Her comment stripped my emotions back like a sharp knife shaving the skin from an orange. I bristled. "Why would you say something like that, Mrs. Marshall?"

"Tikvah moans a lot and she nurses, almost desperately, like she's hungry, but then I've seen her vomit the milk all over you. I'm a mother and I've been a registered nurse for a thousand years my dear, and the way I see it, you are *with* your daughter but you are not *connecting*."

"She's with me all day and all night. We're never separated!" I said, defensively.

"Yes but when she's with you, you are not really with her."

My face burned but she did not back down.

"Mrs. Rahm, I see that you are doing really good work, but you need to think more about your little girl. She is not even trying to walk or talk, and I'm guessing EliTikvah is nearly two years old. There is something going on."

Emotionally, I was dangling by a thread, more like an elastic band about to break. I felt like she was seeing inside my heart.

"She's eighteen months and I just don't know what to do! I try to get her to walk, but she just screams to be put on my back. I can't even get her to eat. They feed her breakfast and lunch at the Red Cross, but in the evening, it's so hard to get her to take solid food from me that I just end up nursing her because my other children need me, too, sometime!"

"I understand my dear."

Then I voiced the thing I feared most. The thought I ran from. Remembering the prayer really the bargain that I thought I had struck with God. That if I found the strength to bear this one last child, she would be born perfect. Was this now a cruel, delayed punishment?

"Do you think that she could be …retarded or something?"

"No, not from what I can determine, but I want you to take Tikvah to a doctor friend of mine. Dr. Guluma is pretty close to where you work and he is very, very good. If there is something wrong, he is the person to tell you what the next steps would be. Make an appointment."

"I will, I promise. I'm just feeling pulled this way and that…" My voice trembled and tears escaped down my face. I felt relieved. I had not condemned my child. At least Mrs. Marshall didn't think so.

"Listen to me, my dear, you are doing a fine job with the Traditional Practices Committee, and I really appreciate that you took on the role of being the secretary of this thing after Zaria left, but I've been watching you, and you look like you are running from something. You had better stop before you sacrifice this pretty baby's health," she said grabbing Tikvah's outstretched hand and smiling at my daughter, as if to say, *There, I have done my best with your mother.*

As she left the conference room, leaving me alone with my thoughts and baby, I felt the bottom fall out from under me. It was not until I noticed EliTikvah's feet moving around my waist that I remembered she had witnessed the entire conversation. I wondered if she knew how scared I was. I *had* noticed that my daughter was not developing normally, and I had tried to bury my fears, but now I had to face them.

The next afternoon, during naptime, I walked into Dr. Guluma's office and introduced myself as Rachael Marshall's friend. His office was crowded, but he had his receptionist call us into the office. After a thorough examination, he told me that he could find no evidence of neurological problems that could account for her delayed speech and walking.

"So why isn't Tikvah walking then?"

"This little girl can walk whenever she wants to. The question you need to ask yourself is *why* doesn't she want to?"

No matter which way I looked at it, all the signs for her delayed development kept pointing back to me. When I said my prayers, I made a silent commitment to do everything I could to help Tikvah walk. Looking back, a quote attributed to Goethe about intention resonates in my soul. It states, "At the moment of commitment, the Universe rises to support you."

I didn't know it then, but an unexpected intervention was coming our way.

On February 28, 1986, I was still living in Monrovia on the Old Road in headquarters. The members that operated our retail business in town, or that worked in Monrovia, lived in this house as well. My husband had been living in town with me, and the children were visiting us from Panesville for the weekend. We were preparing to join the festivities of a Hebrew Israelite holiday, Yom le Mokereem, *A Day of Love.*

The day was a family day, planned to be fun for children and adults—volleyball, soccer, and basketball games, relay races, a feast, and the opportunity to bond with other families. Typically, holidays meant an abundance of work for the Sisters who cooked for well over a hundred people. I had risen at dawn to make 'hand burgers," which were lentil beans soaked overnight, ground in a meat grinder, seasoned, molded into patties, and then pan-fried. Once the food was ready, we dressed the children in their sports outfits, sown by their own mothers.

When my family was ready, I pleaded with Elrahm, "Rahm, can you and the children go ahead? I just need some time to get myself together."

"Why can't you just get ready now? I'll wait a few minutes."

"Thank you for offering to wait, but I need some time. I haven't had a shower, my hair—everything is just a mess! I want to look nice."

"So who is going to take care of Tikvah?"

"Rahm, I need you to take her. Binah can keep up with her until I get there, and if she has something to do, give her to one of the older girls."

He turned and stormed away, then called the children to get in the van.

Our eldest daughter, Binah, had turned eighteen and decided that she no longer wanted to be a Hebrew. She had run away from our Community with Roland, a Liberian boy we had raised in our community, to live in a one-room house without an indoor bathroom in Panesville. I blamed myself for Binah leaving, and since she was the first of the Hebrew children to leave the Community, I bore the brunt of heavy criticism.

Our Binah was so naïve and her life had been sheltered in Liberia. It was routine for Liberian girls her age to ride a crowded bus in the darkness in order to reach Waterside general market to buy bushels of greens to sell on a table in the market. Some young girls had born two, even three children by the time they are Binah's age, spending their entire lives uneducated and working increasingly hard over the years to feed their young ones. I wondered if a cruel twist of fate would cause my daughter to become one of those women. Would she work all day, only to return in the evening to a small room, warm up a little rice over the coal pot, and bathe in water warmed over its dying embers? I had chosen to raise my children in Liberia, and now the advantages offered in America were unavailable here in Liberia, and I was starting to see the negative impact of Liberia and its culture.

I was riding the edge of a double-edged sword, and the cuts kept coming and going deeper.

We had invited Binah to come and spend the day of Yom lem mo kareem with her siblings. We hoped that seeing everyone on a joyous occasion would cause her to miss the familiarity of her friends and family; make her homesick.

I peered through the shuttered window as the other Hebrews, which we sometimes referred to as Saints, took their places in the bus and Elrahm handed EliTikvah to another adult to hold.

Grabbing my bath items, I went and washed my hair and showered. My thick hair required a lot of care to maintain a neatly braided style, and I had recently cut it into a short Afro. Finally, alone with myself, my thoughts and my feeling, the tears came, softly at first, but then long buried sounds escaped from the depths of my soul, and I found myself sitting on the floor of the shower sobbing, until no more tears came. Finally having found my breath, I said, "God I am not happy here. I'm not mad at anybody, but I am not happy. I don't know what to do, but God, today I leave this in Your hands because I cannot carry the unhappiness anymore. *You* take it."

I rose from the shower floor feeling giddy and light. I put on a pretty pink East Indian pant outfit and topped off my cropped hairstyle with a pink barrette. I walked to the Old Road, boarded a crowded bus to Panesville, joined my family, and had a blessed day of fun with them.

As the sun lowered in the sky, we said Shalom to Binah and watched her walk to the road with her old friends, while we walked our other children to their dormitories. As we prepared to leave the compound ourselves, the Mission Leader summoned us into a meeting. At first, I thought we might be expecting guests from the U.S. or Israel, or maybe that we were being moved. I was unnerved. I picked Tikvah up and brought her along. I remembered the incident with Sheryrah in Kakata. Suddenly, a queasy feeling came over me as we all sat together in the dimly lit room. I balanced Tikvah on my lap and nursed her as the Mission Leader began to talk. His words, directed at me, sounded like he was talking through a wind tunnel, yet I heard him perfectly.

"Sister Ahnydah, *you* have always been a troublemaker; *you* have never really been a Hebrew."

When I reflected on all the sacrifices I had made, all of the hard work I had put into trying to fit in, and now to hear from this man that none of it meant anything, I was dumbstruck. My heart pounded. I was trembling so hard I knew if I spoke, my teeth would chatter.

He continued condemning me. "*You* are wicked, and you have always been wicked."

My eyes widened as anger welled in my throat. I longed to shout, *"I know that you've been gambling our money away at Hotel Africa. I despise you for trying to seduce me while my husband was away!"*

I wanted to shout all of that, and more, however, a small voice inside my head quieted me.

"And *you* sit there with your mouth open. Nothing is coming out Sister because there is nothing for you to say!"

Despite the fact that my mouth was dry and gaped open, my eyes were wet and fearful, I said nothing. His mouth continued to move, spouting cruel words, until his voice simply faded. I was deaf.

In the end, the actual charges against me were vague and bogus. My only crime had been sharing my frustration over my husband's extended assignment in Ghana, and telling my mentor, the leader of our Ghana Mission, that two married persons in leadership were having an affair in Liberia that was affecting their judgment. My observations, and the grumblings of others on the Mission, were that the practice of deploying people on missions without their partners was destructive over the long haul to healthy marriages. Nobody had ever blown the whistle. Now our Mission Leader had a beef with me. Sitting in that room, being attacked by the Mission Leader, I realized that my mentor had only talked like a tough guy but he wasn't very powerful after all. I learned that often in organizations, the people who ought to have power, don't. Another life lesson brought the hard way.

That evening, I was humiliated and suspended from the Hebrew Community for seventy days. The suspension dictated that I leave my children, with the exception of my nursing daughter Tikvah, behind with their father.

On the way home, Elrahm, who had sat silently while our Mission Leader leveled accusations against me, was livid.

"What in the hell could you have done to make him put you out?!"

"Elrahm, I didn't *do* anything. This is about something I said in confidence to my mentor. I'm not going to bother to even repeat it because it wouldn't do any good now."

"I don't believe you. You had to have done something more than that! What was it?"

I was not getting through to him, but the question burning my flesh was: *Why didn't you speak up for me, your wife? Why didn't you trust me more than him?*

Woulda, Shoulda, Coulda…

I shoulda seen this coming. My gut had warned me, but I had blown it off. I reflected on the Saturday that our Mission leader had returned from Ghana. I was visiting my children in Panesville and helping several sisters cook dinner. While in the outdoor cooking area stirring a 25-gallon soup pot, I saw him talking to a group of brothers and sisters surrounding him. Suddenly, he spun around and looked in my direction. Our eyes locked, and he cast a dirty look at me that went straight to the pit of my stomach. That look had haunted me until the eventful night of Yom lem mokareem.

Elrahm was assigned to Ghana since early in my pregnancy with EliTikvah. I was battling depression and didn't much care then, but I had missed him during the later months of the pregnancy, and again at her delivery. He had been home only once since her birth and now for Yom lem mokareem. During his absence, I had worked hard to take care of our children, to make him proud of us, and to rebuff our leader's carefully calculated romantic advances.

Before Binah had run off with Roland, I had increased bean sprout sales enough to pay tuition for her, Roland, and her best friend, Aylah, to attend AME Zion Academy High School. I leveraged my connections at Abi Joudi Supermarket to secure a potential retail outlet for the honey Elrahm was planning to bring back to Liberia from a bee farm he had created in Ghana. I had desperately longed for appreciation, not censure.

My head was spinning; I could hardly believe how much my husband had changed. I had stopped considering him my best friend and confident, but I had not betrayed him or even considered it. I still felt intense loyalty for him. It cut so deeply that after sixteen years together, he could allow anyone to do anything to me without immediately leaping to my defense? Even *if* I was wrong, and I wasn't, he should have fought for me. I would have fought for him. Barely coherent, it was all I could do to hold onto Tikvah.

Pain seared through my heart as we walked down the road to get a taxi from Panesville back to the Old Road, but somehow, I knew that the events of this evening had been set into motion long ago, and I knew, somehow, the Unseen Hand was in the midst of this.

Family photo taken in Liberia

OUT OF THE FRYING PAN, INTO THE FIRE

I had seven days to find a place to live. I kept replaying the reasons for my exile, but in the end, the official reasons given were, in a word—bullshit—a veiled attempt to cover a personal vendetta. I was still struggling with censure. I was still reeling with pain that my husband had not jumped to my defense, unwittingly dealing the deathblow to our relationship. Depressed and confused, I suffered.

For six days, I kept my own counsel, daring not to discuss my feelings with Elrahm. He was no longer my life partner, only my children's father. Still, I was paralyzed, unable to do much more than go to and from work and lay sleepless at night while the days, hours, minutes, and seconds ticked by.

On Saturday, the Hebrew Sabbath, I had to leave. I had made no living arrangements, and so, I lay in bed praying a prayer of deliverance. I took a hot shower and dressed in my best business lappa suit. Ordinarily on weekends, my children were brought to Monrovia to visit me, but today, and for the next seventy days, they would remain in Panesville, being cared for by the Sisters that would look after them while I served my suspension. EliTikvah stayed behind, oblivious to our predicament. I left her playing with her father as I walked to the road to hail a taxi.

I asked the driver to head toward town. In the back seat, I prayed silently that God would show me where to stop since I had no idea where I was going. As the taxi neared the YWCA on the Old Road, I thought that might be a logical option, but when the taxi stopped, a little voice inside my head loudly ordered me to get back inside. I was not going to ignore my internal voice this time! I jumped back in so abruptly that the driver asked, "Mommie, what happen 'O?'"

"Keep going Yah, I made a mistake."

We drove another ten minutes until we reached Sinkor where the wrought iron gated grounds of the Methodist Guest House came into view. I will never be able to explain it, but physical warmth embraced and beckoned me through the gates. I stopped the taxi and paid the driver.

Liberians have a phrase, "As God so fixed it," that best describes what happened next. Providence led me to Sister Dorothea, the manager of the Methodist Guest House, a hostel for missionaries and students. I truly cannot remember how I entered her office, but as soon as I saw her heavy frame and round face, so open and maternal, and even after she was abrupt and told me that she didn't have any vacancies, I still continued to talk to her. I knew that I could reach her, because despite her directness, I felt her aura of kindness. She offered me water, and while I drank the cold glass of water and ran my tongue over the small lumps of ice, I measured my words, trying not to sound like a victim. I wanted help, not pity.

"I work for the Red Cross as the Director of the Day Care Center. Do you know Reverend Lloyd?"

"Yes, he is my friend. You work for him?"

"Yes, he is Gbassa, are you Gbassa too?" I asked, though I already knew the answer.

"Yes."

"Sister Dorothy, my husband is not with my daughter and me now, he… is upcountry, but I need to find a place today. I have nowhere to go.

166

I am stopping with friends, and they need the room I have today."

"Even if I had a room, it would not be suitable for you. It isn't clean, and it's probably too small for you."

"Sister Dorothea, I will just need to stop somewhere safe until my husband comes for us. I am at work all day; we just need a sleeping room."

"You have other children?"

"Yes ma'am, but they don't live with me right now. If you could just find a small room, we could manage until my husband comes."

"Children are not allowed."

"I hear you 'O', but my baby is nursing. She goes where I go. She is small, but she does not cry," I said, reeling at having to tell an outright lie.

"We come home late and I promise she will not be outside playing on the grounds."

This was the closest I had ever come to begging, but when she looked at me over her horn-rimmed glasses, I knew she understood my desperation. After mumbling a disclaimer that the room she had probably wouldn't meet *my* needs, she motioned for me to follow her. I prayed silently as she walked me from her office and crossed the carefully manicured grounds. As we walked across the campus, she spoke to several college aged women and men. I followed her to a room she 'found' in a smaller building behind one of the larger ones on the spacious campus. The first floor room was sparsely furnished and had one window that looked into a wild garden. It had its own kitchen and private bath. On the strength of her friendship with my boss at the Red Cross, Sister Dorothea agreed that I could move in that evening.

In Liberia, most clerical and professional positions pay monthly. I had just enough cash to buy food and get us back and forth to work until payday. I promised to pay my rent when I took pay in two weeks. Again, she gave me the 'look,' but reluctantly agreed. As I walked to flag a taxi, my heart leapt in wonderment. The room at the hostel was actually better than the room I shared with my husband at the State House. That evening, my baby daughter and I moved into the Methodist

Guest House. EliTikvah and I were alone. In the evenings, after dinner and our baths, we sat peacefully in the darkness of our room, staring out into the tropical garden, listening to the approaching sounds of night.

We lived at the Methodist Guest House for a little over a month, until once again, divine providence smiled upon us. Friends, former Hebrews, now Rastafarians, were traveling to Ethiopia. Rastas believe that the last Emperor of Ethiopia is the Messiah and in the same way that devout Muslims want to visit Mecca and devout Christians want to visit the Holy Land, Rastafarians want to visit Ethiopia. They needed a house sitter. I moved into their apartment rent-free! Their trip turned into somewhat of a disaster, and they ended up returning after one month, but they knew I had released my little apartment and invited Tikvah and me to share a bedroom with their son while I saved for a larger apartment of my own.

When my seventy days were over, I had been away long enough to feel a sense of freedom and peace. I do not quite remember how I told Elrahm that I would not be returning, that I had decided to make my break from the Hebrew Israelite Community permanent. I do remember his dark, almost black, eyes pleading as he said, "You can't just try one more time?"

I know that meant that he wanted to keep our family together, that he didn't want us to fight over where our children would live, and he was willing to continue the détente that had characterized our existence. But, I had no more "trying" in me. That's not to say that I didn't love Rahm. I did, and I would love him for many years to come, but now I knew that loving him couldn't trump loving me. It had for a long time, but it didn't any longer. I needed a place large enough for my other children to join us. Without my children, I felt like Sampson after his unwanted haircut. My children were the source of my strength. My children were my motivation. Everything was a blur. Perhaps others saw me as clever and self-reliant but I was depressed and afraid. For so long I had surrendered control over my personal life, now I had to climb into the front seat and drive.

It was all I could do to get myself to work while trying to handle the major change in my life. I divested myself of all my outside commitments. I resigned as Secretary of the Traditional Practices Group, and besides growing sprouts, I came straight home after work to focus all my attention and love on my daughter. It finally clicked that EliTikvah was showing, by her refusal to walk and talk, that *she* should be my priority. Within two months, Tikvah walked across the living room floor to me, soon weaned herself from breast milk to ground pea milk, and began speaking her first few words.

Not long after Tikvah started walking, Elrahm mentioned casually that he was taking another wife. He said it as though we had discussed this before, we hadn't. I sympathized a little because I realized that he hadn't known how to tell me. I knew the Liberian sister and she was a good person. In fact our birthdays were close together, both of us Aries. Not that knowing made me feel better, just clearer.

A result of living communally is the voluntary unconscious surrender of control over ones' own life. While I was a member of the Hebrew Israelite Community, everything was based upon what was good for the collective. The transition to being my own decision-maker was overwhelming. Deciding where to rent an apartment, which simply involved how much money I had for rent and a budgeting of my money to cover my expenses was stressful. I already managed the entire budget for the daycare center but the shift from turning in all my money and getting a monthly allowance to managing the entire amount overwhelmed me.

Though I enjoyed and missed the fellowship with Ahavah, Sheryrah and Mahteemia, I had fanaticized about what life outside of the Community would feel like. Friendships I had developed outside of the Hebrew Community turned out to be a Godsend. I was lost without the support of my tribe and soon realized that I had jumped out of the frying pan squarely into the fire!

FREAH MEAT ON LYNCH STREET

Despite not wanting to be with the Hebrew Israelite Community, I wanted to be with my friends. I loved Liberia and her people, but I realized that I would never *be* a Liberian. I felt a terrible sense of isolation and grief. How could I be enough for my children, without their father who showed no signs of capitulating, despite my walking away from him and the very Community that had brought us here. I swallowed the bitter truth that Elrahm *was* a Hebrew and that meant more to him than I did. Maybe most people don't feel that they are the cause of the breakup of a family but I blamed myself for not being able to become the submissive woman that he needed and that the Hebrews wanted; it just was not in me.

Aretha, my daycare supervisor, was now also my life coach. I was so ashamed about the move and the reasons behind it that I didn't share it with my frequent Peace Corps visitor, Ray or any of my other American associates. I approached my housing search as Aretha would have. I focused on finding a clean room with indoor plumbing. I needed to be within walking distance of the day care center, near the heart of town, close to schools, and near the Rally Time Market. I still had two weekly bean sprout deliveries, and I needed to be near the Lebanese supermarkets.

After living on a rubber plantation in Kakata, and navigating the subtleties of using and cleaning an outhouse, I felt I had earned the right to move on. I have never been very materialistic, but as a "responsible woman" and a Director at the Red Cross, I at least deserved indoor bathroom facilities!

Aretha directed me to a two-story brick home a block away from the Red Cross building. It was in the middle of a cluster of houses, some in various stages of construction, set back off the road on Lynch Street. The owner was an attractive Kpelle woman, nicknamed SC. She and Aretha looked like relatives, perhaps because they were both Kpelle women. SC was a shorter version of Aretha, but they were both Botticelliesque, 'thick' and curvy. Both had flawless skin, the color of unsweetened chocolate, perfect white teeth, and oily, straightened raven hair. Both were quick to smile and both, as I recall, were openhearted.

SC's apartment was on the second floor. She was married, but rumored to be estranged from her husband. Her household was comprised of her husband's adult nephew, a spoiled eight-year-old daughter that she doted on, and four other kids she was raising for families upcountry. She sent these kids to government-operated elementary schools, and they earned their keep selling her baked goods, cornbread, shortbread, and sugar cookies in the Market.

The entire first floor of the house had been a nightclub. SC, a Born Again Christian, had re-consecrated the building. She was anxious to rent the largest room, as well as the bathroom facilities and the "kitchen," to me. Aretha negotiated my rent down from $95.00 to $65.00 per month. Her bargaining chip was that SC would be getting her rent, each and every month, guaranteed, something uncommon in Liberia.

SC only had two ironclad demands. First, I must have iron bars installed before moving in any of my possessions, and secondly, because of large rodents that bred in the garbage behind the open market, she insisted that I have a 2 x 4 block cut to keep any stray rats from crawling under my bedroom door. I agreed and was happy to have a room of my own again. I would soon learn that this coveted room would be the most challenging place I would ever live.

During my walkthrough, I saw that the room I would be renting was about 20 x 20 feet, with two windows, one on the east wall and another on the north wall that provided a wonderful cross breeze. The concrete floor, painted red, struggled to provide grounding for the blinding sunflower yellow wall bearing a gaudy bright blue, red, and orange mural on two of the four walls. The color scheme provided a very gay atmosphere in a bar, but as a bedroom backdrop, it hurt the eyes and screamed, "Yikes!" A six-foot wooden table and two kitchen chairs sat in the middle of the room to offset a decorating nightmare that I had neither the vision nor the energy to address.

Exiting the room, a kitchen was on the left and down a short hall. It was small but adequate with a concrete floor and a window with scattered panes of louvered glass. The place boasted a kitchen table and space where our coal pots could sit during rainy season and a small sink with a faucet running cold water. Sometimes, the supply of water in Monrovia was cut off unexpectedly, so most people kept containers to hold water. Following Aretha's guidance, I purchased an empty 55-gallon plastic pork barrel with a top to store extra water.

The bathroom was to the right of my room in the hallway. There was a ceiling socket with a light bulb screwed in with a short pull-chain. Even with the light, the bathroom was cave-like. The walls and the tub were unpainted concrete, and the water in the tub ran, at least it did the day of my walkthrough. I could tell that a bubble bath was not in my immediate future. To bathe, you sat your bucket of lukewarm (if you were lucky) water into the rough-hewn tub and bathed standing with your flips flops on. Across from the tub was a stall with a half wooden door providing privacy for a toilet that was modern but encrusted with filth inside and out. There were smashed earthworms on the floor and a dead roach lay belly-up beside the toilet. The whole downstairs reeked of stale booze.

After my walkthrough, I went back to work feeling shaken. Had my life come to this? How would I ever get that place clean enough to make a home for my children? When I unloaded my feelings on Aretha, she just threw her head back laughing and promised, "Mistress Rahm, we will help you clean it!"

I used a piece of linoleum that I had received as a 'dash' after buying new flooring for the day care center to provide a scrub-able surface for the concrete floor in my room. Until I could afford bunk beds, my children would be sleeping on pallets. During naptime, Aretha had brought her carpenter friend, Seah, to install the linoleum in my room and to cut the required 2 x 4 to fit against the bottom of my door to keep rats out. SC recommended a welder to make the iron window bars.

By Friday afternoon, I was ready to move in. Shop boys brought my new double bed that morning, and everything else was crammed into a station wagon taxi. Binah picked Tikvah up after naptime and took her to Panesville. A toddler would just be in the way while we cleaned that filthy room.

I turned the shiny key in the lock of my new room with Aretha, Ma Mae and Marta behind me. Saah and Andrew filled their buckets in the bathroom preparing to clean and scrub floors.

The door opened onto my new reality.

"Mistress Rahm, the room is big 'O'," declared Aretha.

My staff was kind and affirmed the positive qualities of my new home, yet I felt ashamed that they were seeing me in this situation. After all, I was the boss, the Big Ma, the person who helped *them* problem solve.

"Two windows, you will get good breeze 'O'," Martha chimed in.

"Let's sit all the cleaning supplies on my table and decide who will do what," I stated, feigning control.

After scrubbing my new bedroom, I decided to tackle the bathroom. Three hours later, we were all dog-tired. Everybody left for home and I was left all alone.

My evolving game plan for my family was simple. For now, I just wanted a clean space to live in. Long term, I planned to save enough money to buy some blueprints for a modest home, purchase some land, and then, like indigenous Liberians, build the home in spurts by scraping together enough money periodically to buy concrete to have blocks made. People work slowly to build a home, and the government doesn't assess taxes until the roof is completed.

Aretha was my inspiration. She was building her home room by room. I would do the same.

My knees were sore from scrubbing the concrete bathroom floor, but I was hungry, so after bathing and changing into a fresh lappa, I decided to walk the mile from my room to Broad Street for comfort food—a grilled cheese and fries.

Friday night was party time in Monrovia, and the clubs were alive with hi-life music, laughing, and partying people. The restaurant under the Palm Hotel was crowded, and I waited nearly thirty minutes to buy a grilled cheese sandwich, piping hot French fries, and one icy cold Orange Fanta, which I sipped on the walk home.

I returned to the smell of chlorine and disinfectant in the breezeway, and walked down the clean hallway to my scrupulously clean room to enjoy my snack. The food was worth the wait. The double slices of American cheese were thick, and when I took a bite, the sandwich oozed butter. I sprinkled salt on my still warm fries. Finally unwinding, I drifted off to sleep.

Several hours later, a sudden noise awakened me. I opened my eyes to see my purse floating slowly across the table towards the window. Was I dreaming? I blinked and recognized my purse handle suspended on a long wooden stick. Thieves were attempting to rob me! My eyes traveled up the stick to a well-muscled brown arm. I opened my mouth to scream, I tried repeatedly but no sound came. Instinctively, I reached for the bedside saltshaker and hurled it towards the window. This broke the paralysis of my vocal cords. I screamed, "Rogue, Rogue, Rogue! Rogue, Rogue, Rogue!"

My purse hit the table. Feet thundered away from the house.

I stumbled to the window and stood trembling, gaping at the abandoned mortar stick. My, legs buckled.

"Rogue, Rogue, Rogue!"

Terrified and desperate, I fled into the hallway. I beat on the door of the women who shared the front room. No answer! Bolting up the back stairs to my landlady's apartment, I knocked frantically until a boy of about twelve answered. He said that SC and the others had gone to visit family in Gbarnga and would return Sunday. Men had tried to get into my room. Would they come back?

The wind-up clock on the kitchen table read nearly 5 a.m. SC's son and I were alone in the building. I unlocked the back door and went outside. My recently washed louvered window glasses were neatly stacked on the ground outside the window. The rope that had served as a curtain rod dangled near the window, curtains still attached. There I stood, with a twelve-year-old, trying to wrap my head around what had just happened.

One of my new neighbors, an elderly Fula man, came outside to show compassion. Others had heard me cry out, but he alone had come to see what had happened. Initially, I was wary of him, but he was so much smaller than the massive arm I had seen stretched into my window, that I figured he could be no danger. I explained what had happened, and when I told him I had been asleep in the room with the lights on, he chastised me.

"You slept with the lights on, Ay Yah?"

"I was afraid to be in the dark."

"So you *invited* a Rogue to see you sleeping?"

I was used to living in a Community of people, away from the squalor and crime of the city. I was like a frightened child, afraid of the dark and sleeping with the light on. Talk about an 'Aha!' moment. Reality check! I now lived in a dangerous urban environment, and needed to be aware of my surroundings and actions.

As we walked the "crime scene," the old man told me that there had actually been two men by my window. He had been awakened by voices and heard them talking just before he heard my screams. He told me that rogues prefer to work in pairs to protect each other from a vigilante mob that will often chase, beat, and even kill them before the police or soldiers can get to them.

We talked until daylight, and I was grateful for the company. I am sure my neighbor wondered why I wanted to live in this former tavern in a raunchy part of town instead of with my own people, but he never asked and I never told him. I waited for Rally Time market to open and comforted myself in anticipation of the early afternoon when Rahm would bring my children for a visit. Now was it abundantly clear why SC had demanded the installation of bars before I moved in.

Over time, my feeling of violation from the attempted robbery dissipated. I came to understand and accept that I was living in the middle of poverty and poverty breeds crime. I would feel fear many more times while we lived on Lynch Street, yet I never feared being beaten, raped, or murdered.

Liberia was above senseless violence in 1985, but change was rapidly on its way.

Woman carrying her baby in her lappa

THE HAND THAT ROCKS THE CRADLE

Growing, harvesting, and bringing food to the market are traditional roles that allow women in Liberia to provide the underpinnings of the entire economy, and yet, other than the power they take for themselves by banding together as market women, they are grossly undervalued. In 1986, there were no childcare services targeted specifically for the market women's children, but I set out to change that.

Our Center's enrollment had increased to the point that neither Aretha nor I had time to make a daily trip to the Rally Time Market. Aretha sent word to her contacts in the market to let them know we wanted them to bring us greens, oil, and fish, chicken, or beef. Business savvy market women began arriving at the door of the day care center with their best offerings. Because we were buying in quantity, we received an extra "dash" of food, which helped stretch the budget more. While Aretha was "shopping," the market women stood in the doorway, watching our children play in a clean, safe space with women that looked like them, focused on their care. They saw babies being cuddled and remarked wistfully that they wished they had help caring for their children. Several brought their babies and allowed their little ones to watch the other children at play, but I noticed they never released them from their lappas.

On several occasions, some of the market women asked how much we charged for school, but knowing that the $50 a month price was too much for them, we would simply ignore the question. I repeatedly asked myself why market women, the backbone of Liberia, who balanced wide aluminum pans full of food on their heads with their babies swaddled in lappa cloth on their backs, had no one to help them to care for their children. Whenever I asked others about childcare for market women, they said that the market women would *never* allow strangers to care for their children.

Rally Time Market, with its vibrant commercial atmosphere, was one of the more "modern" markets. The main section of the Market boasted smooth, concrete floors and zinc roofing. The few rudimentary bathroom stalls rarely worked. Around the main market building were rows and rows of raw wooden tables that exposed the fact that the market was not adequate to contain all the sellers. These tables were unsheltered from the sun or rain.

I loved being in the Market. When I had first arrived in Liberia, I made the comparison between the open-air markets and the supermarkets I was accustomed to in America, and considered those in Liberia filthy and disgusting. I later realized that to call the markets filthy is much like calling the fields where vegetables grow dirty. The market was not only part of the economic delivery chain for food, goods and some services, but it was also about relationships. It was a place where people talked, challenged, and negotiated with each other. I learned to bargain in the market, and the thrill for me was challenging myself to get the most I could for the finite amount of money I had. The reward for exceptional bargaining skill was more food at a lower price. Marketers are rough and raw but also big-hearted people willing to "help" you if you had short money. Yet, they could also be shrewd when they knew they could take advantage of your weakness. Shopping in the market was entrepreneurial, and over time, I realized that bartering and bantering in the market was much more interesting than pushing a wire basket at Abi Joudi Supermarket where the prices stayed the same.

However, no matter how much I enjoyed the vibrancy of the market, the children's eyes nagged at me. If they weren't being changed or fed, the babies who came to work with their mothers spent their entire day back-bound. Toddlers played in the debris of the market and were potty-trained right in the market where there was no clean running water. Flies sat on small babies and lay their eggs on their skin, and chiggers from the dirty floors bore into their toes, leaving black spots to mark their entrance. A constant stream of people with various levels of hygiene, would cough, spit, and scratch around the children all day. I have watched a market woman change a runny poo poo diaper, wipe her hands on her lappa, then turn around, fold, fill a recycled newspaper paper cone with palm nuts or peanuts, and receive her payment before completing the diaper change. What else could she do? Even with modern toilets installed in the market, many Liberians see no reason for cleaning them. Truth is most of the market people were unaccustomed to indoor toilets.

Each trip to the market affirmed that a day care center was the best way to ensure that the children of the market women made it through the first three critical years of life disease-free, and until they could start school, receive some education in a safe environment.

My wheels churned. The market women obviously couldn't afford to shell out $50.00 a month for childcare, but maybe they could pay $25.00. I pondered enrolling a few children from the market in exchange for our fish, oil, and produce. I remembered how happy I had been when my eldest daughter was able to attend a very well run day care center because of a sliding fee scale. Could that work here in Liberia?

I shared my ideas with my staff, and they laughed as if their feet were being tickled. Finally, Ma Mae caught her breath long enough to say, "Mistress Ahnydah, you cannot mix the children of market women with the peoples' good children; they will not do it 'O'!"

I had been in Liberia for eight years, and was finally coming to grips with the class issue. Although she had spoken the truth I let her comment go in one ear and out the other, and a few days later, I marched into the new Secretary General's office. Felix W.K. Ireland was a heavyset man with wavy hair and a broad smile. He was Ivorian, well educated, and proud of the purity of his French accent. Although he had a sympathetic ear whenever I needed anything extra for the daycare center, he was also very class conscious and told me in no uncertain terms to focus my efforts on the Red Cross Day Care Center and let the "country people" worry about their own children.

For several months, the desire to create a childcare program that would serve the children of the Monrovia market women lay dormant until I met Beatrice, a retired African American day care administrator from California. She connected me to Rose, the Program Officer at UNICEF. Rose supported my idea of childcare for the market women and suggested that I create a pilot program. She told me that while UNICEF couldn't provide funding, they could provide information and supplies. Bolstered by the promise of support from UNICEF, I bypassed the Secretary General and convinced Reverend Edwin Lloyd, the President of the Red Cross, to allow me to pursue piloting a day care center in the Rally Time Market as potential additional revenue stream for the National Society. The day care center was an economic engine for the National Society and I was constantly pressured to enroll more children than I thought reasonable. In retrospect, I doubt that Reverend Lloyd ever believed we could turn a profit on the market women, but the entrepreneur in him was willing to proceed on the promise that if we could operate child care centers in the market for the Red Cross National Society, we could attract additional funders for other development projects.

We did a small survey in Gbarnga to gather basic data on whether native people would agree to have persons outside their family take care of their children. The survey results were highly favorable and demonstrated both a need and a desire for the service. Reverend Lloyd wrote an official letter to Mrs. Nancy Doe, wife of President Doe, requesting an appointment for me, and behind the scenes, one of Reverend Lloyd's friends, a female cabinet minister, personally arranged the meeting. On the day of the appointment, I took Aretha to lend me some credibility.

The Executive Mansion was majestic and set on lovely manicured grounds. I was nervous and thrilled—here I was, a girl from Chicago, daughter of a postal worker and a hair stylist, walking into Liberia's Executive Mansion to meet with the country's First Lady. The fact that I had never gained any access to government leaders in the United States made me love Liberia even more at that moment. I was dressed in my sharpest lappa suit and 2-inch heels. Mariamou, my Mandingo neighbor, had corn rowed my super thick hair in micro braids so tiny, you could not know I was wearing braids unless you looked closely. Aretha had on her best lappa suit and a fresh hairdo. We looked like women taking care of business.

"Good Morning, I'm Mrs. Ahnydah Rahm and this is Aretha Kollie. We have an appointment to see Mrs. Nancy Doe." I could feel sweat pooling between my toes. The solider at the gate looked at us carefully but did not search us.

"You have no gun, correct?"

"No, we have no gun."

He picked up the walkie-talkie and said, "There is a Mistress Rahm here to see the First Lady. Will someone come and get her? And she have another woman with her." Then he turned to us. "Wait please; her secretary will meet you inside."

Once we exited the courtyard and entered the Executive Mansion, the high marble ceilings, the grandeur and scale of the interior were magnificent. The Doe Administration had taken some care to preserve the Mansion.

The secretary led the way into Mrs. Doe's office. The gorgeous décor faded into the background as I realized I was sitting across from the First Lady. The proposal sat on her desk, but I realized that Nancy Doe was barely scanning the documents. Aretha had already told me that she was illiterate. I was careful to include her secretary, who gave Mrs. Doe both deference and direction, while moving the discussion along. Both Aretha and I shared our thoughts about how we felt about the market women and their children, and how, when the country's children are well cared for, women can work harder and better. Once we moved away from the written proposal and onto "woman-ground," the First Lady warmed and agreed that market women, who she referred to as "my sisters" needed help for their children. She revealed that the original plans for the Rally Time Market had in fact included space for a day care center. Her secretary unrolled a set of blueprints, showing space for the day care. I was flabbergasted! Rally time Market was built before President Doe's tenure, which meant that there had been a plan for the market women to have childcare during the previous administration, plans that had been derailed in the bloodshed of the 1980 coupe.

Our meeting concluded on a very positive note, with Mrs. Doe saying she would pose no objection to the Red Cross moving ahead with our plans to operate a pilot project in the Rally Time Market, as long as the Market Women's Association and John Beh, the Minister of Internal Affairs, agreed.

We left the First Lady's office knowing there was still much more work to be done, but at least we had cracked open the door.

Two weeks later we sent a letter to Minister Beh, the Minister of Internal Affairs and waited for an appointment. Finally, the staff and I met one afternoon about my stalled efforts and the consensus was for me to go and just show up. So that's what I did.

It took months of me sitting in the *outer* office before I was admitted inside of the Minister's comfortable *inner* office, but finally, I sat at the roundtable of men who had come from the interior, listening. I still had not been invited to speak.

The Monrovia Marketers Association was representation of everyone, both men and women, who sold anything in the markets. Waterside was the general market where the market women went to buy their goods. It was the place where trucks and cars from the interior arrived daily with fresh foods and meat from the hinterland.

My most vivid recollection of the General Market at Waterside was my very first time shopping there alone. It was a rainy season, and I was about three months pregnant with Zevah and struggling with morning sickness. When the taxi driver let me out, the sight of a huge brown animal lying on the ground enticed me to move in closer. As I drew nearer, I saw men with knives slicing cuts of bloody flesh from the animal and placing it on brown paper for buyers anxious for the bush meat. I fought to hold my breakfast down, yet that was the beginning of my fascination with the General Market, the Neiman Marcus for goods in Monrovia.

Now, I was going back, not as a shopper but as a seller offering service.

When I arrived at the office of the Monrovia Marketers Association, I explained who I was and told them that the Red Cross wanted to pilot a day care center, free of charge. When I opened the door of the office, a woman was standing inside talking to several other women.

She turned her gaze to me. This was not a place "qwee," meaning "civilized" women came to socialize. She wanted to get down to business. I smiled my most ingratiating smile.

"Hello Yah."

"Hey Big Ma, wha you need?" she said abruptly.

I presented my business card and instantly wondered if she could read it. She stretched over to the desk behind her and returned with her business card. She was the Superintendent of the Market.

"Yawl want to take care of young- young babies?"

"No, walking babies."

"Ain you say it free?"

I knew that the country people didn't want the Red Cross to make any money off them.

"Red Cross day care on Lynch Street?" the market super asked for clarification.

"Yes 'O,' but the daycare for yawl will be in the Rally Time Market itself."

The others in the room were checking me out and talking to each other in their dialect. I was glad I didn't understand so I didn't need to address the insults I felt being hurled at me.

"Will our children get qwee?" they mocked.

I smiled at the joke and turned my attention back to the woman who I had given my business card. "Sister, yawl children will be taken care of so you can make more money."

"We been hearing this Red Cross thing, but let John Beh agree first."

I never understood whether he was loved or feared, but the country people respected the power of his office more than the President of Liberia and I wasn't getting in the Rally Time Market to operate a pilot, even a *free* pilot, unless John Beh said so.

I began the vigil again.

One day, as I sat around the table with representatives from the hinterland, Minister Beh turned to me and said," My people, sometimes it is good to try new things to see if they work. Our people need development and our children need to grow up strong."

I could hardly believe my ears. He was affirming the Red Cross and me.

I spoke to the men about the plans I had for childcare in the Market. I told them if they didn't like the day care center after they let me "try it," meaning hold the pilot, they would lose nothing—only the Red Cross would be the loser. In the end, no one said yes or no, they just asked more questions, and afterward, moved on with another topic. I'd had my chance.

Parents and friends advised me to "find something" for John Beh, which meant finding a bribe to persuade him. However, even if I had wanted to, the Red Cross didn't have any money, so my hope was that somehow, doing the right thing for the right reason would be enough. As I walked back to the Red Cross Day Care Center, I knew I wasn't going back to the Ministry of Internal Affairs anytime soon.

I had been to the leaders, said all I could say and had done all I could do.

Then it struck me that the voices of the Market women counted for something. They should be the ones to say that they wanted a daycare in the market. I enlisted the aid of my staff.

Lunchtime was the most convenient time. I sat quietly in my office eating my lunch. It was time to take my message directly to the market women, but I needed someone with me that would give me credibility.

"Ma Mae, I have finished my rice, let's go into the Market for a few minutes."

"Mistress Rahm, those women will talk 'O,'"

But Martha said, "Let them talk, we will talk too, we are not scared of them!" She joined us.

Martha was feisty and protective of her friends. We left the sleeping children with the others and strolled to Rally time Market.

As we entered the market from the front, Mae began talking with some of the Gbassa Market women. I continued to walk to the back of the market. There was no lighting in the market so the further back in the market I walked the dimmer it became. I would start there and walk my way back towards the natural sunlight. Meanwhile, Martha found some of the Gio women and began talking with them about daycare in the market.

I looked at a young woman sitting on a rickety wooden table, two grimy little children with her. The one sitting under the table on the dirt floor was playing with an old cook spoon, making grooves in the earth and pouring the dirt on her legs and shoeless feet. She was wearing what I assumed had been a bright print dress at the start of the day but was now covered in dirt. Her dress rode up as she turned to pursue an insect on the ground, and I could see that her panties were soiled with urine. Her mother nursed her sibling while pointing customers to piles of ten and twenty-five cent cones of pepper and okra wrapped in old newspaper.

"Hey Ma, I see you got two babies in this market. Would it help you if you had somebody to teach the li'l girl during the day, somebody to take care of the baby?"

"The baby got to suck milk ole ma, I can't leave him 'O'."

"If the place to leave the baby was in this market, you could come upstairs to nurse the baby and come down here to finish selling your market."

"I ain't able to pay money 'O'," she said looking into the distance as though what I was saying was preposterous.

"Suppose it was free."

"I don't know 'O'."

"Think about it my sister because a day care is coming."

Without responding to me, she turned to speak to another woman in a dialect I couldn't understand. The other woman, who was grinding cassava leaves in a meat grinder, just stared up at me as she listened.

Mae came up behind me suddenly and grabbed my arm. "Mistress Rahm, let's go. These women are cussing at us and saying things about you. If that woman says something else, we will fight 'O'. You are easy, but me, I not easy 'O'."

We stopped at several other stalls on the way out. A few women understood, but most didn't.

I was the buzz in the market and on my way out, I heard whispers of things I didn't want to hear. The very women I wanted to help were cussing me out.

We continued lobbying in the market and finally wrangled an appointment with someone in the Market Women's Association. I was hoping to meet with Ma Beh Wreh who was the head woman, but instead met with a woman a few levels down. Ma Wreh was a legend. Supposedly, she was such a shrewd businessperson that she had made enough money to send her children to boarding school in England. I made several trips to meet with the woman a few levels below Ma Wreh, but for some reason, each time I came, the woman that I was supposed to meet with was not there.

Finally, a Kpelle man who had often been the Market Women's intermediary showed up at the daycare center and summoned me to the Market. Aretha and I followed him there, into a building, and to the second floor, and at last, we met with the representative for the Monrovia Market Women's Association. After the meeting, they showed us the space that had been set aside for a day care center. It was larger in real life, and seeing it in person. My heart filled with hope. The "myth" actually existed!

A silly grin spread across my lips, and as I looked at Aretha, whose grin mirrored my own—I felt less self-conscious. There were no windows, only "breeze blocks" arranged in a decorative lattice pattern to allow the warm salty breezes from the ocean nearby to flow through. The room was loft-like and there was a bathroom with a working toilet, a face bowl, and a bathtub. The small kitchen area was too small to cook food in, but large enough for warming food on a hot plate. Dust clung to the walls and floors, and we knew that one of the first things we'd have to do was to get a carpenter to put some fine screening over the breezeblocks to keep out some of the dust. We walked back to work chattering about the cleaning and decorating that would come next.

Back at the Headquarters, I reported to Reverend Lloyd that we had been escorted through the space, but we had not received permission from Internal Affairs.

He smiled saying, "Mistress Rahm, those raw women would *never* have let you in that space if Minister Beh hadn't agreed."

We were in! I couldn't wait to tell the staff and Rose.

My spirits were bolstered by the weekly visits of my children brought by Elrahm. Sometimes he would stay and eat with us and it would feel like family. Several Hebrew sisters would sneak and visit me. I was easy to find. All anyone had to do was take a taxi to Lynch Street near the Red Cross and ask for "the Big Ma for the Red Cross daycare" or "The yellow woman with the plenty children." My neighbors would lead them directly to my door.

In May 1987, the Market day care pilot began. I was a nervous wreck since I had no idea what to anticipate. We were in the Market on Tuesdays and Thursdays. We began our morning at the Red Cross, preparing two lunches, one pot of soup and rice for the children at the Red Cross, and a second for the children in the market pilot. At 10:00 a.m., Aretha, Marta, Saah, our volunteer janitor, and Ma Mae walked with me to the market. All the staff had volunteered time in the evenings to decorate the room with bright posters and pictures of shapes and numbers. We moved several long tables and handmade child-sized chairs around to create activity centers, and in the middle of the floor, we used chalk to mark our UNITY circle.

I love color, and bold colors especially inspired my confidence. I would wear them whenever I felt the need. On this particular day, I had a dark green print top with a matching lappa that I wrapped and tied like a skirt. Most of my work garments had skirts with drawstring or elastic waistbands, but today, I wanted the market women to see that I could 'tie lappa' like them. As we walked into the market, past tables full of busy marketers, we greeted the women and I felt good energy. The Market is pure unadulterated chaos, and we successfully manned our battle stations inside the daycare area. We sent Saah and Ma Mae downstairs to the market floor to invite the market women to send us their children and our very first clients!

As the children shuffled upstairs to the pilot, I recognized that these were special children. Several of the girls and boys balanced trays on their heads containing their own market items. Some sold plastic sandwich bags filled with cold water or Kool-aid, some sold ground peas (peanuts), some sold popcorn or plantain chips in small plastic baggies, and some, in addition to being responsible for themselves, they were also responsible for siblings. These children were so much more self sufficient than the children attending the Red Cross Day Care Center. We gave them space to be children while still providing structure. They were already plenty smart.

Our rule was that the children parked their markets neatly just inside the door and removed their rubber flip-flops. Because the market floors were mainly dirt, we wanted the children to feel a sense of transition. They were required to wash their hands and sometimes their feet when they entered. The first week was completely chaotic. We needed to get in tune with the children who weren't used to our program or us. Nevertheless, we persevered. I had been in Liberia for quite a long time, and although I had accessed the culture on a deeper level, there was no way I could have operated the pilot program effectively without my

Liberian staff. I didn't feel uncomfortable around Liberians, but at the end of the day, people gravitate toward their own, and when a change is introduced, they need to know that it is, at least in part, being initiated or sanctioned by someone just like them.

We created a UNITY circle where everyone was encouraged and applauded. We urged the children to share the songs they knew with us. Most enjoyed being the center of attention. When we broke from our UNITY circle and convened in small groups, I noticed that some of the children were very shy while others were quite outgoing. The age range was wider than typical for a day care center. We had toddlers who could barely walk accompanied by children between six and eight years old. It was our rule, though, that no child would be turned away—they all needed attention and care.

One of the songs that we taught the children was one that I wrote. You would think that after twenty years, the words and the melody would have faded, but I still remember it vividly. I wrote it with a full heart, and it reflects the hope I had for Liberia.

FLOWER OF THE EARTH
Flower of the earth, Liberia
Flower of the earth, Liberia
Land of great worth, Liberia

Westward in the sun, Liberia
Our work has just begun in Liberia
Flower of the earth, Liberia
Glad to live my life in Liberia
Gonna make things nice in Liberia

It's the flower of the earth, Liberia
Flower of the earth, Liberia
Flower of the earth, Liberia

I can only wonder if somewhere, there is a child or a staff member who, like me, still has that song embedded in their heart.

Zefron in Red Cross School Play

A ROGUE BY ANY NAME

After my first brush with Rogues, I was very careful to turn out the lights before going to sleep. I routinely locked the back door of our building from the inside, and I closed the outer front door of the building before going to bed.

I had nothing in common with my housemates and except for my youngest daughter. I would see my older children only on weekends. Deep down, though, I knew that we would be a family again. I had moved into the apartment with the sole purpose of having a place, no matter how small, where the children and I could be together. I prayed for release from the feeling of sadness and utter isolation.

The next day, I was walking past an abandoned building on Lynch Street, right across from the Liberian National Red Cross Headquarters. A note on the door, like a glimmer of light in the darkness, read, "Yoga class inside." At that moment, the beat of my heart quickened, and I realized that the class must be the answer to my prayers.

The desire for exercise was not my motivation. I walked almost everywhere I went and was quite slim, but I remembered the feeling of peace derived from the practice of Hatha yoga learned from a library book. Yoga had helped me break a two pack-a-day cigarette habit in the early 70's. It had brought me into the awareness of vegetarianism, and I found myself happily drawn back into practice. I entered the building, followed the paper signage until I opened a smoked-glass door to reveal a large, open space with wooden floors, sun-filled windows, and about twenty-five yoga devotees—the yoga studio. An Americo Liberian who had traveled, studied yoga, and became a Hari Krishna, taught the class. The fee for the class was ten dollars per month. I signed up on the spot. Most of the students were Indian women with a sprinkling of Peace Corps volunteers, and a couple of white men who seemed to be friends of our yoga instructor.

At least twice a week for the next few months, I spent my lunch hour practicing yoga and meditating. When I was approached to become a member of the Hari Krishna group, I stopped taking classes, able to appreciate the gift of regenerating my spirit through the practice of yoga without wanting to become a member of another group that controlled my life. Thanks, but no thanks!

About a month after I moved into my psychedelic room on Lynch Street, a new renter joined me. Esther was a spunky young woman, about twenty-years old and had migrated to Monrovia from Sierra Leone. She had a dazzling smile and personality to match. Educated by Christian missionaries, she was very polished, and through years of living on missions, was also well organized. Now she wanted a job as an office worker. Her sister, Fatima, later joined her. Fatima was Esther's sister from "one pa." This meant that they both had the same father, but not the same mother. Fatima was about seventeen, frail and gangling, and susceptible to bouts of depression and hysterical outbursts. She came to live with and help Esther, but in reality Esther, who had no job, was responsible to feed them both.

SC soon evicted the Freetown prostitutes in the front of the building, because, despite their frequent gentlemen callers, their rent went outstanding for months. That was fine with Esther and me. A family of Mandingos, Abiba, nicknamed Abby, her husband Marmadou, and Maryamou her cousin rented the room. Abby, I learned, was the stepdaughter of Mandingo Chief Alhaji, Sheriff of the Benson Street Mandingo Compound.

Sharing the bathroom was a major challenge. It was such a rudimentary construction, and as much as I hate to say it, an outhouse would have been more sanitary and easier to keep clean. My constant struggle was to clean the bathroom at a level that we could all share. I realized that I needed to take the lead because I was accustomed to sitting on the toilet, while the other renters came from cultures where they customarily squatted over the toilet rim. Over the years, I actually became proficient at squatting over an open hole, but at the time, my children were very young, and when they came to live with me, I was determined to give them a "civilized" bathroom experience.

Besides the fact that I was determined to sit on a toilet while others squatted, Muslims practice daily ablutions, which is the ceremonial washing of the body before prayers. The devout Muslim prays five times per day. There was no floor drain in our bathroom, and because they weren't aware of mopping up the spilled water, the bathroom floor quickly became covered with filth and muddy water. To make matters worse, earthworms from outside found their way into the bathroom through the tub to wallow in the mud. The filthy water typically trailed under the bathroom door, out into the hallway, and often puddled near the door of our room.

Despite our hygienic differences, Abby's family was respectful and very cordial, and Esther and I became close friends. Every Saturday, the two of us arose early and spent the entire day together, cleaning the hallways, the area in front and back of the house, and the bathroom. When we finished cleaning, we would walk down the back road to the Rally Time market and shop for Saturday's and Sunday's food. Later, we would cook together in the kitchen area in back of the house, and finally, around five in the evening, exhausted from our labors, we shared roasted peanuts or fried plantain chips and a bottle of Club Beer if we had an extra $1.25.

Abby, coming from a family of influential Mandingos, was aware of her rank in society. Scrubbing floors and cleaning up after herself and others was beneath her. Her family never participated in cleaning the hallway, kitchen, or bathroom. They were also curious that a "responsible" American woman would lower herself to clean the floors with a native girl.

One Friday evening, Elrahm arrived with our children. They now spent weekends with me, but this time, instead of him bringing a couple of changes of clothing for each of them, he brought almost all of their things.

He picked up Tikvah, hugged her, giving her to Penemiel, and asked the children to take her outside and go play for a few minutes.

I looked up at him, draped in a bottle-green suit and sandals and pretended that I didn't miss him, when I did.

"Ahnydah, I am bringing the children to stay with you. I don't know if you are ready to receive them, but I'm not around to care for them much and I'm not happy with how they are being taken care of in your absence. Your children are miserable without you."

He was right, I was not prepared to receive three additional children. Still, happiness filled me as I smiled. My prayers were manifesting and soon, everything else would work itself out. Although he was still a Hebrew and I was not, we had made a decision years ago that we would *never* fight over our children, that what was best for them would prevail. Despite everything—it had.

As a gesture of good will and deference to me, Abby brought a servant boy, about eight years old, from her father's compound to help us clean on Saturday mornings. He was so small and as we all rose early, my children and the little Mandingo child were in back, playing before it was time to begin the cleaning. Abby drew a bucket of water and called the little boy to attack the floors, which he did with vigor. The floors were so filthy that it was more work than a child could properly do, especially since she gave him no instruction and only a bucket of water and a rag. When my children saw the little boy scrubbing the floors, they joined him because now he was a friend. Abby was horrified at the sight of my children working side by side with a servant. Things became slightly awkward between my family and Abby's, and it brought to the surface the difference in the way we perceived class. I hoped they wouldn't beat the Mandingo child for being lazy since he was happy to have his newfound friends help him scrub floors.

I cleaned up my children and took them in the market with me. Afterward, we took our time getting back. The next week, I asked Abby not to bring the little boy, and after explaining to Esther what had happened, I returned to cleaning the floors with her help.

Abby and Mamadou never understood why I would scrub the floors and clean up after them, and I could never understand how they could live with the dirt.

I guess we agreed to disagree.

As the only Americans living in the area, whenever my friends came to visit me people in the area would deliver them right to our front door! Generally, this was a good thing, but it also made me a target for victimization. Most people falsely believed that I had money. By my standards, I was poor, but to the average Liberian, I had a job that paid me regularly, I carried the coveted American passport, was well-educated, and even when I didn't have cash, I had friends with money.

Most of all, I had access to areas in society that they only looked at from the outside. I learned quickly that where there is poverty, there are predators.

One such predator was Yah Yah, a handsome young Ivorian of about twenty-five. He was smooth and glib and seemed friendly. He originally approached me for a job with the Day Care Center. I already had two janitors that helped with the cleaning and changing the little boys after naptime. We had a close relationship with both of them and I didn't need Yah Yah. However, he seemed so desperate that I finally agreed to hire him to teach me French.

Yah Yah's visits were sporadic, but I paid him a few dollars for each lesson, which lasted about forty-five minutes. By the time we returned home in the evening, there was little time for anything other than feeding the children and supervising their bedtime ritual. It was very difficult for me to focus on learning French, but I had wanted to help Yah Yah. Then I had an insight that something was amiss about his intentions.

Once my senses were alerted, I noticed that every time Yah Yah was in our room, his piercing gaze swept the room, as though casing the place. We were four lessons in, when I thanked him, paid him the remaining amount I owed, then told him I was going to the French School in Panesville to take classes.

A few days later, on a weeknight, the children lay sleeping on their pallets while I lay in my bed in the dark. I was in that stage of rest, between sleep and consciousness, when a scratching sound across the room snapped me into awareness. My bed was in the corner on the opposite side from where the noise came. There was a window between me and the cabinet on which rested my beige canvas briefcase. Someone had pulled out the top louvered glasses, cut through the wire screen, and was attempting to reach *over* to the cabinet and hook the case with a pole.

Typically, there was a robbery or attempted robbery at least once or twice a week. Having become accustomed to this, I no longer lost my voice, but instead found it rather quickly. I boldly screamed, "Rogue, Rogue, Rogue!" as I ran toward the window.

The pole and the rogue escaped into the night.

I was happy that the burglar bars were intact. The area where we lived was a tight-knit little area; people knew who the good people were and who the bad people were. I needed to make a demonstration to let people know that I was not intending to be a victim. As I lay in bed that night, I was pissed. I lay there with the thought that this Rogue was someone I knew. He went after my case—which contained a composition book with work related notes and several markers, no money. I kept my money in my bra or under the linoleum but the rogue thought there was something valuable in the bag. I realized that unless I made my neighbors respect me, my family and I would not be safe. This was my rite of passage. I needed to transition from being seen as a green American who worked for the Red Cross, to being seen as a "helluva women who wasn't easy 'O'." When Liberians say, "you ain't easy, 'O,'" that's a term of respect. As a sister from the south side of Chicago, I needed to establish that I wasn't taking no mo' shit!

On a number of occasions in the past, when someone had disrespected me and I took the high road, my staff had cautioned me to confront the person. I had been told, 'Ole ma, you too easy O', the people will walk on your head." After tonight, there would be no more walking on my head!

The next morning, as the children and I were leaving for work and school, Yah Yah met us in our hallway, distressed because he said that he had been told that a rogue visited us. He asked if anything had been taken, and I assured him that nothing had been taken. He was overly concerned with what he could do to help. I walked along patiently, listening to Yah Yah's phony ministrations and his alibi of being out of the vicinity until late the previous evening. I continued listening until I was in the center of the clusters of buildings that surrounded ours, and then I snapped—Liberian style.

In flawless Liberian English, I shouted for all to hear that the rogue had to have been someone who had been in my room because they knew exactly what they were looking for! I popped my wrist and slapped my hips, adding that just because I came from America, didn't mean I grew up stupid. For good measure, I added, "From today, I will sleep with my machete, and the hand that comes in my window will stay there!"

I strutted away with my children behind me, leaving a stupid looking Yah Yah behind.

I never saw him again. However, rogues would strike in our area repeatedly, because that is what rogues do. My Vai neighbor next door would come home in the early morning hours and catch a rogue trying to enter her window. Her screams drew a throng of people that beat the man nearly to death.

I rarely felt like I had to bare my teeth in this tenement, most of the people were good people, but where my family was concerned, I would do whatever it took to protect them. I quickly learned to read the cultural nuances that would gain us acceptance and keep us from becoming prey. Living on Lynch Street helped me to cross an important cultural bridge. I learned that if I wanted to survive as a single parent and as a female in Liberia, on occasion, I needed to engage people at their own level.

Yeah 'O'!

My lovely,
Binah

OH NO! I AM NOT THAT WORD!

For years, I had dreamt of Binah being the first of my children to graduate from high school and attend the University of Liberia. My dream shifted only slightly when AME Zion Academy, where she had begun attending high school, opened a college. Because of my friendship and respect for Reverend Umoja, I thought Binah would be in its first graduating class. When she and her boyfriend Roland had left the community, all of my dreams for my beautiful, brilliant honey-skinned daughter, imploded.

The Hebrew midwife and paramedic Baht Ami had tactfully broken the news to me that my daughter was pregnant a few weeks before my suspension. Queasy, weak-kneed, and confused, I was ashamed that my daughter was pregnant, and felt her pregnancy was a reflection on me as her mother.

Roland and Binah had a twenty-five dollar a month room not too far from the beach in Panesville. I caught a taxi and traveled in a sunny haze to the zinc-covered house in. Their room was clean, though rudimentary, and they slept on a single cot. Outside their room was a small kitchen with a concrete sink and one spigot. The kitchen had two windows without glass panes that admitted a welcomed breeze. There was a communal outhouse about thirty-feet away from the back door.

When I arrived, Roland complained to me that Binah had flatly refused to clean the outhouse. He was embarrassed because everyone else had agreed to take turns cleaning it. Honestly, I fully understood her not wanting to clean an outhouse after people she didn't know, but she *had* chosen to live there and I told her that. Even as the reprimand came from my lips, I was wishing with all my heart that she didn't have to live this way.

Roland, a young Kpelle man with skin the color of light caramel with a hint of red in his skin was a few inches over 5 feet tall, he had a round face and slanted eyes. He was the child of rice farmers, and he knew how to supplement the little bit he earned by planting a patch of potato greens and hot peppers behind the house. It was heartwarming to see that he truly cared for Binah, and over the next few months, I watched him struggle to make sure that she had the best of whatever he could provide. The life that Roland was offering Binah was the only life he knew. For now, they were content to be together. Had we been in America, there would have been her grandmother, Yvonne, my sister, Aunt Connie, and Uncle Pete and Elrahm's mother to offer her their support. Here, though, there was only me. I had a lot to figure out for my family.

I visited them regularly, always either leaving money or bringing a gift of food. Binah had been born in Chicago and Roland had been born in Bong County, Liberia, yet in many ways, they were kindred spirits, born just days apart on December 24th and 28th of the same year. Both were stubborn, proud, and determined to make things work out. Unfortunately, they had similar temperaments, tending to internalize and nurture small hurts until they exploded in anger.

Whenever I visited Binah, her eyes lit up and I felt the dilemma wasn't if she'd come home, rather how to get her home. She needed to prove she was just as much woman as I was. She didn't want to come home, as the Liberians say, "wit her mouth dragging the ground." I reasoned that my best option was to be patient and to bait down my desire to control the situation. I was very careful to affirm her choice to be with Roland and to offer to help if they ever needed it. I encouraged Roland as he walked me to a taxi to take me back into town and commending him for taking such good care of Binah. He beamed with pride the way a man does when he's taking care of his business.

Roland would often drop by my office, and on one such visit, I told him I was looking for a bigger place, so if things ever got too rough, we could always make room for Binah. He had never mentioned marriage.

I was more direct with Binah in my attempts to get her to come live with me, but I knew I couldn't force her. I can't say for sure, but she probably felt she would be thrust back into the role of caregiver for her younger siblings, and I didn't blame her for thinking that. Over the years, she had been the main babysitter for her brothers and sisters, living up to the norm of most Liberian girls *and boys*. They grow up caring for their siblings while their parents work. I felt that was a small hurdle to cross compared to the bigger one.

My primary concern was the fact that at nearly twenty weeks pregnant, Binah wasn't gaining enough weight. I didn't know whether she was 'dry' or underweight for physical reasons or spiritual ones, maybe a combination of both. I convinced her to visit us on weekends and I fattened her up with palm butter and rice or beans and rice and greens and sent enough food back with her for Roland.

Sometimes Binah came on Friday, sometimes Saturday morning, but I always awakened on Friday mornings with an air of expectancy, awaiting the knock on our door. Her brothers and sisters adored her and news of her arrival always made them squeal with happiness.

"Your sister is here yah."

"My Binah, My Binah, My Binah'O'," chanted Zevah, the white balls flopping on the ends of her pigtails.

"Our Binah is here 'O'," Penemiel sang, grabbing Binah's delicate hand into his smaller one.

She poured ground peas from the paper cone into each child's hand, and remembering that Zefron was not as assertive as the others were,

"Here, Zefron, here is your part of ground peas," Binah said.

She picked EliTikvah up from the kitchen chair and planted a kiss. "Hey Emah," she smiled.

Happiness filled my heart as I responded, "Morning 'O,' I didn't hear the taxi let you down?"

"I rode the bus to keep money to buy ground-peas for the children. I came down in the market."

A comfortable ride in a taxi cost sixty-five cents and the bus, while only twenty-five cents, was crowded with the sounds and smells of people all over each other and took considerably longer.

"Your bowl is on the table, and there is still a small fire in the coal pot outside if you want to warm it," I said to her busying myself with getting ready to go to the market.

"Thank you, yah," she replied, taking in a spoonful of the food. "I'm alright 'O,' it's sweet."

The children would gather around their sister, the visiting rock star. Zevah would begin with her endless queries, and soon, we would all be laughing and talking. All weekend, we shopped in the market and washed clothes while fighting the rats and cockroaches that crept around our room at night.

The weekends with Binah were fulfilling. For a short time, I had all of my children under one roof, but it made it that much harder to put Binah in a taxi bound for Panesville. My prayer had always been that my children would grow up together and be very close. Growing up, another family had raised my brother who was from, as they say in Liberia, 'one ma and one pa.' My sister, from 'one ma,' and I had a terrible case of sibling rivalry that wasn't reconciled until we were teens, and at twenty, I learned that my biological father sired a son by another woman. Life hands you what it hands you, but I wanted better for my children.

Binah was an admirable big sister, not that she wasn't guilty of the occasional abuse of power, but I always knew that she would never let any harm come to her siblings. They, in turn, adored and respected her; and still do. We had to find a way to convince her to come home.

On one visit, I suggested to Roland that he consider what was best for his unborn child. Finally, at his urging, Binah agreed to come live with us, just until she delivered her baby. I was quietly saving and planning so that once the baby was born, I could afford an apartment or rent a small house with space enough for all of us. Nightly, I spoke affirmations and drew pictures of a small house with a front porch and a yard for my children to play in. I taped the drawing on the wall over my bed.

A broiling hot Saturday morning Roland brought Binah and her belongings to share our room on Lynch Street. The children were elated to have their big sister home. They knew that Binah was having a baby and Zevah asked a never-ending stream of questions about where babies come from. Penemiel just pointed to her stomach and asked her if she had eaten too much because she was getting a big belly.

Even though we were struggling financially and cramped into a small, ugly room, I was relieved. I identified my feelings with how Samson must have felt when his hair had regrown and he regained his strength. I had my children, all of them, with me under one roof, and we could finally move forward.

My main concern for Binah's pregnancy was her physical and emotional health. She just looked too small and vulnerable to be a mother. While I busied myself by focusing on her health, I was in major denial about being a grandma. Every time someone reminded me that I was about to be one, I cringed. After all, I was only thirty-seven. In my mind, grandmas were old women that had already raised their own children, and now had the luxury of spending time spoiling their grandchildren. Yet, here I was about to be a grandmother with four young children of my own to raise! I just couldn't wrap my mind around this new title, this new responsibility…*grandmother!*

Fattening up the baby ma was the task at hand! Every morning, we either cooked parboiled rice and palm oil, or sent the children upstairs to our landlady to purchase freshly baked, thick hunks of corn bread or shortbread for breakfast. When I left with the smaller children for the day, I gave Binah money for snacks of ground peas and plantain chips until she cooked our main meal of the day. Since she had nothing to do but sleep and her appetite was growing, Binah was happy to cook rather than wait for me to arrive home in the evening.

One of our fondest rituals from our time on Lynch Street was putting the younger children to bed and asking Esther to watch them while Binah and I walked over a mile to Broad Street to the Lebanese owned restaurant where they served the best grilled American cheese sandwiches and fries. That was our time to talk, alone as mother and daughter. It was during these walks that I attempted to nourish my daughter's spirit. I realized that I had taken Binah's loyalty and love for granted and I valued our time together as a gift.

Unfortunately, the midwives and trusted friends that had delivered my last three children had all left Liberia. Although I felt I could have delivered my own first grandchild if it came to that, I didn't think it was a good idea. Binah should experience a hospital delivery. As the projected delivery date drew near, Binah enrolled in the prenatal clinic at St. Joseph's Catholic Hospital and we continued to make ourselves as comfortable as five people could be in our small room while we began to prepare for the arrival of her baby.

Meanwhile, I consulted Aretha and asked for her advice on matters of family protocol in the Kpelle culture since both she and Roland were Kpelle. I had mixed feelings and felt torn. I was an African-American, a former Hebrew Israelite, embedded in Liberian culture, and wasn't sure which culture I wanted to embrace. In America, women usually have custody of their children, but in Liberia, the children belong to the father's family, and I knew that Roland's family was obliged to help us. According to Aretha, if I wanted to, I had every right to take Binah to her in-laws and leave her and the baby with them. Obviously, I didn't want to do that, but I did want help.

Aretha urged me to get on a bus to Bong Mine and meet the family, but I was resistant to that idea. After all, the baby was Roland's and I didn't understand why I needed to go any farther than him. Aretha smiled and let the matter drop. I had Binah draft a list for Roland of things their baby would need so that they *both* could grasp the seriousness of what they had embarked upon. The idea fell flat. I was told that he had no money, so obviously, he would be unable to provide what the baby needed. I was frustrated. Finally, I took Aretha's advice and went to visit his family in Bong Mine to "settle the palava" or "dispute,"

Roland had alerted his brother Edward to meet me at the bus stop. In the event that I missed Edward, Roland had written directions for me to find his father and mother on my own. I was unsure of what I would find, but I boarded the bus to Bong Mine with high hopes and the best intentions.

In the tribal system, Roland's father was a town chief, a local official. The town chief's responsibility was to make decisions in tribal disputes and to divide the farmland between families. Everyone in Bong Mine would know where the town chief lived.

As I sat on the crowded bus and enjoyed the lush scenery of Liberia, I wondered what would happen if Roland had misdirected me, or if when I got to Bong Mine, his family turned on me.

It is hard to capture how embarrassed and isolated I felt during this period of my life. People believed that because I was an American citizen I had it all, when actually, I was broke, exhausted, and afraid. I remember being very cautious about who I talked to about my situation. Although I desperately needed help, I was also *ashamed* that I needed help. A Liberian proverb says, "When you have your head in the lion's mouth, you have to be careful how you pull it out." My head was definitely in the lion's mouth, I could feel its teeth scraping across my forehead.

Bong Mine, famous for vast iron ore deposits, is one of the regions in Liberia that boasts a large concentration of members of the Kpelle tribe. Oprah Winfrey has traced her DNA back to the Kpelle tribe, the largest ethnic group in Liberia. The Bong Mining Company, a German corporation, founded the town of Bong Mine in 1957. Bong Range is a range of hills covered with tropical forest. The Kpelle people migrated from Liberia from the Sudan in the 16th century. They are rice farmers and highly practical. Knowing that Roland came from a family of farmers, I understood how, in addition to hustling for a living when Binah ran away with him, he also immediately began to grow a patch of greens and peppers to feed her.

When the bus pulled into Bong Mine, I asked several people if they knew Mr. Brown, the town chief. Everybody knew him, but since I didn't speak Kpelle, and no one I met spoke English well enough to give me directions, I stood at the bus stop and waited. One thing I had learned by this point in my journey was that Africa gives you the gift of patience.

After about thirty minutes, Edward found me and I felt more at ease. He was a familiar face that I knew from his visits to Roland in Monrovia. He was a handsome young man. Roland's skin had a reddish cast, but Edward's was the color of milk chocolate. He had blazing black eyes and he grinned a lot. I perceived him to be an elder brother but I didn't actually know his age.

We fell into an easy stride down a dusty path that eventually became thick bush. Edward took the lead snatching at the thick branches that obscured parts of the trail. I was in a strange town to handle a family beef with a tribal official. We walked, and walked, *and walked* in the heat. Finally, we came to a dusty clearing that housed their village. All the houses were small and just a step above hut status. My heart sank.

Edward went inside a small house on the right side of the road and opened the unlocked door, emerging quickly to report that no one was home. I didn't know whether I should feel insulted, but mostly I was hot, tired, and thirsty. He brought a sturdy straight-back wooden chair to the porch, and I sat while he went to buy a plastic bag of cold water for me. I bit into a corner of the plastic bag and let the cool water flow inside my mouth while Edward made a few inquiries of their neighbors and learned that his ma and pa were working their rice farm. He left me to go fetch them.

As I sat on the porch, the neighbors came discretely by to see the yellow woman who was visiting their town chief. Word had spread that one of the brothers was having a baby by an American girl and her mother was coming to see their parents. I was aware that typically, the man of the house handled this type of family matter, but Binah's father and I were separated. I had to do what I had to do.

Passersby greeted me with "Hello Yah" and "Hello Mah" and I responded with a simple "Hello Yah." I sat, growing more and more impatient. These people were farmers and the farm was the family livelihood. I must have marinated on their porch for over an hour when finally I spied a small man with a fragile looking woman walking a couple of steps behind him.

Roland's father was a wiry man, not quite five feet, who weighed scarcely 100 pounds and his mother weighed ten to fifteen pounds under that. The thing that struck me most about Roland's mother was that her natural hair braided loosely hung to her waist. She had no perm, no weave, just long, healthy hair. I also noticed that when she smiled, her teeth were filed to points. I had not seen this in the city but had been told it was very common with traditional Kpelle women. I wondered if the Kpelle had once been hunters. Why would farmers need sharp teeth?

Both of Roland's parents had leathery skin tanned by long hours toiling in the sun, and I took note that his mother's reddish color was the same as Roland's. We embraced, and they sat with me on the porch. Roland's mother smiled but never spoke, letting her husband do the talking for both of them.

"Mrs. Rahm, Hey yah, you alright?"

"I'm alright 'O'."

"We are sorry for your time, but we were on the farm."

I guessed that they had probably walked the better part of the hour to come back and wondered what work they had left undone. He sent his wife for water, and I noticed it was not cold, but it seemed clean so I drank from the cup she provided and thanked her.

Liberians are such polite and generous people. Even if this was their last clean water they would still have offered it to me.

"How's Binah and the chilren?"

"They alright 'O'." I responded. "The town is nice, your people are friendly." I continued to set Mr. Brown at ease and give him respect.

"Yes, these are my people; they know how to treat everybody good."

We made small talk about the weather and talked about our children, until I felt it was time to get to the point.

"Mr. Brown, I came to you. You know my daughter's situation."

"Yes, Roland has told his mother and myself."

"The children can make problems for themselves," I said. "I was trying to send them both through high school, and now look at this kind of embarrassment." This was a reminder that I had not only paid for my daughter's schooling, but Roland's as well.

The mother was silent but I hoped she understood my dilemma.

I continued, "Roland has no job, no money. Why must he make a baby. I already have plenty chilren, so what will I do?"

"We will help, when I get rice Mrs. Rahm, I will come to you and bring it. Edward told me you don't eat chicken so I can't bring that, but I will bring all the rice I can, and anytime I get something, I will help you."

I thought about the long list of baby needs that I had in my purse and realized that the couple that sat opposite me on the porch could not fulfill those items. Even though they were agreeing to help, we all understood the truth. I didn't even smell food in the air, although evening was approaching. I wanted to leave before they would be obliged to find food for me.

"Thank you plenty."

"More water?"

"No, thank you yah, I'm all right. It's getting late and I don't want to leave those chilren alone for too long, ain' you know?"

We laughed the gentle laugh of understanding.

"Edward will walk you back to the bus," offered the chief.

I hugged and kissed both cheeks of Chief Brown and Roland's mother, feeling the frailty of each one's tiny bodies. We had given each other respect and that was all I could ask for.

Edward and I began the long trek back to the bus station. I didn't realize it at the time, but my visit to Roland's family home would be the only time I would meet his mother, and the last time I would see Edward.

How could we know that a little more than two years later, the Liberian Civil War would rob my grandchild of paternal grandparents.

I felt lighter on the ride home. Even though I had no additional resources, at least I had clarity. Whatever support my grandbaby needed was my responsibility.

A few weeks before the delivery, Roland's father visited us on Lynch Street and met Binah's sisters and brothers. He brought a half bag (50 pounds) of rice from their farm, for which I was grateful.

That was the last time I saw Roland's father.

"The Belly," as they say in Liberia, continued to grow, and Binah began to radiate health. It had been good for her, physically and spiritually, to come back to us. Roland visited regularly, sometimes they got along, and other times, they didn't. Roland had grown up in a home where, when his father was frustrated, he beat his mother. He told me once that his father had knocked his mother unconscious. Violence is a learned behavior, and when Roland lost his temper, he also wanted to hit. Binah, who is every bit her mother's daughter, wasn't a receptive target. They fought.

On the evening of September 3, 1987, Binah began to feel contractions, and immediately, she was frightened that she was about to deliver. Roland happened to be visiting, and "as God so fixed it," we had a neighbor with a car willing to take Binah and Roland to St. Joseph Catholic Hospital, about ten minutes away by car. I was relieved that she wanted to go to the hospital early.

During Binah's pregnancy I experienced a 'letting go' that can only happen when the realization sinks in that there are events swirling about that are not always under one's control. After many nights of tossing and turning, I finally came to a place within myself where I was able to relax, wait for things to happen, and respond as best I could. Some people might call that reactionary, but I called it waiting for "De Lawd," as the elders say, to give me some direction. I was adrift from any real cultural anchor, making my way in a new life, my daughter was having a baby and I was becoming…a…a…a *grandmother!*

Binah and Roland left for the hospital about ten that night. Part of me wanted to be with my daughter, but my intuition guided me to realize that "baby pa," the father of her baby, was the appropriate person to support her. I stayed behind with my other children. Roland was thrilled at the prospect of experiencing his first child with Binah and as nervous as any new father I've ever seen. After seeing them off and getting my other children to sleep, I lay awake the entire night, silently praying that my daughter and grandbaby would have an easy delivery.

Barely past sunrise the next morning, Roland knocked on our door and announced that at 5:00 a.m., on September 4, 1987 my granddaughter, Yohanna Jartu Brown, had been born.

Roland had come to retrieve the sanitary napkins and other personal items that they had been so certain would be unnecessary the night before. I awakened the children who asked me a barrage of questions, especially Zevah, while Roland took a nap on my bed. I hurried to the Rally Time Market to shop for food to prepare so that he could take a nice meal back for them. I prepared a thick soup of brown lentils to accompany country rice, the most nutritious kind, and potato greens with lots of palm oil. I packed everything in a basket and covered it with a cloth dishtowel. Before long, the new father was off to the hospital with provisions for his small family. I would give them some bonding time and go later in the day to bring mother and baby home.

That evening, on the taxi ride to the hospital, it finally sunk in that I was actually that word I had never wanted attached to my name! I was still young and a head-turner, and I certainly didn't want to be placed in the category of fat, old, braless women who were toothless and unattractive. I had real difficulty embracing the title of grandmother, especially when I had a three year old of my own. As they say in Liberia, I was still "full of juice!" All of these thoughts raced through my mind as I entered the Maternity Ward of St Joseph's Catholic Hospital.

The ward was plain, the beds had a combination of whitish sheets and lappa cloth brought by the patients, and the marble floors were clean. The windows were open and sunlight flooded into the room. The attending staff, while not polished in the Western sense, was caring and efficient.

Binah was in a crowded room with eight or nine other women. One bed bravely held two pregnant women. My guess was they were close to being discharged, and the hospital was short a bed for an incoming patient. There was another woman lying on a pallet on the floor who was asleep with her back turned. The women didn't seem to mind the over crowdedness. In fact, despite the stress of expectant mothers, there was an air of conviviality in the room. I was dizzied by the fact that my daughter was in the hospital with other women, not in the girl's dorm. She had taken her place among women, some her age, some younger, that had just delivered babies. The conversation in the room was in familiar Liberian patois, peppered with words from various indigenous dialects.

When she saw me, Binah sat up on the side of her bed and glowed. She looked happy and she began sharing every detail of her delivery with me.

"Hey Yah, Binah, you are woman now! The nurse said you did well." I felt really relieved and wanted her to realize that despite not choosing the path of motherhood for her, I felt she had handled herself well.

"I was so scared, I was wishing for you."

"I know baby, but you and Roland needed to go through this together. That is your baby pa."

Even saying the words, I still couldn't wrap my head around the fact that my daughter was now a mother. I desperately wanted her and Roland to realize that they had a *joint* responsibility, and it was my greatest hope that having him present during the delivery would finally make that click for both of them. I asked the typical questions.

"Did they cut you?"

"A little. I had three stitches, and it hurt when they sewed me up, but I'm all right now, just very sore."

"Well, I'm going to take you home. The children are waiting for you and the baby."

A nurse came to take her temperature and soon after, another nurse entered.

"You the grandma?" the second nurse asked.

"Yes, I am," I said, the word grating on my nerves like fingernails dragging across a chalkboard.

"The baby is fine 'O,'" said the admiring attendant as she handed her to me wrapped in a soft pink blanket.

Awed, I looked into the roundest face I had ever seen. Her skin had the same reddish overtones as her father, and she had a head full of hair. Her little eyes were tiny slits, and she looked more Asian than the mixture of African American and Kpelle. She was light as a feather, so small compared to my younger children, but heavier than her mother had been at birth. Binah had been a little over four pounds at birth; my granddaughter was almost seven pounds.

Binah's chatter and smile broke my reverie, which was different from how I had ever seen her smile before. She looked older than she had when she had left for the hospital. There is that magical something that happens when a women goes from being a woman to being a mother.

"Emah, when they came to shave me, the nurse took out the razor and shaved me so quick, I thought she was going to cut me 'O?' Emah, I wanted to scream, but you told me to breathe deeply, and I did, but oh, I wanted to scream!"

We laughed and talked, and she seemed so confident, so strong. Giving birth is a rite-of- passage that raises a woman to another level of femininity. She took me on her journey to motherhood, detailing her fear and pain, Roland's nervousness, and when he was asked to leave. Binah relishes in the tiniest of details, so she relayed every nitty gritty thing that had happened that night.

In the back of my mind, while I was thankful that she had been able to deliver at St Joseph's Catholic Hospital rather than JFK (also known as 'just fo killin,') Hospital, I felt a tinge of sadness that there weren't any sisters that I trusted to help my daughter bring her first baby into the world. Delivery stories for women are like war stories for men. They bind us together, and in at that moment, I felt a closeness that had been piecing itself together over the past months, suddenly click into place.

The baby had started rutting. "She wants to eat now," I said, handing Binah her prize.

The nurse said she was a few ounces over six pounds and was perfect in every way. I sat on the side of the bed marveling at the merger of both families that I saw in the baby's countenance. I was overwhelmed as I watched our newest family member nursing at her mother's breast. And yet, I still didn't want to be called her grandma.

Perhaps it's because I have never had a grandmother active in my life. My maternal grandmother lived in Alabama, and I remember seeing her only twice. We were more like life-long pen pals than grandmother and granddaughter. My father's mother died in an asylum for the insane, and my stepfather's mother, though residing in Chicago, was a virtual stranger to me. Grandmother was a role I simply did not understand, yet I had fallen instantly in love with the small person that my daughter held in her arms—my granddaughter.

Binah was anxious for the triumphant taxi ride home with her new baby. Her clothes were folded neatly on the bed just waiting for the discharge order. However, when her doctor made his rounds, he made a notation on her chart to keep her for an additional day. The confident baby ma I had just been conversing with disappeared, replaced by a young girl who just wanted to go home with her ma. She cried, begging me to sign her out.

I strolled to the nurses' station with every intention of doing just that, until a nurse explained that because of the stitches required after her delivery, and the fact that this was her first child, they wanted to watch her in case she developed an infection. She warned me that if I signed her out, she could develop a fever, they wouldn't accept her back as a patient. I considered the advice and realized that although my daughter would be vexed, to be on the safe side, she needed to stay.

When I delivered the unwanted news, Binah's hormones and all the fearful emotions she had suppressed overwhelmed her and she began to bawl.

"Ma, I've been brave through the delivery and everything. I just want us to go home now!"

"I understand, but you have to think of the baby," I replied softly. "If you get sick and she can't suck, how will she eat? She is small, not eight pounds like your sisters and brothers were."

"I don't want to stay here, can't you see? They will move me to the floor or into the hallway," she cried, and I couldn't argue with her on that fact. She was probably right, but at least if something happened, they would care for her. If she became sick, and I had to take her to JFK Hospital where the level of care was not as good, and they might also turn her away. She was *my* baby, and I wanted her home, but I had no resources to cover us if she became ill, no community of women to help me make decisions, and no one to support me if I made the wrong decision. She had not cried through childbirth, yet she was crying softly now, a defeated cry. To make matters worse, I understood exactly how she felt.

"Ma, I'm eighteen. I can sign myself out!"

"Yes, and if you get sick, they won't treat you. Then what? You are at the better hospital now, but suppose I have to take you back to JFK?"

"I don't want to stay here! I stayed last night, it was bad, but I didn't complain, I know we are jammed, but I just can't take it another night. I want to go home with my baby!"

"You have to listen to me!" I shot back. "I hear you, but you have to think about this little pie faced baby. This isn't anything new; they don't discharge patients with a fever. There could be an infection; you could *die* from a complication from your delivery. After I delivered you and I was supposed to go home, I awakened with chills and a fever. I was sick, and it took an extra week of recovery time before we could go home. Binah, I had the same option of signing myself out, but I thought about what would happen if I did. I might have died, and then what would've happened to you? So I stayed, and I'm asking you to stay."

"Hey yah, Emah," she said, tears rolling down her cheeks.

She stayed.

Thankfully, Binah and my very first grandbaby were able to leave the hospital the next afternoon, but our adventures on Lynch Street were just beginning. Now there were seven of us!

On many occasions, I thought about women that had been my friends in America and how differently they had experienced the phenomenon of grand motherhood. They shopped and spent a fortune on their grandchildren and shared photos of their grandchildren with friends, and maybe even strangers.

But I would not do these things. I was in a time warp, estranged from one culture and a stranger in another, and struggling to make sense of the distance between.

*Zefron and
sidekick Tikvah*

GO WITH YO GUT

One of the strengths that helped me in Africa was that, on important matters, I learned to trust my instincts, even when they appeared to contradict my logic.

Once Binah had delivered her baby, my focus turned to moving us out of the crowed room on Lynch Street. Conditions had deteriorated and due to the demolition of old buildings in the area, there was an influx of rats the size of kittens. On several occasions, when one of us accidentally forgot to place the 2 x 4 block against the bottom of the door, we arrived and had to drive rats out of our room. Just before Yohanna was born, I had come home during the naptime at the day care center to find a huge black rat standing in my bed. When I entered the room, it lifted its head and looked at me as if I was the intruder. *On my bed!* I didn't have time to wash and dry my sheets in hot water before bedtime and was silent that night when my children asked why I was sleeping on the bare mattress. Things were coming to a head.

Now that I had a new baby and a woman recovering from a delivery, I had to make some new living arrangements, and fast. While SC had gone "up country" to visit her people, the toilet broke. Raw feces, toilet tissue, and rags used in lieu of tissue covered the bathroom floor. In this condition, it was impossible to use, and the stench blanketed the hallway outside of our room. The children and I used the bathroom at the Red Cross, and at night urinated outside. Unfortunately, Binah was unable to squat and go to the bathroom because of her labor, and so she used a plastic covered bucket, which needed to be carried and emptied at a government (as in public) toilet. Fortunately for me, Roland made it his responsibility to come every day, retrieve the bucket, empty, rinse, and return it. This unpleasant responsibility provided him with a big incentive to help us find another place to live. While the people in the surrounding area were used to living without an indoor toilet, I was embarrassed believing that people knew I was from America and possibly wondered why I would tolerate such a situation. I lay awake at night, planning how I could take my family from this awful situation into a better one.

One day, Roland came to my office excited to have found a room for us in Panesville for seventy-five dollars a month. It was close to the room that he had in Panesville, and he had talked to the man for me. All I needed to do was take a taxi ride there, look at the place, and if I liked it, could close the deal. I left work early that day, and as I rode from Lynch Street to Panesville, I felt hopeful and as if a weight had been lifted from my shoulders.

I stopped to pick up Roland, and he walked me to the house, inhabited by simple market people, the house was recently made from cast concrete blocks and had a shiny new zinc roof. The interior was clean and the floors were raw concrete, but I knew I could warm them up with a nice piece of linoleum. All the other tenants were native Liberians and was sorry that I wouldn't even have a peer who worked at a government ministry or taught school. I was lonely for companionship, but figured I had friends in town and didn't really have that much time to socialize anyway. I decided that I could adjust and deal with not having many people to talk to in return for clean surroundings.

I had brought Tikvah with me, but because she was still barely walking,

I picked her up to make the walkthrough simpler. When I met the owner, a thin Gbassa man who weighed all of 120 pounds, he seemed cold, almost condescending. By now, I was tired of hauling Tikvah around and stood her temporarily on her feet. I followed the owner into the actual room he was renting and looked around. It was four drab walls and a concrete floor. All I could think was, "God, is this what it has come to?"

Finally, I asked to see the bathroom and was shown to an outdoor bathhouse where tenants could bring a bucket of bathwater and two-yard lappa cloth to cover the doorway. On the other side of the bathhouse was a built up hole in the floor to squat over. There was no indoor plumbing. Tikvah had been stumbling along behind me, and as I turned to pick her up, the Gbassa man said in a breathy voice, "The baby *fine* 'O'."

"Thank you yah," I said, but there was something about him that seemed odd. As we left the small zinc-covered house, I was resigned to the fact that this room would be my next home. I told him I would send 'baby pa' back the next day with the $100 deposit. I would move in Saturday with my children and provide a month's rent at the time.

I felt relief over leaving the squalor of our building on Lynch Street. So what if the bathroom was outside? I had taught my children to manage difficult situations and at least the smell of the toilet would not be able to come into our room. The Panesville area, like any suburb, was cleaner and more spacious than the city. My children would have open space to play and ride bikes, and the crime of Lynch Street would be left far behind. These were definite pluses. The only minus was that I would have to pay taxi fare to ride into town daily, instead of walking a few blocks to get home. This would decrease the amount of money that I could save for our house, but for now, it was more important that my family have a clean place to live. That evening, I shared the news with the children that we would be moving Saturday. Our struggle with the rats was over.

However, that night I couldn't sleep. I kept thinking back to the owner of the house, his eyes, and the way he looked at my Tikvah. The coldness I felt when he entered the room chilled my heart. I tossed, turned, and tried to shake the feeling, but by morning, I knew that despite what I had said, I would not give 'baby pa' the rent deposit. I was going to listen to my intuition and not move my family there. I have always lived by my intuition, and although it hasn't always made sense to me, it has always steered me in the right direction.

Roland stopped by the Red Cross later that day to get the deposit, and when I told him that I did not want the place, he was vexed. He ranted on and on about how I was embarrassing him and making him look like a small boy. I understood and sympathized but refused to give in. He stormed out of my office, and later that evening, he came to our room and took Binah's bucket of water and feces away, emptied it for us, and left quietly. I didn't see him much the next week or so. He came to visit my daughter and his baby while I was at work. I only knew he had come because my Binah would tell me.

Meanwhile, I still had my feelers out for a place to stay. I was desperate and feeling stupid about not accepting the room in Panesville that would have resolved most of our immediate housing problems. It was hard for all of us, and I held myself responsible for the deplorable conditions in which we lived.

Several weeks later, Roland arrived at the Day Care Center saying it was urgent that he see me. Aretha sent him back to my office where he shut the door in a conspiratorial way. Once I entered, he began telling me a story. The night before, a child had come up missing in the area of Panesville where we were supposed to move. It was the time of the year, when those that believe in "African Science" carry out ritual sacrifices. Heart men cut the heart from a living person and offer it as sacrifice. Some say the heart is eaten, some say it's not, but whatever happens with the heart, the victim is dead. The abducted child was a Kpelle, like Roland. All the people, and particularly the Kpelle people in the area, were alerted to call out the child's name all over the area. He told me it was called "making noise" for the child. In this way, the person who has abducted the child knows that the child is highly valued and that many angry people are looking for the child. This can cause the kidnapper to release the child and flee. According to baby pa, searchers found her safe near a local swamp. She identified her kidnapper who, it turned out, was none other than the man that had tried to rent the room to us!

This once again validated my reliance on my instincts. I continued to pray, knowing that something better was on the horizon.

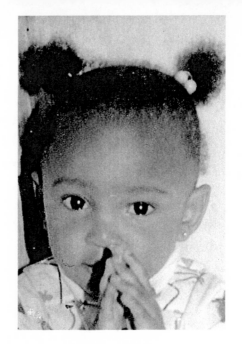

Yohanna Jartu's First Birthday

FINALLY, A HOME

You can find your family wherever you need them because when it comes down to it, we are all spiritually connected.

In 1987, despite my challenges, I had no thoughts of returning to America. I certainly was not interested in returning 'wit my mouth dragging the ground.' Seven years away from America, and I missed my family but not the racial climate in America. Nothing that I had heard or read about, during my time in Africa, gave me the impression that people of African descent, my people, would ever be valued beyond the legacy of chattel slavery. Despite the eventual election of a man of color to the White House, which was beyond my wildest dreams, there is a pathological tarnish related to America and its racial worldview.

Elrahm had taken a second wife and they had moved to Gbarnga. Ironically, several months into the marriage, his wife came to visit me to tell me that she had left him. She felt he was harsh with her children and had never felt her affection returned. I wasn't even jealous when they married because I didn't feel he really loved her, not in the way a

220

woman wants a man to love her.

As God so fixed it, Seah, a carpenter I often hired at the Red Cross, was the one who eventually found our next home. In addition to working for me, he was a handy man for an elderly nurse on Chubor Road. The widowed nurse worked for the Ministry of Health. She wanted to rent space in her house to bring in extra income.

The home on Chubor Road was spacious and bright, although anything was an improvement over the pervasive darkness in the former tavern we lived in.

I paid Seah's taxi fare and we rode to the Market at the top of Chubor Road. "My daughter, you must be Seah's friend. He told me good, good things about you. I'm Elina Seeton, but dey call me Ma."

"Ma, I'm Ahnydah Rahm."

Ma had sparkling, white even teeth that were all her own, and her hair was died coal black. She looked to be in her 60's but I learned that she was mid-70. Her back was erect, and gait was strong and rapid as she took me to the rental area. She flung open the door and I knew immediately it would be our new home.

The suite consisted of two bedrooms and connecting bath. This was deluxe accommodations compared to our room on Lynch Street, and finding it forever carved Seah a place in my heart. Ma showed me a huge kitchen with granite floors, a sink with running water, and ample kitchen counter space. There was an electric stove that worked (at least it did that day), built in kitchen cupboards, and a large white refrigerator. Outside the back door lay mango trees, a breadfruit tree, palm nut trees, and butter pear (avocado) trees.

"Ma, the trees are plenty 'O'," I said.

"My daughter, we planted those trees when my mulatto children were babies. We never wanted them to have to beg for food."

It had been a good plan.

Because the Ministry of Health sporadically paid its employees, Ma demanded $175 a month in rent. I had to have the rooms, so I resorted to begging and cajoling, pointing out that our move further from town caused me to incur an additional $100 a month expense in transportation fees. For a few moments, things looked doubtful, but what I was unaware of at the time was that Ma wanted her grandchildren, Gabby and Rico, two thoroughly spoiled little curly-headed boys, kept away from "raw country children." Having my children as playmates insured that. Her son-in-law, Abiti, served as an attaché to the Embassy of Zaire, a title without a regular paycheck. Her daughter had moved to America, leaving Abiti and Ma to raise the boys. Ma finally gave in and rented us the two bedrooms, a bath, along with space in the living room and access to the kitchen for $125 a month.

I chose the smaller room because it had two windows, one to the north and another facing west. I would have a good cross breeze and view of the backyard. My children needed the larger room in order to accommodate their double sets of bunk beds, as well as a bed for Binah and Yohanna. Our greatest joy was the bathroom. It had a porcelain tub, sink, and a *working* toilet! Outside our bedroom suite, Ma urged us to place our own sitting room furniture, which I was ashamed to tell her we didn't own yet.

I was overjoyed at the prospect of purchasing furniture. I belonged to a Liberian Savings Club and had "five hands," or five savings passbooks, corresponding to the names of my children, which I contributed to monthly. Our membership meeting took place the second Sunday of each month. We would discuss the business of the savings club, then socialize over snacks and Club beer. Liberians saved to build a home, purchase a table in the market, start a small shop, or pay for the unexpected funeral of a loved one. There were no credit cards. Our Club was composed of upwardly mobile native Liberians, a few bi-racial persons of Liberian ancestry mixed with Lebanese, Chinese or Indian ancestry, and me. If you wanted to save money in Liberia and be in the company of others who had the same goals, the support of a savings club was essential.

We moved in that Saturday, and because the space required very little cleaning, by Saturday evening, I was unpacked, settled, and able to sit up late talking with Ma. She was a wonderful storyteller and a fountain of wisdom. For the first time since I had left the Hebrew Israelite Community, I felt at home.

Binah was still breastfeeding Yohanna, and doing quite well, except that during the excitement of the move, she developed a touch of malaria and that, coupled with sore nipples, caused her to want to slow down the nursing. I implored her to continue breastfeeding, but she was reluctant, and her breasts became even more tender. Several days later, she came into my bedroom and bared her left breast. There was an obvious reddish lump, and she had a raging fever. She had an abscess on her breast. I was terrified. I put her to bed with a hot compress over her breast and sought Ma's help. Ma brought aspirin for the pain and then pulled me outside to talk.

"It will hurt her 'O,' but she must continue 'O.' If she stops nursing, and you can't afford the milk, the baby will be sickly. You have to be strong for her. Whenever she cries, tell her to keep feeding and help her to take deep breaths while she is nursing. If we keep putting the compresses on the abscess, and she keeps nursing the baby, the abscess will bust and we can drain and pack it, but otherwise, she may have to be hospitalized."

Ma was preaching to the choir. I had worked the Well Baby Clinic and seen what happens when babies are placed on a formula that baby ma can't afford. My grandbaby had to be breastfed. Pain stabbed in the pit of my stomach, but I told Binah what Ma had said. Binah wanted to be a good mom to her little daughter, Yohanna, whom she nicknamed Nookie. She appreciated our family's predicament, and having watched me nurse her siblings, she understood the value of breastfeeding. However, she was afraid of the pain. Never one to lie to my children, I admitted that nursing with the abscess would be very painful, but that she needed to trust me and to trust Ma, who was after all a nurse. I must have looked a little shaky, because Ma looked directly at Binah and firmly said, "We are women; we do what we have to do for our children.

I will help you, you ma will help you but you *will* do it, 'O.' You got to feed you own baby. See how small she is? She needs *your* milk!"

And that was that.

Every day for over a week, I sat with Binah through as many feedings as I could.

"The baby is crying for milk."

"I *know* Ma. Bring her, I just need to drink some cool water and take some breaths."

I diapered Yohanna with a diaper retrieved from the clothesline. It smelled clean, the faint scent of bleach clinging to the white cotton. I wiped perspiration from the fat rings under her neck with a damp towel, wiped her face, and brought her to her mother. She was hungry and rooting for milk. I stuck my finger in her mouth to help calm her so that her first draw at my daughter's breast would not be so painful. Meanwhile, Binah massaged her breast to start the let-down reflex. She took a deep breath as I handed her the baby.

"Oh God!" she sighed loudly, whistling through her teeth. She closed her eyes and her head arched backwards. Yohanna grabbed at her mother's full aching breast. Another deep breath and a few tears later, the baby was sucking nicely, milk had begun to flow, and Binah was breathing rhythmically.

"Hey, yah this is hard 'O' Emah." The pain in her eyes pierced me.

"I know, but you are doing well. You are a strong woman."

Binah knew the pain would come, and ultimately go. She just needed to breathe through the discomfort, and she did. If I could have nursed my granddaughter, I would have, but my job was to have a cooling towel ready to apply once the nursing was over to help ease the pain.

One evening, as I lay in my room nearing slumber, Binah burst into my bedroom crying. "Emah, I have a big hole in my breast!"

She had startled me, and I shouted, "What? Does it hurt?"

"No, man, but when it busted it felt good 'O.' The pain stopped!" She was both excited and relieved.

I thought she was over-reacting, but when she bared her breast, I saw that an abscess the size of a golf ball had risen, burst, and was leaking thick yellowish pus down her side to her slender waist. I'd never seen anything so gross before.

"Binah, please sit on the bed and calm down. Don't be so darn dramatic!" I said, nervously closing the door behind me before bolting across the living room to Ma Seeton's rooms.

"Ma, something is wrong with Binah's breast, she has a big hole in it!"

Ma came with me immediately. I had hoped that since the abscess had opened, we could just clean it and everything would be over, but it wasn't that easy. It never is.

Ma calmly responded, "It busted good, but now you have to get all the infection out. I'm going to press it and make sure the core is out, or it will come back. Then we can dress it." My knees buckled. Binah was experiencing the only relief from pain she'd known in over a week. What Ma suggested sounded Medieval; however, the confidence in her voice told me she knew what she was talking about. I went back to our rooms and told Binah, this time with authority, what our next course of action was.

Her voice was sad and resigned as she asked me to mind the baby while Ma handled the procedure. I took Yohanna into my bed and held her close, while the children and I heard Binah screaming as Ma tried to remove its core. I wept, wondering why this was happening to my daughter. Zevah, Penemiel, and Zefron sat sadly on the edge of my bed with their feet dangling as I promised them their big sister was going to be all right. We waited.

Finally, Binah's ordeal was over, and she climbed into her bed and slept until it was time for the next nursing. While Binah slept, I went across the Great Room to thank Ma. She was also exhausted, looking her age, and yet, she had words of comfort for me.

Binah couldn't nurse on the injured breast that night, and for several days, she discarded the blood-tinged milk, but finally, she was able to return to nursing on that breast. This was a character-defining moment for her, and I realized through this ordeal that she had truly become a woman capable of putting the needs of her child before her own.

Despite the challenges we faced, we felt deeply embedded in the culture of Liberia and I always looked at the upside. Here, I had stumbled onto a woman who, while she could not replace my own mother, was such a grounding, loving spirit for my children and me, that I was sure her presence in my life was divine. I was certain that we could forge lasting ties in Liberia, and we had options beyond the Hebrew Community or returning to America in order to have family. I was learning that family could be anywhere.

My dream expanded. It was hard to hear my mother's voice on the rare occasions I went in town to Telecommunications to make a transatlantic call. The few times we spoke, I felt worse after hanging up, and so, I mainly wrote long expressive letters. Letters allowed me to share my life without hearing the unspoken question of, "Why won't you come home?" on the other end of the line.

It was during this time of my life that I began to think of ways that I could work harder or smarter in order to figure out a way for us to visit America every couple of years. I did not allow myself to think of how happy I would be to visit my mother, sister, my Uncle Pete and Aunt Connie, Aunt Sara and Uncle Mike, for fear of being disappointed if my plan failed. I desperately wished to establish my family in Liberia, as well as go back and forth to America. If I could do that, I would have everything I wanted in life.

Eight months into the Market Daycare Center pilot, Reverend Lloyd summoned me into his office. He had the reputation for being a short, Gbassa tyrant, but today, instead of an outburst, I felt him measuring his words.

"Mistress Rahm, I know you and your nurses are doing a lot of good for the children in the market, but those raw country women will never give the Red Cross any rights to operate a child care center in the market. We are suffering for money and I cannot continue to pay staff without getting more money in return. If we can't get money from those people, we can't give them services.

"But Reverend Lloyd, we are making progress, the children..." He didn't let me finish.

"Mistress Rahm, You will *please* shut down the pilot at the end of the week." Then he quickly added, "Mistress Rahm, this is all I have to say about this market thing. I am directing you to use your charm and enthusiasm to work with our very large International Community to produce a money-making Bazaar."

Despite my feelings, I knew he had correctly assessed reality. The Marketers would never allow the Red Cross to collect money from a day care center in their Market, and at the end of the day, Red Cross had to make payroll. Case closed.

When we shut down the pilot, we were mad as hell with Reverend Lloyd, and we were shamed in the market. The pilot had gone well, the population of children had grown to the point of our having between seventy and eighty market women's children attend the part time day care center. We had even arranged for the Well-Baby Clinic nurses to come and provide inoculations. Now we had to leave! In an act of rebellion, I refused to remove any of the tables, chairs, or materials we used from the pilot site in the market. How could we take anything away from the market women? We had come to give. Reverend Lloyd knew I was bitter about his demand, and for a few weeks, he cut me a very wide berth. He didn't come into the child care center. He didn't send for me. We just ignored one another.

The market women asked Aretha and my staff why the Red Cross had left the market. Some would stop by the day care center and ask if we would be returning. I tried not to be the one to respond to those inquiries because I felt we had let the children of the market women down. However, the unintended consequence of our increased interaction with the market women and our work in the market was that the Well-Baby Clinic experienced an upsurge of women who trusted the Red Cross to provide care and inoculations for their children.

First Bike
Zevah, Penemiel and Zefron

SHIFTING GEARS

For my new project, I had the Red Cross van and driver, new business cards, a budget for personal expenses, and a mandate to make the Red Cross International Bazaar happen in a big way. I threw myself into my new task of visiting the fourteen various embassies and seeing an entirely different side of life. The embassies were set on beautifully tended grounds, and I basked in the opulence, each embassy more beautiful than the next. I wanted to represent the Red Cross as best as possible, and so, I had my Mandingo tailor sew several Europeanized lappa suits, and heels became a regular part of my uniform. I enjoyed developing new relationships and picking up nuances of various cultures during my visits, and some of the embassies were kind enough to load up the Red Cross van with gently used toys that benefited the children of the Red Cross Daycare Center.

The Red Cross International Bazaar, held in a large hall on Ashmun Street, was an amazing success. It boasted the participation of most of the foreign embassies represented in Liberia. Some countries mounted replicas of their flags behind their display area, while others decorated their tables to reflect their culture. Because the embassies wanted to strut their national pride, they made every effort to impress the crowd with the many unique things they brought for sale. Each embassy highlighted their specialties—Portuguese wine, French bread, wines, and cheese, Lebanese deserts and food, Indian jewelry and fashions—it was a cultural overload with two dozen countries represented.

By noon, the place was crammed with people of all nationalities. There were games for children, raffles, food, clothing, jewelry, small pieces of furniture, and crafts from the many countries present. The Red Cross was the beneficiary of the sales, and as I walked the tables, each table captain informed me they were competing with other embassies to give us the most money!

My personal highlight was a spectacular fashion show given by the Indian Women's Association. Fascinated by the beauty and elegance of Indian garments during the Bazaar, I purchased a couple of Indian pants suits with long tunic tops. During the display of the gorgeous garments, I was awestruck that the cloth from Southern India, where the people tended to be darker than many Africans, was of subdued colors, and coarsely hand-woven like the highly valued 'country cloth' in Liberia. The similarity of the cloth and the dark-skinned people that spun it were clear connections between the cultures of Southern India and Africa.

After the Bazaar, I was completely exhausted. I hadn't slept in my bed in two days. To my credit, though, I had charmed my way into the pockets of just about every Lebanese or Indian merchant and every embassy that would make a donation. Red Cross was popular in the foreign community because each of those countries had a National Red

Cross or Red Crescent Society operating in the respective represented country.

One of the very wonderful, touching things I learned about Islam from my Lebanese friends is that despite the fact that I was given thousands of dollars in cash and merchandise, very few of the Lebanese merchants would accept acknowledgement as donors. One of the largest merchants at Waterside Market refused to have his name listed as a donor saying "In Islam, if you do good, this is between you and God."

The Red Cross International Bazaar was the first of its kind for the Red Cross, but it was not the last. I left the Bazaar that day with over $10,000 in profit. The President of the Red Cross asked me to take the money home pending the final report. As I reflect on that now, I realize that either I was truly trusted or that others knew that they were very corrupt. I also realize how much money there was in Liberia during that period. I kept the money in a shoebox at the back of my closet and there it stayed until I returned to work. Besides the childcare center, all of the other services of the Red Cross were free. The funds raised from the bazaar would help with the National Society's programs. We received a certain amount from the International Red Cross (ICRC) but were expected to raise money in Liberia to pay our dues to the ICRC.

In all my time working for the Red Cross, except my month in Voinjama, I rarely took all of my vacation. In the early years when I struggled to improve the quality of the daycare I felt I couldn't afford to be away for an entire month, and I was paid for my leave. Sometimes I'd take few days off or leave early, but I loved what I was doing, and without even realizing it, my designated vacation time would pass me up. But now I was emotionally drawn and exhausted. Exhausted from the market pilot and the Bazaar, exhausted from moving my family to a new residence, and exhausted because my estranged husband was sick in Gbarnga and visiting him had stirred up the turmoil from our relationship.

I treated myself to a wonderfully rejuvenating month at home with my children. For the first couple of days, I didn't get out of bed for more than a few hours. I held court in my bedroom where my children shared my bed with me, and also shared with me all the things I had missed while I had focused on the Bazaar. I happily acknowledged the bond they had developed with Ma Seeton and her family, and I would sit up late at night soaking up her wisdom and encouragement.

I also struggled with the realization that my relationship with Elrahm was beyond salvaging, and I was terrified of having to raise the children alone. Ma, a member of the Grebo tribe, had worked, struggled, and sent all five of her children to boarding school in England when her husband, a Lebanese trader, died suddenly. She had feared for the future of her daughters.

She said, "Mixed race women become whores in Liberia." Here I had thought that *all* uneducated women became whores, but I got her point. Mixed race women were often chosen to become the mistresses, rather than the wives of foreigners, who bore children by them, then returned to their wives in India or Lebanon. She epitomized pride, strength, and incredible determination that inspired me then and still inspires me. Ma had quietly watched my strained interactions with Elrahm and without saying a negative word about him, I knew she understood that our relationship was at its end, and so she, like the mother I had left behind in America, fed my soul and gave me confidence. "When my husband died I was just a scrawny country girl, he did everything for me. My child I cried to him in heaven asking how I would raise his children. His spirit sent me to his Lebanese friends and often they paid the tuition. Trust Gawd my daughter, he will make a way."

Liberia is a slow place and my vacation took the form of walks with my children, watching them play soccer and games in the yard and resting. I loved being home every day and taking naps with my granddaughter in the afternoon.

Several months after the success of the Red Cross International Bazaar, one of my caregivers returned from the market shouting that there was a day care center open in the Market! Not believing, I rushed there to see for myself, and sure enough, it was true. I wept tears of joy because something good had come from the tremendous sacrifice my staff had made. They felt such pride that their own country people, not foreigners, had put the Market Day Care together. The thrill of the opening of a daycare center created an atmosphere of excitement and fulfillment that lasted me all afternoon. That night, I fell asleep knowing that a few people with an idea can work together to accomplish just about anything. It was then that I finally felt a profound sense of belonging. It was as if I had just earned my place on this earth.

The model that the market women and their partners developed was very different from ours. The fee was only thirty dollars a month and only one-third of the children enrolled actually belonged to the market women. The other two-thirds were children of other low-income, but upwardly mobile parents, including clerks, girls in college, and other individuals who understood the concept of day care but were unable to afford the prevailing fees in other established centers.

The Ministry of Health provided some support for the long-range goal of providing childcare services, health care services, and information for the children and mothers. This was a wonderful start, and I felt encouraged by it. One of the highlights for me personally was when I was selected to be a presenter at a two-day training session hosted by UNICEF at the site of another market day care in Sinkor. In addition to my invitation to present a paper on childcare, I received a cash honorarium of twenty-five dollars that I earmarked to purchase an extra one-hundred pound bag of rice for my family. The reward was both spiritual and economic.

The workshop was held in April 1989. My staff received invitations, and with the invitation came an opportunity to see the fruits of their hard work. I was delighted and honored to speak after Mrs. Inonge Mibkusita-Lewanika Ph.D., who was Regional Advisor for Early Childhood and Women in Development and an international advocate for the development of African women.

I experienced a surge of absolute joy seated around the conference table with other childcare center directors, savoring, what at that moment, seemed to be an important milestone. The country finally appeared to be on the path of understanding that the health and welfare of its children, at *all* levels of society, was important. We took great pride in knowing that we had helped play a role.

While I lived in Liberia, I had seen many so-called development efforts end in frustration and watched some very bright people undertake very ill advised projects—projects that represented work *they* wanted to undertake, but not work the people of a town or village really needed. This project, however, had survived because women needed and really wanted daycare.

I felt that I was moving forward fast, in May of 1989 I was asked to represent the Red Cross at a two week Aids Workshop in Nairobi Kenya hosted by International League of Red Cross and Red Crescent Societies. Besides learning about AIDS, a disease that Liberia was in complete denial about was inspiring and informative. I met delegates from all over Africa and listened intently to the various scenarios presented. I enjoyed having money to shop in the markets for gifts for my children and especially remember the Kenyan drum that Zefron treasured and my beautiful soapstone chess set. Two weeks away from struggling to make ends meet, with a generous per diem, living in a luxury hotel and having every meal prepared for me was comparable only to my time in Voinjama in terms of relaxation and time to connect with my spirit. I returned to Liberia renewed.

In November 1989, the economic conditions in the country had taken a downturn, and government ministries became slow and irregular at paying their employees. One month, we'd get paid, and then the next, we never saw a check. The Red Cross, which had been very timely in paying me up until his point, had begun to pay us sporadically. I had no idea how my staff was making ends meet. It was hard for me to miss a paycheck for two months—I had bills to pay and food to put on the table. The bean sprout business was an asset, but I needed another form of income. I decided to start a business selling used clothing, called ducofleh in the interior.

Of the two Red Cross janitors who I knew needed the extra money, I did not even consider Saah for this assignment, because despite real improvement in his surly attitude, he lacked the people skills to sell anything. Instead, I chose Andrew, who had brought Saah to us in the first place. However, to appease Saah I confided to him that while Drew would be handling the selling of the old clothes in the interior, Essie and I were going to be leaving the Red Cross to start our own business, and we wanted him to come along as a our janitor. He beamed at his assignment as the first janitor in our new school.

I was confident in Andrew and his capability to charm money out of our customer's pockets. He was a good hustler, and I could already see the profitability in this venture. I had worked briefly for Janet Williams, an African American expatriate, operating a ducofleh business across the bridge. I had contacted her and carefully selected $500 worth from

Janet's finest ducofleh. I knew this was a new business, and I coached Drew as much as I could, but in the end, I had to trust him to do his best. I reasoned we could learn the business over time and eventually make a better profit. Janet would be our supplier, and Drew could sell used clothing to the north of Monrovia in Gbarnga located in Bong County, and eventually push further into the interior. He was Krahn and I felt once we were well established I might be able to send him to his home in Nimba county, near the border of the Ivory Coast.

Drew loaded up the taxi at my house, then we all held hands, Drew and my family, and prayed before we sent him off. He was gone for a week, and during that stretch of time, I had nothing but faith in his ability to sell clothes.

When he returned, instead of him coming to me, I had to look for him. Oddly, I couldn't find him for several days after he should have reported to me. He finally showed up at the Day Care Center and swore that despite the fact that all of my best pieces were gone, he was ripped-off. He reported just over $200. I didn't even have enough money to buy more clothes in order to continue the business. But the real killer was that I knew in my gut, that Drew had sold the clothes, and for some reason, kept the money. I was persistent in trying to get him to open up and tell me what really happened. I rationalized with myself that if he would just admit the truth, I'd feel better, but in the end, I knew the truth would still hurt.

It was Aretha who said, "What do you want him to say? You are like his Ma. He can't tell you it."

"Why can't he just tell the truth?"

"Mistress Rahm, the truth must be sorrowful, and he can't tell you it because you trusted him."

I stopped asking about my money, but I could no longer stand the sight of Drew or have him near me. I told him so and he left. I heard rumors that from time to time he came to see Aretha and Saah when I wasn't around. I had no intention of ever seeing Drew again.

This small stab of disappointment would soon be surpassed by another, even stronger betrayal.

WALKING IN FAITH

My experiences in Liberia served to strengthen my faith in ways I could never have imagined. By the time I was in my mid-twenties, although I didn't know what the term meant at the time, I was Agnostic. I believed that there is a higher power, but I did not feel an authentic connection to any of the denominations. Now I am comfortable with that, but then, I was not.

One hot summer day, long before my life in Liberia, I reflected on how I was lying on the 57th Street beach on Chicago's lakeshore wearing

236

a hot pink backless swimming suit and reading a book recommended by my drama coach at Ebony Talent Association. The book, by Frederick Bailes, was called *Hidden Power for Human Problems*, and the phrase that resonated as truth to me and started me on my spiritual journey was Bailes assertion that, "We are where we are by right of consciousness." I remember reading the words repeatedly and desperately wanting to understand what he meant. If that was true, then, race, financial status, who you knew, your IQ, none of it was *the* defining factor. Instead, your consciousness was the most important indicator of success. That day, with the sunshine beaming on my bare back, I quietly prayed, asking my Creator to place me on the spiritual path, and with my words, I selected my world and experiences for a long, long time.

In June of 1988 I legally changed my name from Susan Peters, the name my father had given me at birth-the name on my passport, to Ahnydah Rahm. No one ever called me Susan and it was always uncomfortable to have to use that name when cashing my paycheck at the bank. My long-range goal was to become a Liberian citizen and this was a first step. There was a brief court proceeding, and a fee of fifty dollars paid after which the judge pounded the gavel and my legal name in the Republic of Liberia was now Ahnydah Rahm. All forthcoming paychecks would reflect that name. My hopes for a prosperous and happy future were invested in Liberia.

An odd climate filtered throughout Liberia in 1988. Rumors of a coup were in the air, a coup that many Liberians welcomed with open arms. It was common knowledge that Head of State, Samuel Kanyon Doe had stolen the October 1985 election after repeatedly promising the return of Liberia to civilian rule. Liberians had watched the "election" process unfold in disbelief as they realized that Doe's promise was nothing more than a lie. An unblemished peaceful change of power, from military to civilian rule, was impossible in Liberia.

General Thomas Quiwonkpa, who had been with Doe during the April 12 coup and one of the original members of the People's Redemption Council (PRC) advocated strongly for Doe to step aside and allow civilian rule. His disagreement with Doe, and Doe's fears of his popularity, spurred Quiwonkpa's flight from Liberia and life in exile abroad. Quiwonkpa had an advantage that most leaders of military coups do not. He was not an unknown, and he was somewhat of a legendary figure in Liberia. He was "a soldier's soldier," and lived a disciplined life and had controlled his troops after the coup. He is reported to have made his troops refrain from abusing civilians, even the targeted Americo-Liberians and he continually spoke against corruption in the evolving Liberian government.

From the very beginning, one of the stated aims of the Doe regime had been to seize Liberia from the hands of the Americo-Liberians and eventually to return Liberia to civilian rule by all of its people. In 1984 the ban on the forming of political parties had been lifted and elections were scheduled for 1985. However, although eleven political parties were formed only four of them were "allowed" to enter the election.

On November 15, a month after the election was stolen, Quiwonkpa returned leading a small force bent on overthrowing the administration of the now President Samuel K. Doe. Because they were extremely popular, masses of Liberians openly rejoiced in the streets when the takeover was announced. According to political analysts, Quiwonkpa made several tactical errors. First, he did not seize and hold control of the communications systems. Most importantly, it was said that he didn't have the stomach to kill President Samuel K. Doe.

President Doe moved quickly and ruthlessly to regain control of the radio station and control the message. He declared that he had put down the coup, then immediately moved to capture the more idealistic Quiwonkpa who met with a horrific death. Doe struck a further note of fear when he seized all cameras and footage of the 'rejoicing' during the coup attempt and had his soldiers hunt and kill anyone who was identified rejoicing. The stage for future conflict had been set.

Many civil servants who were not members of the Krahn tribe, Liberia's politically astute progressives and foreign nationals, sought a change in power. The perception at the time was that the removal of Samuel Doe would allow Liberia to finally right itself and move forward. At the time, Liberia was teetering on the ragged edge, existing each day on the manna of our faith.

Despite the slow-and sometimes non-payment of employees, my student's parents, many of whom were government employees, were loyal to us. They struggled to pay us regularly, and when they learned that the Red Cross had stopped paying us consistently, they urged us to open our own school, pledging to follow us. I wrote a proposal for my own childcare facility, First Steps Child Development Center, and mailed it to friends in the United States that had previously lived in Liberia, asking for financial support. Perhaps my friends were overwhelmed with the reconstruction of their own lives because they never sent any funds.

Meanwhile, I had grossly underestimated the value of my relationships in Liberia and the high-level contacts of Essie, my Red Cross head teacher. Essie had shared our proposal with a Liberian executive that we both admired. The executive met with us and reviewed our proposal, agreeing to loan us $5,000, which we secured with a verbal "ladies agreement." Essie reached out to an old friend, the owner of an abandoned bungalow in Sinkor, and set up a meeting between us. After cookies and soft drinks, this woman gave us permission to use her house as long as we reconnected the water and lights. With verbal agreements between four women, the financial backing and the building that would house First Steps Child Development Center had been born. I deposited the money into our newly opened account in the Bank of Liberia and realized that our dream was about to come true.

Progress was in the air. It was time to leap forward. I was anxious to leave the home we shared with Ma on Chubor Road and relocate my family in our own home. I hadn't figured out how to do that but I was working on it.

Sometimes I have a sixth sense of something that is about to happen. One evening after getting out of a taxi on the old road and taking a leisurely stroll home I began to feel Elrahm's presence. I passed it off as just missing him, he was in Gbarnga and so I continued on my walk. As I turned onto the short road and walked past the old man's house next door, my children ran toward me, their eyes shining. "Abba here 'O,' Abba here 'O!'

"O.K.! I see you are all happy that Abba is here." I did not know what had brought their father to visit and I braced myself.

Binah walked up behind them and stuck her arm in mine. I could sense that even though she was older, and had disappointed him when she ran away with Roland; she was still at heart a daddy's girl.

"Abba said he was sick, Emah. He's really lost weight. I fixed him some rice and he went to sleep. He's in your room," she said quietly as if she wanted to keep me calm.

She smiled a smile I hadn't seen in awhile. I knew she was happy her father was back with us, even thought it was probably only temporarily. When she was a tiny girl in Chicago he took her everywhere, even to play basketball with his friends. The children loved their father, I couldn't dampen their happiness.

Entering our house, I saw Ma sitting on her gold French provincial couch. "Mr. Rahm is here, 'O,' a fine looking man, I can see why the children so fine, 'O.' You and Mr. Rahm both fine 'O.' "

I smiled and went inside our rooms. Elrahm was lying on my bed, fully dressed and sleeping soundly. I knew that he loved his children and there was still love between him and me, and I found that I was happy not to be alone.

For the next several months, Elrahm lived with us, and I found myself fantasizing that we could be a happy family again. He seemed relaxed and spent time playing with our kids, and on top of it, he was a good cook! Life took on an air of normalcy. Their father supervised their homework and made sure they sat down together and ate as a family, even if I was working late.

Yet, there was still friction between us and none of it had to do with his having taken a second wife. I continued to hope, in vain, that he would leave the Hebrew Community, but even if he did, we still didn't make sense as a couple anymore. For the sake of peace, and to allow my children to experience the presence and love of their father, I kept my mouth shut and walked on eggshells. I knew it was only a matter of time before he went back to one of the Hebrew compounds, even though he professed to have "reservations" about the management of the Liberian Mission.

The weeks moved on, for the most part, uneventfully. The children went back and forth to school, and my eldest son Penemiel began to play soccer at the large field near our house. Initially, the other boys who were older and rougher than him had bullied him. Thankfully, his father was there to walk him back to the field to face his tormenters. It took some coaxing, but finally Penemiel was comfortable making friends and playing soccer with the other boys. Every Sunday after dinner, the citizens of Chubor, along with my family, went to the soccer field to watch the boys play soccer. It was good to feel the children's happiness at having their father there and the boys that wanted to date Binah were always more respectful when they saw her bearded father towering over them.

I allowed myself to wonder what it could be like if Elrahm left the Hebrew Community and found work, or started a business, and we were able to keep things the way they were. Unfortunately, Ma began to pick on Rahm, making remarks that I felt were disrespectful. She was a controlling person. She controlled Abiti, her son-in-law, and to the extent that I let her feel in control, she even ordered me around. Elrahm was a Hebrew, used to being given deference by women. He appreciated that she had helped me, but felt in general, that she was becoming overly involved in our family business. I didn't disagree, but my way of resolving this was to move out and be the woman of my own house. I yearned to have our own space and entertain people I liked that were not necessarily friends of Ma's or even Liberians.

I had met a teacher at a conference who lived farther down the road on Chubor and who had a home he needed to rent. The perfect solution had just dropped into our laps. My kids and I would still have Ma in our lives, but without her constant overbearing influence. Unfortunately, it would be a financial challenge. The rent for the house would be one-hundred dollars more than I paid Ma, but I couldn't say no. It was the perfect house with the right amount of space—three bedrooms, a large living and dining room, a working bathroom, and a kitchen with a working sink. The large front yard was perfect for the children and the broken wrought iron gate just needed the attention of a welder.

Elrahm and I discussed the move. There was this lingering part of me that wanted to hold our relationship together, but his vision was of us remaining as members of the Hebrew Community, turned me off. After I left, several of his friends—the Brothers that had worked security at the State House when I was summoned for those late night "discussions," others who knew that the money was being gambled away—told him that I was railroaded. On a number of occasions, Elrahm shared his remorse at not coming to my defense. I accepted his apologies but my mother has a saying "that ship has sailed." There was nothing more to say.

During my weeks at the Methodist Guest House, and on Lynch Street battling rats and cockroaches, I had visualized building a lovely home for my family. I dropped out of college, left America, had endured back-to-back pregnancies, put my heart and soul into being the best wife and mother I could, only to be unfairly punished and literally forced out. I had tried to live *his* vision. Now, if Elrahm wanted to stay with us, he needed to fit inside this new vision—*my* vision. However, a few simple words brought everything into sharper focus.

We were cozily lying in bed, a nice cross breeze coming in the windows and I thought this was the perfect time to talk about the future.

"Rahm, I'm sure you know we're going to get the place down on

Chubor. It's more expensive, but I talked to the man and I think they will agree to $225 a month. I'm going down there after work tomorrow. Walk with me so you can see our place. I'm hoping to be able to move in at the end of this month when I take pay. I'm sick of Ma's fussing right now, aren't you? And I know—"

"Ahnydah, I'm going back to America."

Reeling as though I had been gut-punched, I managed to formulate my next words. "What! I don't understand. What are you going back to America for? Are you being sent on an assignment?" I turned away to face the door and to hide the tears that were forming in my eyes.

"I…I need to get a job."

I was happy that he understood that we needed him to contribute to our well-being, but scared because he would be leaving me alone with five children. He was abandoning the "big family," the group that could sing five-part harmony. It was one thing for him to be a Hebrew living on the compound while we lived and worked in town; it was another thing completely to have a co-parent an ocean away.

"And so what brings this on?" I asked, angered that he had already made this plan without even discussing it with me. And realizing that this visit all along masked a deeper intention. The betrayal ran too deep to mention.

"Come on, you know I'm not happy cooking and cleaning up behind you and the children," he countered. "Besides, the school fees for these people are a lot, and I see you working on all the different hustles you can come up with to make money—the bean sprouts, selling ducofleh. There isn't any work I can do in Liberia and I'm sick of watching your back coming and going down the road every day."

"So how do you plan to get back?"

"Jeffrey is sending me a ticket."

Jeffrey, Elrahm's younger brother, had lived with us as a teenager, and was reported to be doing very well for himself. It crushed me that while I was figuring out how to find another place *we* could call home, so that *we* could stay together to raise our children, Elrahm had been plotting his exit strategy. I felt a knot developing in my chest that matched the one growing in the pit of my belly.

"I'm just going to earn some money and then I'll be back."

We both knew he was lying.

He said goodbye the day before we moved to our new home. He helped us pack up everything, and even packed his clothes, allowing the children to believe him when he said he'd be back for them. We packed them in a big straw basket with a lid so that the children could still see and smell them and feel close to their father. The clothes he left behind were not clothes one wears on a job search in America, we both knew that, but the children didn't.

And so, one humid Friday afternoon as we hugged for the last time on the porch of Ma's house, our children gathered around their father to give him a hero's departure. He lovingly hugged each of them, telling them the lie that he was going to America to find a 'good job.'

The yellow taxicab zoomed down the dusty road, taking with it all the innocent love our five children had for him.

Saturday morning, we moved into a little house about a half-mile further down Chubor Road, a house whose backyard opened onto a swamp, with a broken wrought iron gate and a large front porch.

The last home we would have in Liberia.

NEW BEGINNINGS

We had met discretely with parents at the Red Cross Day Care Center and explained that Essie and I were opening our own childcare center. I would leave behind half of the staff I had personally trained, including Aretha, who could lead the Center in my absence and help train a new Director. I don't know if the milestone was lost on her because we never discussed it, but she was really ready to take on the role of interim director. She was no longer just the cook and supervisor! My more progressive parents vowed to follow Essie and me to First Steps Day Care and Child Development Center, and with that support, we felt confident to move forward with our plans. This was our time!

We recruited Marta, Ma Mae and Saah, as our new employees, to help us clean and decorate the space, but there were challenges afoot.

One morning, I arrived to do some painting, and instead found the toilet and face bowl missing! Rogues had broken in during the night and taken them. Essie and I repurchased the items at a discount only to have them stolen again. This forced us to hire an old Kru man, who was trusted by one of our friends, to sleep in the building at night. Finally, rogues stopped stealing the window glasses, and we began to feel that our investment was secure.

Moving to the house on Chubor gave us privacy but still allowed us to be close to Ma, who was, after all, like my children's grandma. Binah and Roland had parted ways, but they continued to co-parent Nookie. Binah had a couple of other boyfriends after Roland, including a professional soccer player, then a brief stint with a moron that Penemiel attacked with a mortar pencil when he caught him roughing up his big sister.

After our first couple of weeks in the new house, there was a new face hanging around my front porch. His name was Chris. He was young man of mixed American and Liberian heritage with the same last name as my mother's maiden name. We had a running joke that perhaps he and Binah were distant cousins. I actually wrote my mother to check with relatives to see if his father's name was familiar. At any rate, soon Chris became as close as family. I loved the evenness of his temperament, and he became an elder brother to Penemiel and Zefron.

With all that was going on, and Christmas nearing, I started to feel anxious. I have never been much of a holiday person since I could never understand the connection between the Nativity story and the commercialism of Christmas. Before coming to Liberia, we had stopped celebrating Christmas and adopted Kwanza, an African American holiday, as our tradition. During my first seven years in Liberia I followed the Hebrew Israelites' lead and ignored Christmas altogether. Once outside the Hebrew Community, however, I was in a country that had so much Christian influence, I felt slightly pressured to begin a modest celebration of Christmas. I wanted the children to fit into their environment. They had already begun attending church at the Haywood Mission School on Sundays, so Christmas was a logical extension. We celebrated four Christmas' together in Liberia, but no matter how hard I try, I can only remember our last Christmas Eve in 1989. I think it is easy to remember mainly because it was Binah's birthday, but in hindsight, the day that began joyfully as my daughter's 21st birthday, also marked the beginning of the end of our lives in Liberia.

A married man, the husband of a friend, angled to have me as his mistress. He handed me a white business envelope containing two hundred dollars, "an early Christmas gift," he had said. I wasn't about to turn the money down but I also wasn't going to bed with him. Shame on him if he thought two hundred dollars was getting him anything but my perennial smile! In the privacy of my room, I touched that envelope to my forehead, repeating this affirmation, "Every good and perfect gift comes from God." I planned to use the money to buy a small television set for the children.

In Liberia, there was television programming on for only a few hours each evening, but on Christmas Eve and Day there were daylong reruns of *I Love Lucy, the Brady Bunch,* and *Fred Sanford*—I thought it was a creative and different way to introduce my children to American values.

Thankfully, media hype about Christmas in Liberia did not exist— no commercials, no constant reminders that you needed to spend money to be happy. People on Chubor Road were, for the most part, easy-going folks who planned to cook and share food with family and make friends happy. If they belonged to a church, they planned to attend and be thankful. Some people would, 'go walkabout.' There was simply the enjoyment of being together. I was enthralled with the anticipation of sitting around the television with my family and sharing a sweet family day.

I bought a gift for Essie, who was by now my dear friend, and some small simple things for my children. What warmed me most was the fact that my children were grateful for everything I was able to provide for them. They were my strength and inspiration.

To celebrate Christmas Eve, we had invited a fellow Chicagoan, that I had met through friends to share dinner with us. Ron Watkins was witty, urbane, and attractive. He had recently come to Liberia to run a diamond mining expedition. We had struck up a conversation when I had shared the mining plans of the Hebrews and I also had a Portuguese student whose father was in mining. His swagger reminded me of what I missed about the Black men in America. There was obvious, instant chemistry with Ron, something I had not experienced in a very long time. I was still raw from the breakup with my husband, but Christmas Eve dinner with my children and a handsome Black man was exactly what I needed.

Talking with Ron was as easy as turning on a faucet and running water. Finally, there was nothing to translate, nothing to misunderstand. He was probably feeling a sense of cultural isolation as well because he seemed equally excited about sharing a vegan dinner with five children and a 'date' with a grandchild. How brave was that?

I remember laboriously and lovingly preparing savory, hot palm butter (sans meat) with Binah hovering over me to ensure that the Country Rice was perfect. We also prepared potato greens and there was soda pop for the children and a couple of icy bottles of Club Beer purchased for the adults. After dinner, Ron and I talked comfortably as the children kept a watchful eye on their mother, who they hadn't seen in the company of a man in quite awhile.

I honestly cannot remember whether there was an announcement on television or the radio, but that evening, along with the rest of the

Republic of Liberia, we learned that Charles Taylor's rebel troops, reported to have been training in Sierra Leone, had crossed Liberia's northern border. Thus, December 24, 1989, marked the beginning of the rebel incursion that what would eventually spiral into the hellish Liberian Civil War.

Common folk had limited information, and truthfully, many people who were not Krahn hated President Samuel Kanyon Doe and wanted him overthrown. The coup in 1980 removed the head of state, cabinet members, and those closest to him. While not anything to be ignored, a coup wasn't a war, and definitely wasn't a civil war.

As Ron and I sipped beer and flirted, Zevah and her little friend played NaFo in the front yard, my boys walked to the soccer field to watch the games, and all over, people fellowshipped. Yet, while most of Liberia enjoyed a sweet day with their family, life-altering changes rode towards Liberia leaving behind a trail of blood.

MY WILL BE DONE

In January 1990, I requested a six-month leave of absence from the Liberian National Red Cross. I decided against officially resigning until I knew that First Steps Child Development Center was on firmer ground. The Secretary General was a friend, and while I had purposely not discussed my plans about First Steps with him so as not to strain his loyalties, I knew he had gotten wind of it. Yet, he didn't bring it up when I presented him my request and I was grateful. So with Essie and Ma Mae, we opened our daycare center and kindergarten, and as promised, we took Saah along as our janitor.

On January 13, 1990, I walked down dusty Chubor Road to take a taxi to First Steps Child Development Center so that I could attend to final details before the opening. I was wearing a green and cream-colored garment made by a seamstress that sold many of her creations in Cote de Ivorie, or the Ivory Coast, which, because of the French influence, made her a fashion leader. The skirt was just over the knee with a deep slit in the back. The top had balloon sleeves that fitted right under the breast to the waist, and had a deep scoop neck that fell off one shoulder. I wore a matching jaunty little cap slightly to the side. For the occasion, I wore my hair, which was normally either braided or tied in a ponytail, in loose curls framing my face. This day, the opening of First Steps, was the culmination of all my dreams. Essie and I were finally going to work our plan and when we did, both our families would be able to live a good life in Liberia.

I arrived to find that Essie and her little daughter had beaten me there. Essie was fussing over the refreshment table, and I immediately began checking the set up of the room and rehearsing my opening remarks. I had invited my closest Black American friends, Lydia, an elementary school teacher, her teenage daughter Lynn, and Lydia's legally blind mother. My good friend Reverend Umoja was giving the consecration. I was ecstatic and although my family was thousands of miles away in the United States, I knew my mother, sister, and Uncle Pete would have been very proud.

When I had a few quiet moments that day, I reflected on my journey the past ten years. I had come from America with the Hebrew Israelite community, found work at an internationally recognized agency, and successfully navigated another culture. But I hadn't stopped there—I became a director, a fundraiser, helped to develop the talents of other women, managed to educate my own children and developed and sustained a retail sprout business. And now I was co-founder and co-owner of a day care and kindergarten. I distinctly remember looking at Binah during the opening ceremony and watching her socialize with our guests, owning her status as the eldest daughter of the owner. I looked around me, and felt exhilarated to be standing squarely at the beginning of a road leading to the realization of my family's legacy in Liberia.

Due to the specter of encroaching political upheaval, cash flow was drying up. We were optimistic that when the political situation in the country stabilized, First Steps could break even in the next semester, and perhaps turn a profit the semester after. To stabilize my financial situation, I continued selling bean sprouts in the Lebanese grocery stores and pursuing my other entrepreneurial ventures. While Essie and I intrepidly moved ahead with First Steps, the level of violence in the country was escalating.

According to one of the leading newspapers in Monrovia, *The Daily Observer,* the headline read: "MRU Leaders Discuss Rebel Activity," and also "Mano River Union Leaders, General Lasanah Conteh of Guinea, President Joseph Momoh of Sierra Leone and President Samuel K. Doe Meet to Discuss Rebel Activity of Charles Taylor's Forces in Liberia."

I felt so close to success, nothing was going to stop me. I divided my waking hours between working at our school and hustling to cover the bills, not leaving much time for my children. There were often days when I came home so drained, that I barely greeted my family before locking myself in my bedroom and turning on my noisy fan. I cried, prayed, planned, and wrote in a little red journal that I used to contain all my thoughts. When I wasn't writing, I was asking for divine assurance that I would have the resources to support us. I was struggling to pay private school tuition for five people, consoled only in small measure by the fact at least Yohanna, attended First Steps.

While we had lived on Lynch Street, Zevah and Penemiel attended CDB King Elementary School, a government school near the Red Cross, and Zefron and Tikvah were with me at the Red Cross Day Care and Kindergarten. Government schools were free and the education was rudimentary. My employees at Red Cross warned me that I wouldn't be pleased, but at the time I was trying to get them in school quickly while I figured out our finances. I realized I had made a mistake when I walked into Penemiel's third grade class and realized that there were only a few children in the class that were the correct age. The third and fourth grades were together and many of the children, mostly boys, were fourteen- and-fifteen years old. Zevah was in a similar situation in second grade.

As soon as we relocated onto Chubor Road, I transferred my children from CDB King and enrolled them all in the Haywood Mission School on the Old Road. Binah decided to finish high school at Assemblies of God evening school. I was broke but realized that this was the price of educational progress. I still dreamt of building a house for us, a house large enough for all of us to live in comfortably, a house we could entertain in and where my children could grow up and call home.

Now the children spent most of their time with Binah and Mommie, a Gio woman, really little more than a girl that I hired as our housekeeper and cook. I began noticing that, although my children were being educated in decent Liberian schools, they were sorely lacking in social skills. They spent their afternoons playing clapping games and soccer with the children in our area that they were familiar with, but because we rarely attended any social events outside of school or church, they were never forced to mingle with new, different children. Not only were they not behaving like well-raised Americans, they were not behaving like properly raised Liberians. They were not rude or destructive, they were polite and spoke when spoken to, which was the way children behaved in Liberia, but their table manners and their speech wasn't as articulate as I would have liked. I knew that they were not going to get that kind of polish without more effort on my part.

Friends with the Peace Corps and USAID and several individuals in the small Bahai community were forming a group, the African American Association for Development in Liberia (AADAL), to promote cultural exchange between Liberians and Americans. I sensed that they too were feeling culturally isolated and this was their response. Joining the AADAL brought me into a social network of people who had built roots in Liberia. Some members were Americans in long-term marriages with Liberians, some were those who had originally come to follow a job and decided to remain in Liberia, while others were retirees who just enjoyed Liberia's climate, people, and culture. I became friends with Ginger Davis, a Peace Corps volunteer who had met and married a Liberian attorney. She and I talked about how I wanted my children to be more socially adept. We discussed boarding schools, the option many busy Liberian parents chose.

Initially I was resistant, but as I began to make comparisons between my children's behavior and the children of other members of the AADAL, I was embarrassed that they only knew rudimentary table manners—no one's fault but my own since that's all I had taught them. For example, the spoon is the informal fork of country folk in Liberia, and we had so strongly identified with the people in our area, that we didn't even own any forks! I felt ashamed that I had neglected that and other details of etiquette. I sprang into action, purchasing forks and knives to go with our spoons and began serving our food on dinner plates rather than ceramic bowls. I even purchased cloth napkins and found a piece of lace from the Market to use for a tablecloth. Sunday became our day to sit together and eat at a formal table. I taught my children to take turns blessing our meals. After years of eating with spoons, they were uncomfortable eating rice with a fork.

For Sunday dinner, we closed our front door and refused to have any interruptions. This was our special time. I often served collard greens, somewhat a delicacy, instead of potato greens or cassava leaf. I favored country rice, and so, I would slice fresh cucumbers and serve them with a lime juice dressing for salad. We would have either ice water or orange Fanta in tall plastic tumblers with our meal.

Sunday dinners were the beginning of me retaking the reins of my children's upbringing. I would no longer surrender them to the tide. I needed to set a better course for them, and I reluctantly agreed with friends that a good boarding school could help.

For the most part, churches and missionary societies support the boarding schools in Liberia. But the process of finding the right school was rather painstaking. I began to network with both Americans living in Liberia and Liberian friends to look for affordable mission schools that would give my children what they needed academically, along with some much-needed social polish, while I worked out our economic issues. I sifted through recommendations, and Konola Academy, a Seventh Day Adventist School, emerged as a favorite. It was located behind the town of Kakata, in an area not far from the rubber plantation where our Hebrew Community had lived. Coincidentally, popular Liberian radio personality, and Liberian hunk, Dougba Caranda, was a Konola alumnus.

I took a taxi ride out to Panesville to ELBC radio to see Dougba and discuss the school. He provided a strong endorsement for Konala Academy and said the children would be well cared for, academically well prepared, properly socialized, and well disciplined. Those words were music to my ears.

Once again, I found myself silently battling depression. Emotional paralysis had reclaimed me after the end of my twenty-year relationship with my husband, and the stark realization that I was going to be raising our children in Liberia, alone. Overwhelmed, I avoided facing my fear with work. In hindsight, I realize that during the period that I abdicated my parental role, Binah ran the household. She decided what we ate, paid our bills, managed Mommie, made sure the children made it to and from school, and supervised their homework. She also helped make deliveries and collections for our sprout business.

In the tropical heat, frequent rinsings were needed to keep the sprouts from rotting. I was sleep deprived from getting up and down during the night to rinse the bean sprouts. I left for work around eight in the morning and rarely came home before late in the evening.

I wasn't sure that I had done right by Binah. She had a daughter of her own to raise, and had become a typical Liberian girl. I had initially thought I wanted this for her and for all my children, but soon realized that not all things Liberian are good. I bristled at the sight of her brushing her teeth outside, instead of in our bathroom, and spitting frothy toothpaste over the side of the front porch, or watching her clumsily try to handle a fork. I saw the outworking of my error. I should have inspired her to a higher standard of living.

I had been so enthralled with learning every nuance of Liberian life that I had forgotten that African-Americans were the legacy of a strong people, striped from their homeland, enslaved and disenfranchised, who had built an entire nation with their backs and their intellects. A remnant of those same people had returned to Africa to found what would later become the Republic of Liberia. How had I neglected to share the richness of that story with my children?

The Hebrew Israelite community focused on the connection between the ancient Hebrews and Africa while culturally living the virtues of the Old Testament. In retrospect, I wonder if I sacrificed the important story of our people, the Africans lost in the Diaspora, to my desire to blot out the stain of chattel slavery and assimilate, escape, into the Liberian culture.

Conflicted by my failure to transfer the pride in who we were, and the legacy of those enslaved Africans stolen from African to my children, I realized that my children, ignorant of their own culture, were being absorbed into another— the culture of Liberia. I sobered up in the midst of our identity crisis. The question that begged an answer was exactly who did I want to be and who did I want my children to be?

Zevah had turned ten exactly two months after Charles Taylor's forces crossed over into Liberia from Sierra Leone on my eldest daughter's twenty-first birthday. Zevah longed for a pink and white aluminum tea set she had seen in town. She wanted to play tea party with EliTikvah and her little friends from across the road. Given what was taking place in the country, it seemed ridiculous to even contemplate a tea set, but my Zevah was only nine years old and could not have grasped the severity of what was taking place in Liberia and in our lives. I kept my sanity by taking my periods of solitude and on February 25, 1990, I lay across my bed looking out over the swamp and wrote the following poem.

"In Lieu of a Tea Set"
written for Zevah's 10th Birthday, February 24 1990

Never saw a baby girl like Zevah, soft and clinging
Warm and demanding, determined to drink up all her mama's love

Playful and willing to be held by everyone!
Carried everywhere lovingly
Always waking…always peeping…Zevah
Mama's baby Zevah

Never saw a little girl like Zevah
Testing and questioning all of life's corners
Keeping all of us busy looking for answers to questions,
Answers she will never accept as anything but reasons
To go ahead and do it her way anyway!

I never saw a face like Zevah's
Strong and weak, bright with sunlit curiosity
Eyes of almond slanted wisdom
Closed to fear and lack of confidence.

Never saw a face pretty like Zevah's
Nose of grace and beauty, brows thick with ambition
And dignity, a delicately pouting mouth, jaws powerful
With subtle determination

Never saw more charm than in Zevah
Smiling brightly, doin' her magic for and on you—
And before reality hits you—you're busy doin'
for her
First born on African soil,
Splendor of God she is called

Daddy's princess Zevah
Mama's Madam Zevah
Yohanna's Aintee Zevah
Happy Birthday Zevah!

Unfortunately, Zevah did not get her tea set.

Haywood Mission School was overcrowded, so they offered morning sessions and afternoon sessions. My children attended in the afternoons, and I felt as if the level of teaching in the afternoon was not as good. With the thought of eventually sending all my children on mission, in February of 1990, I transferred Zefron and EliTikvah to the Seventh Day Adventist Elementary (SDA) School in a town near Camp Johnson Road and prepared to send Penemiel and Zevah to Konola Academy. Despite the increased expense, my rationale was that SDA had a good reputation as a feeder school for Konala Academy, and besides, friends had recommended Konola as a perfect school to send Penemiel and Zevah.

One evening, as we sat on the steps of our front porch, I broke the news. "Penemiel and Zevah, I've decided to send you both on mission, to Konola Academy."

"Emah, where is that?" Zevah inquired.

"Behind Kakata."

"Are we all moving back to Kakata?"

"Zevah, here you go asking plenty of questions!" Penemiel said, withholding his own queries.

"No, we are staying here in Monrovia."

The fact that I was sending my children away was so hard for me that I think the only way I could get through it was by being harsh. The part of me that didn't want them to go was fighting with the part of me that knew that letting go for a time was best for everyone concerned. But we loved each other and Penemiel wouldn't just let me off the hook easily.

"But Emah, just because I rode my bike off Old Chubor Road and you couldn't find me?" Penemiel asked, visibly upset.

He was a rambunctious boy, always exploring some new area, never content to stay close to home. I had recently punished him for peddling away on his bike alone for almost an entire day. I had canvassed his friends' homes to look for him, only to discover he had gone off with a new friend I didn't know. I hated that he thought that I was sending him away for being adventurous—one of his most endearing qualities. I knew that someday he would become a very self confident man but in the interim it caused me some anxiety.

"No, that's not it! I want you to stop behaving like grunna children. But I'm sending you because you are not getting a good education on the Old Road. Maybe it's the teachers, but I feel like I'm wasting my money. I need you to be in an environment to focus on school more."

Zevah looked up at me, her almond shaped eyes clouded, but she was silent. Thankfully, Binah injected the logical argument that sealed the deal.

"You know Emah is always working, and right now she does not have enough time to run behind you. Myself, I do not have time, and Penemiel, you are all over the place! I have to see after Yohanna, the bean sprouts, *and* the house. Emah wants a good school for you. Dougba Karenga went to Konola and he works at the radio station. They say Konola is a good and a fun place. At mission schools the children have fun 'O.'"

"But Emah, I wet the bed," Penemiel nearly whined as he waged his last argument.

"So it's time for you to stop wetting the bed! I need you to try hard for me, man, for all of us," I replied, angry that the bedwetting could be a deal breaker.

"Penemiel, you piss at Konola and they will beat you 'O'," Binah said, in her most threatening voice.

"Emah, I don't want to go!" Penemiel pleaded through his tears. He was a mama's boy and I knew he didn't want to leave.

"You *are* going! I'm not sending you alone, man," I countered. "Zevah is going, you don't hear her crying."

However, when I took a moment to look around me, I saw that there was no support for my argument. Zevah had quietly left the porch.

"Penemiel, we have to work together. It is just us right now. If you can just go for this year, once Essie and I get First Steps on its feet, you can come home. By then, our money will be better. Right now I need to just worry about the little ones, man."

I felt like a bad mother, but I was trying my very best to secure our future while having some support to help my children focus on scholarly pursuits.

The start of Konala Academy and Seventh Day Adventist's semester was only in a couple of weeks. I hustled, pulling all of my resources together to get their combined initial first semester payments of $754.00, plus two 100 pound bags of rice as well as the textbooks needed for class.

I remember the day in February when I traveled to Konala Academy with Zevah, who was nine, and Penemiel who was nearly eleven. I gave my last thirty dollars to Kromah, a Fula taxi driver and neighbor, to drive us to the Academy for orientation and enrollment. I loaded the trunk of the taxi with their first semester requirements, and their cloth suitcases containing their essentials and four carefully pressed school uniforms each. I was stoic during the three-hour drive. I really wanted my children at home, but right now, they needed a better education and environment. And I needed some time to get myself together.

We moved through the formalities of orientation, touring the facilities, and visiting the dorms where my children would live. I was surprised and delighted to run into Soniyah, a young Liberian girl whose mother was a friend of Don's, our Hebrew brother with LCADP. She was fourteen and resourceful and seized the opportunity to declare herself Zevah's big sister. I was relieved. Although Zevah was the type of little girl who always knew how to 'work' people, to get what she needed, she had always been around people who loved her.

Penemiel, even with his wild streak, was the question mark. He was an outgoing child, considerate, and well liked, but he was also a chronic bed wetter. I was terrified that his secret would be uncovered. So why did I take him there? The answer was desperation, plain and simple. I just hoped that his own fear of discovery would keep him from pissing his bed in a room full of strange boys. *I just hoped.*

At any rate, I took care of all the formalities and hugged my babies tightly before saying goodbye. I promised to send them money or snacks weekly when Konala's provisions were delivered from Monrovia to the school by van. Visiting day was Sunday, but they asked that parents not come for the first few weeks. I couldn't have come any earlier if I'd wanted to. I was hoping that I would have taxi fare by the time I was allowed to see them.

I sought refuge in the taxi with Kromah behind the wheel. I had barely paid him enough to cover the gas, but I was his regular customer and his neighbor so he empathized. As I wept in the back seat of the taxi, he consoled me, trying to comfort me by telling me the children would be just fine. My prayers lifted to the heavens asking that they would be safe. Little did I know that bloodshed was on the way. Those prayers would need an answer sooner than later.

Besides leaving my children behind in a strange environment, I had left only one cup of rice for my family at home. That was all that we had. We had never been so broke. I knew Binah would stretch the rice to feed the children; I could do no more. Tomorrow would take care of itself. Despite the fact that I was doing all that I could for my children I knew that they could have had more materials things in America.

Kromah dropped me off at the taxi depot and I walked the rest of the way alone. When I arrived home, Binah told me she had borrowed twenty-five cents to buy a cup of country peas to cook with the rice for Zefron, Tikvah, and Yohanna. She pointed to a small covered bowl of beans and rice for me. I lied, saying that they had fed me at Konola, knowing that she had surrendered her portion of food for me. I locked myself in my bedroom and turned on my fan.

I lay in my bed, uncertain and prayerful, until the next morning. I only had taxi fare to get me to the day care center. The children would miss school today. Ashamed, I left quietly without leaving money for food or waking anyone.

I moped about at work until I found the courage to share my situation with my ever-optimistic partner. While busying myself teaching the students, Essie scanned our books. She handled tuition payments and kept a mental note of each family's payment status. She tracked the paydays of every government ministry and knew which ones had taken pay and which hadn't. She also had her ear to the ground and knew who had money coming in from other sources.

I considered Essie a friend as well as a business partner. We shared the dream of founding the best day care center and kindergarten in Liberia. Our gifts were very different—Essie was practical, business minded, and politically astute, whereas I was creative, innovative, and stubborn. My American citizenship lent an international flair to our operation, which we hoped would help us to widen our demographic to include the children of expatriates when we were ready. We had the elements of a winning team.

Essie could "squeeze blood from a turnip," and by close of business that day, she pressed twenty-six dollars into my hand. She had collected some tuition, set aside the Center's weekly grocery money, and had split the rest between us. My heart leapt! Essie and her husband Fred, a union organizer, dropped me at the junction of Old Road Market, about one-and-a-half miles down the dusty road to my house. I planned to stop in the market to pick up some groceries. My walk home would be a lot easier now that I could bring home food. As Essie and Frank's car pulled away, I saw Binah. She was carrying a market bag and smiling as she walked toward me, proudly handing me a fistful of money.

"Where did you get all this money?" I asked.

"Emah, when you left us with no money, I was scared. You never did that before. We always had *something* and when you left without telling me anything…" Her voice lowered to a whisper. "Chris told me he had heard you crying in your room last night. Emah, I knew you were really jammed."

She was proud of herself and I was angry at myself. "So *Chris* gave you this money?" I said holding the fistful of dollars up.

"No, he hustled up my carfare and I went across the bridge to Miss Janet's warehouse."

My dignity took a swan dive. *"You asked Janet for money?"*

She nodded, but remained silent and looking down the way Liberian children respond when questioned by their elders.

I bristled that she had gone to Janet. I had worked part-time for Janet months ago but stopped because I just had too much going on. In Liberia, it was customary for a "responsible" woman needing money to save face by sending a child to ask for money. Binah told me that Janet had given her one hundred dollars without blinking.

I had mixed feelings. I was ashamed that Binah had needed to beg on my behalf, yet warmed by the knowledge that if anything ever happened to me, my eldest daughter would do whatever it took to take care of her daughter and her brothers and sisters. I had raised my children to be proud, to look out for one another, and above all else to always stick together. She understood that. We walked home in a distant silence. My heart hugged her that day, but somehow my arms could not.

The next day, I taxied across the bridge to see Janet. I needed her to understand that I wasn't a beggar, just caught in the grip of unfortunate circumstances, and that I would work out a payment arrangement. While I had not wanted my daughter to ask for the money, it had given us a cushion and I was willing to work to pay it back on time. I made sure to look put together and prosperous—every hair was in place and I was dressed in business-like African attire, looking my part—that of a co-owner of a private school.

Janet was a fast talker and a multi-tasker. After greeting me warmly, she continued with several simultaneous business transactions with men waiting in her office. Business meetings in Liberia are highly collaborative and nobody's business is private. At first, the lack of privacy offended me, but after awhile, I understood the respect given to the opinions of others. However, on this particular day, I asked to speak to her privately.

She was a big woman, in spirit and in build. At five foot, six inches, and just under two- hundred pounds, she was thick. Her wavy black hair gave her the appearance of having American Indian ancestry mixed with African stock. She had large hazel eyes with lashes so thick they looked fake. Girls in America paid for their lashes to look so good. Despite being dressed in baggy pants and a loose blouse, she looked like a commercial for Ebony Fashion Fair makeup. A Washington D.C attorney by profession, she was a trader and adventuress by passion. I loved that about her.

Once alone, I explained that I had not sent Binah to get money from her and offered to repay her. She looked me straight in the eye and said that I could repay her by returning to work for her and helping her control the people who were stealing from her.

On my taxi ride home, I reflected upon the first time I met Janet Williams. One afternoon, after Elrahm had left Liberia, he'd called me at the Red Cross to check on the children. When I mentioned that my paydays were sporadic, he told me that a woman named Janet owed him money. He had worked for her and her Liberian partner in Gbarnga. The women had gotten into a business dispute, fell out with one another and in the midst of the conflict, had never paid Elrahm the money he was owed. He gave me the address of her warehouse in the Freeport and suggested that I go to her and attempt to retrieve his salary and use it for the children and myself.

We had a long private conversation, and in the end, she, with some support from her Controller, convinced me that she didn't owe Elrahm as much as *he* thought. I was prepared to take her at her word, what choice did I really have? However, she acknowledged that raising five kids in Africa was a challenge and citing cash flow issues, she was willing to pay me a portion of the money. I liked her so much and admired what she was attempting to do and ended up working for her for several months and we became friends.

I went to Janet's warehouse every Saturday and Sunday, and if she had a new shipment of clothes in, I'd come several days during the week. My job was helping her manage the workers that constantly stole the used clothing she was selling, and helping protect her from unscrupulous locals with clever swindles. I also served as a compassionate ear for Janet who was aiming to become a large-scale importer. Women who dealt with old clothes were mainly market women; Janet was higher up the food chain. A natural dealmaker, she did not always know the correct person to offer the bribe, and was bleeding money. It was critical to bribe at the top level of the food chain, but you also had to spread some dollars to the operational level to get results. A crooked Pakistani was helping her at the government level, and based on what he delivered, he was demanding too big a cut from her.

Janet's Controller and the Controller's husband, African American converts to Islam, were both expats with a houseful of children. The Controller was a hard-nosed dollars-and-cents person. She watched the books like a hawk and attempted to keep Janet, an expansive thinker, from spreading her cash reserves too thin. Her husband was the warehouse manager—a tall, scholarly, and sensitive man who was always trying to rationalize the Liberian workers' stealing. Our job was to spot stealing and stop it. The truth, which we debated on a number of occasions, was that many of the workers came to the plant with the intention of taking the low wages and increasing their "take home" by supplementing their salary with stolen clothes they would sell later. That was the ducofleh game. The workers were going to steal, it was part of the equation. The wages were low and even paying more money would not have resolved the issue. You just had to watch for stealing and know when to fire people.

Now, after the "clear the air" visit following Binah's conversation with Janet, I was working with Janet again. She had surrounded herself, like the Lebanese and Indian's traders, with a team of her compatriots helping her. The most interesting new member was a big red African American, a former Detroit drug dealer, married to a public schoolteacher. He had been one of the fortunate men in the drug trade who had managed to avoid jail time, bank his money, and retire from "the life" in one piece. His dream had been to turn his bad money into something good. As he shared his life story, I understood him to be a good man with expert business skills that would have been successful in any avenue that was open to him. Unfortunately, the only avenue he had found open to him in Detroit, 'back in the day,' was the streets. He had arrived in Liberia with a quarter of a million dollars worth of mining equipment that had, over the first eighteen months, either broken down or been stolen. He was heartbroken and ashamed to return to his wife empty handed. Eventually, he embraced his ill fortune, and as he so eloquently put it, "you can't turn bad money good." He was the third man that I personally knew that had come to Africa to get rich mining gold, only to learn that it "just ain't that easy."

Even though we were working hard, weekends together were enjoyable as we shared our memories of America and all things

American. Embedded in a culture that was completely unraveling, we shared rumors about the rebel incursion and wondered how long we would be able to stay afloat.

Eventually, the soldiers closed the road that the Controller and her husband took to work. Our friend from Detroit became ill and for a while, it was just Janet and me, still stubbornly trying to hold on. Her business was very near the Freeport, and we both knew that soon, because of spontaneous security checkpoints, I would be forced to stop traveling to the Freeport, and she would not be able to travel across the bridge to my side of town. We worked as hard as we could when we were together. During these times of uncertainty and escalating violence, I often wondered why she did not just go home to her son in DC. I'm sure she thought I was crazy for staying in Liberia with my young children.

Ends up, we were two women cut from the same cloth!

Janet somehow got the notion that I needed a Liberian protector, and she decided that through her business and political contacts, she should introduce me to an influential man. When she found one, I couldn't help but see the irony—this very man had rescued me on the way to my house in the midst of rainy season several months ago.

One day, as I walked home from work, it began to unexpectedly downpour. In under a minute, I was soaked to my panties. Suddenly, this guy pulls up in a big black Blazer and offers me a lift down the road. I recognized him from around town as a government official and was flattered that he would stop to help me. I had casually mentioned this to Janet which inadvertently fueled her desire to see me mated with this powerful Liberian. She arranged for him to meet us for lunch.

He was Krahn, the group that was attempting to avoid ouster. On the afternoon of our lunch, I dressed in a beautiful deep purple and tan print lappa suit. The pencil skirt had a top with puff sleeves that fell off my shoulders. My hair was styled in a French roll and I wore pale pink lipstick and black pumps. I looked like I deserved the best! Our rendezvous took place at the Mandarin Chinese restaurant on Benson Street, my long-time sprout client. I was a person of some importance there. The headwaiter, Alfred was a friendly, very effeminate guy. I hadn't seen him in awhile, and today it struck me that he looked scrawny, and his behavior teetered on insanity. When he saw me, he immediately became his warm self, but as I looked at him closely, I knew better than to inquire into why he looked so ravaged. In Liberia, it was called "the slims," we know it as AIDS.

Mr. Government Minister joined us and we began our lunch. I ordered fried rice without egg, vegetable spring rolls and tea. We ordered a couple of bottles of red wine and chatted a bit about the war. Every other breath Mr. Minister took, he managed to say something hateful about "the Americans." I vividly remember him talking about the American warships that hovered close to shoreline.

"President Doe should bomb their asses with rockets."

Janet tried to engage him. "Mr. Minister, why is that?"

"Because they cause all these things that are happening here. The American's put Charles Taylor up to his tricks, how he escape from prison in America? That's a lie."

We continued to drink wine. I was reluctant to talk about what I was working on while Mr. Minister went on and on, spewing his hatred of America and Americans. I thought him ignorant and disgusting for talking like this while wining and dining two fine American women. Janet eventually got him involved in conversation about her business, and he gave her some tips on how she could get her shipments more easily into the country. He intermittently flirted with me between sips of wine, but his hate-filled statements had hurt and alarmed me. I didn't necessarily hold America harmless in the internal intrigue that had brewed and finally erupted in Liberia, but America, with all its flaws, was still my port of origin. When I looked into his eyes, I saw nothing in this man that made me feel that he would protect me and my children, rather my instincts alerted me that this man would use and discard me.

Good food, smooth wine, yet neither could distract me from the angry man seated next to me. I had not worked all these years to rebuild my self-esteem only to become the kept woman of a man who didn't deserve me. Moreover, even if I was for sale, this short, bitter man didn't have my price. As he left to return to his office, I was polite as he gently massaged my hand. I had the presence of mind to look him squarely in his eyes and promised to contact him soon. We waved goodbye as he pulled away in his shiny black truck. I hoped that he would forget that my house was on Chubor Road.

I told Janet to hang up her matchmaker's cap. True, I was bone tired from struggling to make ends meet, and I desperately wanted to be rescued, but even broke, I had my standards!

I made a ritual of gathering supplies for my children on Thursday evening so that I'd have treats to send to them on Friday morning. Before work on Friday, I would go to the Seventh Day Adventist School and drop off the supplies with notes from Binah, Tikvah, Zefron, and me. I recycled cardboard oatmeal containers with plastic snap top lids as airtight containers for bene (sesame) seeds that I roasted in a cast iron skillet and pounded them with table salt in a mortar to make a tasty but nutritious food supplement. Binah labored to make granola with raw oats, a few raisins, ground peas, and sugar. We worked together to send whatever would make Penemiel and Zevah more comfortable. Even though we were struggling ourselves, we wanted them to feel our love. Their absence saddened me, but I recognized that Liberian parents routinely sent their children on mission, and I had determined that my children would have the best education I could give them, no matter the sacrifice.

Then came the fateful day in April 1990 when a messenger came to my office with a letter requesting that I go to Konola immediately to pick up Penemiel. They had learned that he was a bed wetter. I was devastated! When I had taken Penemiel to Konola, they made specific reference to the fact that they would not accept a student that wet the bed. Of my five children, three were nightly bed-wetters. Penemiel, who had been so sickly as a child, had clung to me more than my other children. I knew uprooting him from his home was going to be very hard on him. When I had left him at Konola, he had looked at me with his big black eyes and promised me he would try his best to stop bedwetting. According to the letter, he was expelled, "Because he had been wetting the bed and after being talked to by the Dean of Boys, he still cannot overcome this habit."

It wasn't until I actually went to pick Penemiel up that I realized how much I had missed my children. I was uncertain whether to leave Zevah. She was, after all, younger than Penemiel, and he had always been her protector. However, Soniyah had embraced her role as Zevah's "big sister," combing her hair, helping her keep her possessions in order, and she assured me that with her brother gone, she would continue to look after Zevah. Zevah seemed to adore Soniyah, and appeared to be adjusting well, so I hugged her and promised to send enough treats for her and her big sister. Penemiel and I returned with Kromah to our home on Chubor Road.

When we arrived home, Penemiel received such a warm welcome from his siblings that I knew he was secretly glad they kicked him out of Konola. Until I figured out what to do about his education, I'd have to take him to work with me while the other children went to Seventh Day Adventist School.

During the rest of April and most of May, I continued sending food and treats every Friday for Zevah. Keeping my word, I was lavish with the treats I sent her and her "big sister" Soniyah.

As the days and weeks passed, the tone in the country became sinister, and yet hopeful at the same time. There was a feeling by many everyday citizens that it would be good to have the coup happen as quickly as possible, have Doe either be overthrown, or rebuke those seeking to overthrow him.

Samuel Kanyon Doe was not a man without cunning. After the 1980 coup, he had somehow, been handed the presidency of Liberia. According to sources, the U.S. Ambassador to Liberia was purported to have said that Samuel Doe had stolen the presidential election of October 1985—which would have returned Liberia to civilian rule. He crushed a subsequent attempted coup in November staged by his former comrade, People's Redemption Party comrade, Thomas Quiwonkpa. Quinwonkpa was killed, mutilated and cannibalized after which over 500 Liberians, mostly from the Gio, and Mano ethnics groups who were rumored Quiwonkpa's conspirators, were slaughtered. For the next four years, despite civilian rule, corruption had abounded, and the country continued to flounder.

Like the majority of Liberians, I took no interest in politics. My priorities were the price of rice, whether we received our monthly paychecks on time, and the health of my children.

Underneath the calm exterior of Liberia, the daily papers reported an escalation in the senseless and quiet killings of civilians, particularly upcountry in the areas where the Gio and Mano lived.

On Chubor Road, people began locking front gates and doors that were typically left unlocked. I prayed nightly that the rebel incursion, which was becoming a war, would end.

Our Center's night watchman, Mr. Teh, an old Kru man who traveled to work from the Freeport, became sporadic despite Essie's persistent pleas. He lived with his daughter and the twenty-five dollar bus fare he received from us each month helped him to survive. However, rumors of soldiers killing citizens under cover of night abounded.

Teh was supposed to patrol the Center for the entire night, and was not supposed to leave until either Essie or I arrived to relieve him. On this particular morning, my taxi pulled up at the same time as Essie and her husband. I walked into our office to put my briefcase down and Essie went to talk with the old man. Several minutes passed before I heard her calling me.

"Mistress Rahm, come. You must hear this 'O'."

I came outside into the short hallway just in time to hear Teh tell his story.

"Ehh Yah, I will not come agin 'O' the soldiers were not easy last night."

"Huh!" I was irritated, we had finally found a solution to having our bathroom fixtures stolen by rogues and I was anxious to hear why Teh didn't want to return.

"Old Ma, last night I was here in the window looking out. I saw dem; they were ten, everybody the same size as their friend, all carrying their gun and their cutlass. But Mommie, not all were soldiers 'O,' I recognized one of our government ministers, I can't say that Krahn man's name but that man not solider 'O' that man government minister."

"What was he doing with the soldiers then?" Essie chimed in, a half smile on her face. I could tell she thought Teh was being overly dramatic.

"They were gone to kill! I heard screams, bad screams last night Mommie. I not sleeping here agin. If they see me or bust the lock and come inside, they will kill me, I don't wan die without my head 'O.'"

"So who will watch our place against the rogues?" I said surprised that those words escaped my lips.

"Rogues? There is no stealing in Sinkor this time Ahnydah, only soldiers. Rogues sef is scared," Essie said in a sobering tone. She reached into her bra and took out five dollars handing it to the old man. "Come after the end of the month, and we will fill out your money. Good friend, thank you Yah."

"Ehhh Yah, what is happening to our country 'O,'?" said the old man as he walked down the steps of our school.

The Daily Observer, Tuesday, May 22 1990, carried the headline, "3 HEADLESS BODIES FOUND!" According to the paper, "The men had been bound by the hands and were shirtless. Their heads were placed on display so that relatives of missing persons could come to identify them while their bodies were in the Morgue of JFK Hospital."

I forced myself to look at the three heads. They all had their eyes closed, all were handsome young men. I wept that morning at the school. That same issue of *The Observer* announced that Reverend Leo Simpson and his wife, who ran Haywood Industrial Mission School where my children had attended afternoon school, were leaving Liberia with mixed feelings. Unfortunately, I was staying with mixed feelings.

Zevah was still at Konola and I knew that she was temporarily all right, but I wondered how long Kakata would be safe. Friday morning I planned to drop off supplies at the Seventh Day Adventist School for Zevah. When I arrived, the pastor of Konola called those of us who were dropping off parcels in for a briefing and a prayer session. The news of the rebels drawing nearer was frightening, but at the same time, the administration was very confident that the children were safe. I didn't want to be an alarmist, but something inside me was saying they were not telling us everything.

When I prayed that morning, I prayed that Konola would be surrounded by God's perfect peace and that God would keep the school and all the children well. My prayer was intense and while I prayed, I could see my little Zevah and her smiling big sister Soniyah clearly. Some of the oddest things stick in my memory, and on that day, while joining my prayers with the others in the room, I remember wearing the yellow and white dress that I wore when I needed to feign cheerfulness.

The remainder of the day went quickly, and during my taxi ride that evening, I resolved that the following week, I would travel to Konola, behind Kakata, to visit and probably retrieve Zevah. I know that people kept saying that everything would be all right, but I wished that my baby was under *my* roof. I dozed most of the way home, and when the taxi dropped me off at Old Road Market, I strolled the rest of the way home, speaking to neighbors along the way.

When I opened the wrought iron gate to my front yard, I was surprised to hear Zevah call my name and in seconds, she was hanging around my waist!

"Emah, we heard at school that the rebels are coming and Soniyah decided we should come. She packed our things and we took a taxi. She brought me!" She took another breath before continuing, "Head master said they will come for all the children with the bus but Soniyah said we should not wait. Are you mad Emah?"

I certainly was not mad. I was paid back ten-fold for every kindness I had every extended to Soniyah and elated that Soniyah had the foresight to get herself and her "sister" out of there.

"No, no, I'm not mad! Where is Soniyah?" I wanted to thank her and see that she was alright.

"She is gone to her ma. She said she wants to go to her father in America but her ma couldn't prove it! Zevah said.

I recalled a previous conversation with Soniyah where she had told me that her and her brother's dad was an American citizen but she didn't have any documentation to prove it at the Embassy.

"She almost took me to the Red Cross, but I said she must bring me home."

"You and Soniyah did well." I hugged her, thankful that Soniyah had lived up to her word.

That evening as I watched my daughter playing with her brothers in the front yard, I was so grateful that Soniyah was a strong-willed girl who took her role as my little girl's big sister seriously and protected her. I never gave a second thought to any possessions Zevah had left behind, especially when I saw the headline on that following Monday, May 28. The Standard read, "REBELS ADVANCE ON KAKATA." I later learned that most of the children were able to get out before the rebels converged, but unfortunately, several members of the staff and their families were trapped at Konola Mission.

When I think about the hundreds of thousands of families torn from their children or other family members during the war, I have to acknowledge that I did, and to some extent still do, suffer from survivor guilt.

As the mood in the country became more somber, people focused on their survival. After our matchmaking episode at the Mandarin Chinese restaurant, Janet and I would see each other only a few more times. The last time that we were together, I received a tip on where we could purchase 100 pounds bags of rice. Janet owed me one hundred dollars in salary, and we decided to purchase rice to stockpile. We bought four bags, two bags for her and two for me, and hid them, under blankets in the trunk of her small car.

As we drove along on the road from the Freeport through Panesville, the traffic had slowed for a makeshift checkpoint which had been erected. Fifty-five gallon pork barrels had been placed across the road to narrow two-lane traffic into one lane. As we approached a checkpoint the traffic crawled. We witnessed a scene that would become commonplace—armed Liberian soldiers accosting private citizens.

"What the hell is going on up ahead?" I said, getting nervous.

"Gosh! Did you just see the soldiers pull that family out of their car?" Janet shouted. "How are we gonna get through?"

I listened to the angry plava and the pleading. Like others, I was too afraid to help the family with two young children protect their belongings.

"My things, my things inside the car 'O!'" We heard the man hollering and the woman screaming.

"Never mind yah mommie," I heard the soldier mocking as their car was confiscated.

People seemed to be migrating toward the city, and I imagined that the family had their important papers in the car. Two stone-faced soldiers, barely more than teenagers, got into the car and drove away without looking back.

"Sis, if they see this rice it's gone!" she said in desperation.

"I'm saying that they won't see this rice. We just have to pray hard that they won't stop us or notice it, Janet."

The truth was I was so afraid I didn't think my legs would hold me if they pulled me outside the car. I cared about the rice, but not as much as I cared about getting home. Watching the soldiers beat a man with their gun butts, I knew that the rice was a secondary matter and so did Janet.

"Hell, if they take it, they take it. We got that and Sis, we'll get more."

She spoke with her normal bravado, but I saw the fear through her heavily lashed hazel eyes fear which mirrored my own. Janet's car sat idling in the line creeping slowly towards the soldiers who stood on either side of the road, randomly poking their rifles into car windows. We faced one of three possibilities. They could jack the car and put us out on the road; they could just confiscate our rice and maybe let us keep the car; or they could wave us through the checkpoint.

My heart fluttered and I could barely breathe, but Janet, oddly energized by the whole scenario, projected a rising confidence that stabilized me. Soldiers hijacked the car in front of us. The owner got out and walked away with his hands atop his head while the soldiers laughed at him. These same soldiers looked into our car, still laughing at their most recent victim, and waved us through.

I had almost peed my pants as the car behind us was pulled over. Perhaps we got a pass because we were women, but either way, I was just glad we got a pass.

Our tone was somber for the rest of the ride. Conditions in the country were worsening.

There was no telling where the fighting would break out next, and I wanted to be with my children.

"Janet, I won't be coming back to work until this is over."

"Sis, I know," she replied softly. "You take care of those kids,"

It was late eveing when she backed her car up to the front porch and unloaded the rice. Binah and her boyfriend Chris greeted us, helping to move the rice as quickly as possible, taking it into our house.

Meanwhile, Janet and I embraced. "Take care of yourself Janet, thanks for everything."

"Sis, don't worry about me, I'm a trooper, I'll be alright.

She honked her horn as she left our yard heading across the bridge. I watched her car through the gate as it receded down the dusty road.

PART III

THE COUP BECOMES
A CIVIL WAR

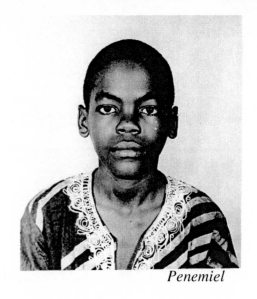

Penemiel

PREPARING FOR WAR

The shift from a rebel incursion to a Civil War was subtle. When in the midst of turmoil, it's hell so most people don't pay much attention when it becomes harsher, they just want it to end. I wanted to reopen First Steps Child Development Center, to continue working with women and children in Liberia. I didn't want to struggle for my life and my children's lives, but like everyone else in Liberia, I had no choice.

On Friday, June 8, 1990, *The Daily Observer's* back page the headline in bold block read letters, "ALL AMERICANS ASKED TO LEAVE AT ONCE." The article stated, "The United States Embassy […] has announced that because of the 'deteriorating security situation and the potential threat to lives' in the country, all Americans should depart the country immediately. […] The Marines, according to the U.S. Embassy, will play no role in the fighting going on between government troops and Charles Taylor's rebels, called the National Patriotic front."

On Sunday, June 10, after much soul searching and prayer, I reluctantly sent Binah, Yohanna, and Penemiel back to my mother in the States. Binah, a beautiful young woman, was rape bait, and I constantly worried that Penemiel might be kidnapped and forced into soldering. Everyone else was under voice control. I felt if I could secure Binah and Penemiel until the end of the coup, then once the violence ended, I could send for them.

My most difficult task after their evacuation was to tell Roland, Yohanna's father that I had sent her to America without consulting him. I understood that the rule of departure for a child of mixed parentage from the country was that the Embassy required written consent from the Liberian parent. However, due to the extraordinary circumstances in the country, the priority of the U.S. government was to ensure the safety of American citizens, and so I was simply asked if the Liberian parent agreed, and of course, I had said yes.

Roland and Binah, who had once been so devoted to one another, had, as young lovers often do, grown apart. Yet, because they had grown up together, they remained friends, and Roland was a good father. He always managed to hustle up money to bring Binah for Nookie. He came regularly to take her out for the afternoon, and his eyes lit up whenever he saw her. I felt that his little daughter was a symbol to him of something beautiful that he had helped create, and now when he was alone in Monrovia and scrapping for his life, she too was gone.

A few days after the June 10th evacuation of Binah, Penemiel and Yohanna, Roland paid me a visit. As I watched him walk through the gate, I felt the crushing weight of my decision.

"Hey Old Ma, you alright?" he asked lightly.

"I'm alright."

"I came to see Binah and Nookie."

"Roland, she is gone, I sent her and Binah to America."

"Old Mah, you sent *my* daughter? *My* daughter! You never asked me, that is *my* daughter 'O,' that's not your child. You can't do that!"

"I did it for all of y'all, Roland, can't you see what's happening? She is so small, the food business is hard, everything is hard! I sent her with her mother and Penemiel so they can be safe. We couldn't keep Nookie safe here."

"But she is *my* daughter. I could have taken care of her if you don't want to take care of her. I'm her pa!

"I hear you, Roland," I replied sadly. "I know you would give your life for her, but you need a chance to live too! At least, if it does get much harder, you will have a reason to live Roland, you will know that you have a little girl safe in America. When things improve, she will come. I don't want to leave. Don't you see me still here? But I know that Binah is a fine woman and soldiers would try to rape her. If they take over our area, you know Penemiel is just like a grunna boy. They would kidnap him and make him a soldier. I understand you are vexed but it's safer for them in America."

He was a respectful boy, and didn't cuss me as he might have. He knelt in the yard, and I saw his head bowed. I heard him sobbing as he arose and stumbled in circles around the yard, his hands atop his head. I had ripped his heart out, and the mother in me wanted to comfort him. As I approached, he recoiled.

I walked into the house, past my remaining children who sat in the living room with Chris who tried to console me by telling me I had done the right thing. I headed for my room and heard Chris leave, the front door closing behind him.

Moments later, I heard him speaking softly to Roland. I closed the door to my room and turned on the fan.

As the news of Liberians fleeing areas where the rebels were invading circulated, Essie and I had no choice but to close and lock the doors to First Steps Child Development Center. Families wanted to be together to face whatever forces had been unleashed in our country.

Reverend Umoja and his wife stopped by my home and brought me books and other educational materials so that I could home school my children. I suspected that he and his wife were leaving Liberia and just as several other departing friends had done, wanted to leave me fortified since I had chosen to remain. I had never felt so alone, and yet I was in such a place of resolve.

The days progressed in slow motion. I longed for my eldest children, and each night I prayed for them. I knew they were with my mother and that she would take care of her grandchildren and great grandchild. How did I not realize that *we* were really the ones that needed prayer? My family in America received more news footage of the war's progress and the atrocities taking place than I did. Sure, the rumors of atrocities horrified us, but fortunately for us, we were only directly aware of what was happening on Chubor Road.

I scrapped for food daily in the market, hoping that the soldiers didn't take it from me as I passed through the checkpoint that stood between the market and the road I walked to get home. The only reason the children went outside our wrought iron gate was to draw water.

Toward the end of July, the U.S. Embassy sent another alert, this time advising, "All Americans, due to deteriorating situation of the country, depart Liberia immediately."

The coup to overthrow President Doe had now become a full-blown war. Once again, I revisited my decision to remain with my three youngest children, hoping that things would normalize soon in Liberia. I still hoped to send for Binah and Penemiel. Somewhere deep inside, I should have realized that it was time to walk away, but I didn't. Knowing that I should walk away and disobeying my inner guidance would almost prove to be my undoing.

One morning, shortly after I returned from the Market, I looked up to see my former janitor Andrew walking through my wrought iron gate. Drew was Krahn and I instantly noticed that he was wearing a Liberian Army uniform. I froze as I saw Drew and another soldier approaching. The soldiers loyal to Samuel Kanyon Doe were mainly Krahn, and they controlled our area. They hunkered down on the Old Road to await the arrival of Charles Taylor's rebel forces.

Drew had an AK47 slung comfortably over his shoulder. I tried to breathe as I stepped forward, not knowing what to expect, but knowing I had to protect my children somehow. However my children were fearless. Drew was like an elder brother. They ran to him, oblivious to the gun he wore around his shoulder.

"Andrew! Andrew!" my children called, admiring the figure of their big brother wearing an army uniform. To them, it was no different from when he visited us to play soccer.

His face was stoic, intense, and unsmiling until he reached the step beneath me and pivoted. I held my breath trying to look fearless.

"Hello old Ma," he said, veiling a measured smile

"Hello Drew, so you soldier now?" I queried in Liberian English.

"Yeah 'O', I soldier now." He introduced me to his comrade, a young man close to his age, but a few inches taller who only nodded.

"This is my old Ma, she's like a mother to me. She and her children should live on this road and not be disturbed, ain' you hear it?" The companion nodded and smiled at me.

Turning back to me, Drew continued to explain his new life. "I'm the bodyguard for President Doe's Shaman. If anybody humbug you, or you need anything, come find me." He gave me directions to the Shaman's house on the Old Road. As he turned to leave, he motioned for the other solder to wait outside the gate, and he pressed a carefully flattened $10.00 bill in my hand. He looked me in the eyes and said, "Old Ma, if I get more I will bring it to you."

Drew was attempting to repay me for the money he had swindled from me. As I closed my hand over the money, I realized that nobody had $10.00 to give away during a war. Drew had used the most influence that he had ever had in his life to protect my children and me. In my eyes, we were even.

We embraced warmly, and in my heart, I asked God to keep him safe. That was the last time we ever saw him.

The Children of God in War

Danger heightens my senses,
The smiles of my children are especially touching and sweet to me.
Their trusting eyes are a delectable promise at a time when danger hovers near.
How can they smile and play so innocently while I am wracked with uncertainty?
They play NaFo as if tomorrow will surely come,
Their every rhythmic clap gives me hope.
Somehow amidst this danger
I feel DANGEROUSLY happy!
How can the big-eyed boy eat so lustily his rice, greens, and beans?

I call him "boss man;" he asks me if his bath water is on the fire. I say, "Yes boss man,"
I'm hopelessly in love with you" (I chant under my breath)
Every family needs a boss man and the big-eyed boy is ours.

The girls tell me they are "all soaped up," how else can I tell if they really bathed?
One daughter is taller than 9 years; she is boss man's twin, and the small one with no teeth is a whimsical bit of fluff; a brown Pollyanna with palm oil stuck to her one front tooth.
I selfishly appreciate not being in this war alone
and each night and early morning, I ask God to spare us all.
NaFo is a clapping game reminiscent of "hambone" that is played by Liberian children. Written June 18, 1990

First Steps
staff and student

ALL GOOD THINGS MUST COME TO AN END

People have asked me dozens of times why I didn't just leave Liberia when the storm clouds first began to gather. I had been totally enthralled with my work in Liberia for eleven years, had witnessed my own growth from an impatient, volatile, self-centered young woman, into a patient, more thoughtful, woman specializing in women's development programs. I effectively navigated a culture very different from my own, and had used my skills to support and encourage the development of others. Spiritually, I came of age in Liberia.

Building a future in Liberia was a seductive goal that I had clung to by my fingernails, ignoring everything that was happening around me until I could look away no more. I so desperately wished to overlook the sour bitterness that strangled Liberia, and instead dwell only on the sweetness that I had known for so long. But then, that wouldn't be very accurate.

After eleven years, I was a chameleon, blending casually into the landscape of Liberia. It was difficult, if not impossible to tell that I was not a Liberian. Mandingo men often mistook me for a Fula woman. My burnished skin reflected years of unfiltered sun, my speech was now the local patois, except when I needed to sound civilized or qwee. There was the typical slowness to my stride, which I still have not shed. Each day, I wrapped my lappa and tucked it into my waistband, my feet were clad in rubber flip-flops, and my hair braided in the style of the local women.

Yet for the first time in all these years, when I walked the road to the Market, fear weighed heavily upon me. I had come to realize that it was possible that the children and I could lose our lives in Liberia, not of old age or sickness, but from the crack of a bullet or the strike of a machete. Traveling through the Old Road Market checkpoint became increasingly terrifying. The soldiers at the checkpoint were young men, hungry and afraid. When I heard the rumors of atrocities taking place locally, I envisioned the soldiers as predators guided to their next victim by the smell of fear. Each time I approached the checkpoint, I prayed, thrust my shoulders back, and walked the cadence of confidence. Soldiers stopped me several times, but I was never detained or harassed.

Life settled into an abnormal kind of normal. We knew something terrible was approaching but it was something we'd never experienced before so we really didn't know how terrified to be. What normalcy we had managed to maintain was completely destroyed the day that Chris's friends busted through our door—in a hysterical state. They told us of a family on the road that had been hacked to death and left in the swamp behind our house. I didn't know the family personally, but I had seen the wife on the road. I remembered thinking that she was pretty every time I saw her. It seemed that someone had "called their name," an enemy with a grudge against them had placed them on a death list. As they shared the details with Chris, I fought the urge to tell them to be quiet. They were upsetting the 'normal' life I had settled into. I excused myself, and once safely inside my room, I took my red journal from under my mattress and lay across my bed, covering the pages with my fearful thoughts.

That evening, I closed the wrought iron gate and locked it. For the first time in my life, fear paralyzed me. I never wanted to go outside of the gate again. I stayed away from the market for an entire week, choosing to buy chicken and greens from women passing on the road and using much of our supply of dried beans. I was terrified of what lay beyond the gate. I listened to the radio and the reports on the BBC. All reports said that Charles Taylor's men were fighting their way towards Monrovia, closer and closer every day. Liberians prayed for American's intervention. Surely America would come. However, at the same time American warships hovered off the coast of Liberia, in the Middle East, the BBC reported trouble brewing in the Gulf between Iraq and its neighbor Iran who had just concluded eight years of war. With oil being such an essential commodity, obscenely juxtaposed with human lives, I prayed that the U.S. would help.

Liberians looked upon America as a child looks to its parent. Traditionally, the U.S. had been Liberia's strident ally and Liberians felt intrinsically that the U.S. would intervene. I hoped so, but I didn't expect it. If America didn't stop the factions converging in Liberia, I prayed that no anti-American sentiment would arise that could cause my family to be in more danger than we presently were.

One night, as I stood on my front porch, I felt the weight of being responsible for my family. I had no plan, no next move. Essie and I had closed First Steps, and Abi Joudi Supermarket, while still open, was not accepting bean sprouts. After all, its customer base was pouring out of Liberia, heading back to India, Lebanon, China, Britain, France, Portugal, Switzerland, and other places around the globe. My income had dried up.

The children were sleeping, and instead of taking one of the long evening walks that always put me back on track, I stood staring out into the night praying silently.

God, I have no money, no one to protect me and my children, but I want to stay. I'm not ready to go back to America, not yet. Then, I was still.

The coup, which everyone knew was inevitable, had morphed into something much more ominous. I didn't fully grasp what was happening, nor did anybody on Chubor Road. Instead of one faction overthrowing the government, there was yet another group of soldiers, led by Prince Johnson, on the horizon. I had mixed feelings. I didn't have loyalties for anyone. As an expatriate, I had grown, learned, and struggled in Liberia for years. I was happy with the contribution I was making to the lives of Liberian women and children, but I had no interest in politics. I wanted to help accelerate the development of the country and continue to make it our home. I longed for the type of financial stability that would allow me the ability to travel back and forth to the States to visit our family, especially my mother and my sister.

Experience has a way of reshaping you, and as my perspective broadened, I realized the importance of instilling in my children the knowledge that they had a history beyond Liberia. They would be citizens of the world, who would comfortably transverse wherever they wanted. As for me—I had fallen hopelessly in love with Liberia, with the people, and with the pace. I felt that I could easily live the rest of my life in Sweet Liberia.

My mind was a jumble of information, some of it real, some of it innuendo, and some of it speculation. Most civilians stayed very close to home, clinging to news delivered by people fleeing other areas of the country. Charles Taylor and his rebels were fighting their way closer to Painesville. Soon they would reach Old Road. Prince Johnson and his forces were closing in on Liberia from the sea. Everybody's goal was to dethrone President Doe and take over Monrovia, the capital of Liberia.

Not ten minutes after "Amen" did Don, my kindred spirit, stride confidently through my gate, bringing closure. With a few words, he became the answer to my prayers.

"Look Ahnydah, I have a contract to serve as the bodyguard to a high ranking female foreign contractor; I need a favor. I want Kizzie and my family to stay with you."

As he explained his plan, which included dispatching a trusted employee to guard my home, money, and other logistical support, I remembered my mother saying "When you pray believing, God is as instant as you are."

Don and his wife, Kizzie, a Liberian National, who had joined the Hebrew Israelite Community, had a little girl together in addition to the two children, a boy and girl, Kizzie had from a previous relationship. They lived in a small apartment on the old Road near the market. Kla, the teenage boy, had declined the move, but Kizzie and the girls joined our household.

Kizzie's family slept in Binah's bedroom and Don visited Kizzie several times a week during the day. Don sent James, a young West Indian man, to protect our house each night. I never saw a gun, but I believed he was armed, and his presence made me feel safer. He left each morning at dawn.

Don installed a bar to secure the front door, explaining, "It won't keep 'em out but it will give y'all some extra minutes to escape through the back door into the swamp if you need to."

I felt secure.

We stockpiled food and bottles of malaria medicine, penicillin, worm medicine, and vitamins. There was nothing more to do.

Managing the temperaments of two strong-willed women under one roof was tough, but we took a stab at making it work. I created a schedule that kept us grounded in a predictable routine. We arose between 6:00 and 7:00 a.m. and after cleaning the bedrooms, we gave the children bread and tea. From 9:00 a.m. until noon, Zevah and Zefron worked through the outdated SRA reading laboratory color-driven reading modules. I focused on teaching the children math and reading, and in the afternoon, they played safely inside our gate. They only left our yard to draw water from our Ghanaian neighbor's well, and that was only if the water Don had paid him to deliver to us daily ran out. If we heard machine gun fire in the distance, one of us ran to fetch the children.

Kizzie was a determined but painfully shy woman in her twenties when we met. Her own mother had died giving birth. She carried a pain that stemmed from her being an orphan raised in the homes of people that had worked her like a slave from the time she was old enough to sweep floors and light a coal pot. She had become pregnant when she was very young, twice, and various relatives had raised her children, a boy and a girl, until she had come to live with the Hebrews. When she talked about Don her eyes lit-up and I got the distinct impression that she had never felt anyone had ever really loved her, except him. A woman of few words, I had a sense that if I could ever break the ice with her, there was intensity and warmth. However, I sensed she was jealous of the friendship between Don and me. Occasionally she "threw hints" that there was or had been more between us, there wasn't.

The real issue was that Don wasn't an affectionate husband and he was rarely home. Don being gone was "his" normal and I didn't blame her for feeling jealousy, but it caused her to become increasingly unhappy living in my home and away from the certainty of her own environment. I needed our living arrangement to work, but it was like walking on glass. It was the fear of displeasing Don that made her stay in the safety of my home.

The terrifying events unfolding daily validated the painful decision I had made to evacuate Binah, Penemiel, and little Yohanna. Every day we heard new rumors of missing boys presumed kidnapped and forced to become soldiers. I cringed at the thought of Penemiel, a gangling mama's boy, holding a gun. More than a daughter, Binah had become my companion. I missed the feisty temperament that often drove me to my limit, but I was glad that now she could go to college and enjoy being beautiful and young. I felt confident that Elrahm would help my mom take care of our children once he knew they were back into the

States. I tucked warm thoughts of Binah, Penemiel, and Yohanna into a corner of my heart.

As the war progressed, the looting and harming of citizens on the Old Road increased and spilled down Chubor Road. The irony was that the rebel incursion that the Liberian soldiers were defending the country against, hadn't even made its way to the Old Road. Doe's own hungry soldiers descended upon our communities. Armed, they took whatever they needed from civilians to keep their own families from starving.

Then there were the revenge killings. Innocent citizens, even whole families, slaughtered simply because of an old grudge, or worse, because of jealousy. The rule of law was shattered. Many of us murmured under our breath that we wished for the invading rebels to come and subdue the current intruders.

Rumors circulated that the ruthlessness of the raw soldiers in our area was because there was no commander. For days, we watched as many of our neighbors, their belongings bundled atop their heads, fled to other areas for safety, until eventually, we packed our essentials and fled to Don and Kizzie's apartment on the Old Road.

I fought hard to understand the violence swirling around us. Repeatedly I asked myself why Liberians couldn't just band together and develop their country with the intention of making everyone prosperous. I felt like a visitor from another planet because I couldn't wrap my head around hacking people to death because they were of a different tribe or murdering by innuendo. That just didn't seem like a rational solution. Tribal violence was bringing Liberia to its knees. This senseless ethnic violence was killing the spirit of nationalism that could have ignited the people of Liberia.

We lived with Don and Kizzie for a little over a week, until one morning, Chris came to give us the all clear. He had stayed in our home to protect it from looters. Now that residents of Chubor were returning, we felt it was safe for us to return as well, and so Chris helped us carry our belongings back down Chubor Road. Kizzie refused to return, deciding that whatever fate the coup held for her and her children, she would meet it in her own house.

The trip back would have been uneventful except for soldiers that jumped Chris and knocked him to the ground. As he lay on his back, I saw the gun butt coming down towards Chris and screamed. Don's cried diverted their attention.

"Stop, we beg you 'O'!" pled Don. "He has done nothing 'O!'".

We were carrying a bag containing twenty-five pounds of rice. Don seized the moment to strike a bargain, rushing to Chris' side he opened the bag Chris had been carrying and offered them each the equivalent of two or three day's worth of rice, begging them not to take the entire bag.

"Hey yah, I got big, big family 'O,' I beg you take your own, you can dip it yourself but please leave enough for my women and chilren."

"Rice business is hard 'O,'" said one of the soldiers, distracted from harassing Chris, as he took the cup we stored inside the bag and began repeatedly pouring rice inside his helmet.

"My friend, my peopo plenty 'O,' I beg you yah," Don said, trying to curtail the assault on our rice.

The other solider poured rice into a small plastic bag that he had pulled from the pocket of his khaki pants. No one stopped to see our trouble; this was not a time for caring.

The soldiers glared at us, and made a few menacing movements with their guns, but allowed Chris to slowly rise and pick up our bundles. Chris easily dwarfed the soldiers who were at least a full foot shorter than him, yet that didn't matter at the moment. They had guns and we didn't.

The rice had been cushioning my prized pink and white soapstone chess set purchased in Kenya while attending an HIV/AIDS workshop. I saw the Rook broken on the concrete, and I passed without picking it up. We walked the rest of the way in silence, focused on getting off the road and back to the familiar surroundings and familiar smells of our home.

Liberia was isolated from the entire world. Roberts Field, the country's airport, was closed. Our only contact with the outside world was the news broadcasts of the British Broadcasting System on the short wave radio band. My children were terrified of the constant gunfire that rang out across the swamp behind our house. From my bedroom, we listened to the nightly shooting that began after dusk and lasted until dawn--the newly established curfew. We developed the ability to differentiate between the sounds of an AK47, used by the government troops, and the Italian made Beretta, issued to Charles Taylor's rebels.

Each night before retiring our household gathered in the living room for chess, conversation, and prayer. One night, fed up with being afraid, I prayed, "God, take away this awful fear. I love Liberia and I want to stay, but I'm afraid and I don't know what to do. I couldn't live without my children, so if you take them, please take me too. But God, if you want me to go, please send me a sign. I know I'm hard-headed and I never draw back once I make up my mind about something, but if it is ever really time for to me to take my children and leave Liberia, please send me a sign so clear that I will know that you mean for us to go. Meanwhile my family and I will place all our trust for our safety and deliverance in you. Selah."

I prayed that prayer from the deepest place in my soul. As I reflect, I realize that my prayer linked me to God as never before. That night, while we lay in darkness listening to the gunshots, instead of tossing and worrying, I finally slept.

The next morning, I walked out into the sunlight, through our gate, and down Chubor road to the Market.

December 23, 1989, the day before rebel invasion, Binah gets her hair braided by Buah

EXODUS

Chris now slept in Binah's old bedroom and my children played in their own bedroom during the day, but spent their nights in my bedroom. Their room was in the front of the house and I wasn't comfortable with them sleeping in a room with so many windows facing the road.

Zevah slept in my bed and I began to notice her grinding her teeth—it sounded like she was cracking ice in her mouth, or chewing on rocks. She complained of a sore mouth, and as I lay awake, I knew the grinding was her body's response to her internalizing her fear. Thinking of what I could do to help stop her from grinding, I finally tied a big knot into a cotton scarf and placed it in her mouth, tying it in the back of her head at bedtime so that it would stay in place. The knot prevented her teeth from touching and allowed us both to sleep. At night, Zefron and EliTikvah's vinyl-covered mattresses lay at the base of my bed. It was my vain attempt to stop the increased bedwetting.

On August 2, 1990, 100,000 Iraqi troops invaded Kuwait. As we listened to the BBC report this on our radios, I knew that the U.S. would never choose to rescue Liberia—perennial ally or not—over the defense of its oil interests in the Persian Gulf.

On August 5th, or somewhere thereabout, I lost the ability to taste my food, and I could not sleep. I didn't take off my clothes that night, but instead, lay next to my children, fully alert, fully clothed. It wasn't that I was afraid, but it was as if I had risen to a level where I was an observer of all that was going on. I think the phrase is, "In it, but not of it."

I rose early the next morning knowing with absolute certainty that it was time to go! The U.S. Embassy had evacuated all Americans, short of the essential Embassy personnel, and I had no idea how we would even get out of Liberia, but I knew that I had to try. Once I decided we had to leave, I went into overdrive. While the children slept, I used a flashlight to pull together our important documents, their school records, and our identification in a manila envelope.

I still hadn't told anyone about my planned departure, nor did I have any reason to expect that we could actually leave, but I knew we had been living on faith, and now more than ever, I just needed to believe and take one-step at a time. Our only hope was to get to the American Embassy or to find a way to get them to come for us.

The best way to approach the move was on a need-to-know basis and I crafted a careful lie that would get the children packed without alarming them or sharing my real intention.

"Chris, have Zevah and Zefron pack a bag of clothes in case I decide we go back to Don's house. The gunfire was too plenty last night. They should pack this morning 'O.'

"I couldn't sleep mysef. Emah, are you going in the market?" Chris inquired.

"No, I'm going to Don's to talk with him, but I will bring the greens back for dinner."

"If you got five cents bring pepper yah." He called out after me.

I left Chris unaware of my plans. I had become his mother figure, and while I planned to leave with my children, I would be leaving Chris, who had been like an elder son, behind. I had no choice.

I walked quickly down the sandy road to Don's house on the Old Road. I knew that he hoped we could all ride the war out. He thought that once it was over, those of us who had stayed would be in a better position to take advantage of economic opportunities that the international community would make available to the incoming regime. I felt guilty for wanting to leave. I valued Don's guidance and friendship, he was like my elder brother. But I now had direct inner guidance telling me to leave, and I needed Don to help me find a way to get my family the hell out of Liberia. I knew he was going to be disappointed in my decision. We had never had an argument, but walking to his house that day, I prepared for one.

When I entered, Manke, Don's little girl, was sitting on a small chair between her mother's knees, getting her hair braided. I greeted them with a smile and wave. The apartment was small but neat, an obvious result from Kizzie's days of serving the family she had stayed with as a child.

"Don, I need to talk with you about something. Can we walk on the road?"

We left his house and walked east on the Old Road until we reached the American Cooperative School, nicknamed ACS, run by the U.S. government primarily for children whose parents worked at the Embassy or the Liberian elite. The closed iron gate provided shelter and haven for refugees fleeing violence in other areas.

"Don, America is about to go fight for oil in the Middle East. They aren't going to assist Liberia. I need to take my children and go." I spoke quickly and definitively feeling like I was in the emotional calm before the storm. My hands were wet and clammy so I wiped them on the grey and red lappa skirt I was wearing.

Don was his usual confident self, but instead of revering his words as I normally did, today he seemed almost like a fanatic. "I know things look really bleak but just wait."

"No waiting!" I shouted, and was almost to the point of trembling.

"I am going with my gut. I know that we need to go, right now, today if possible!"

"Are you crazy? Do you think the Embassy is going to send soldiers to come and get you? Come on, Ahnydah! I just think you are panicking," he said unaccustomed to my opposition. I believe he was on a short fuse from lack of sleep and my stance was more than he could take.

"Don, I am not panicking! I'm not even scared anymore, but it gets to a point where hanging on is stupid. How long will we keep moving from your house to our house and then from this area to another area? What is the point? I didn't give birth to my children to let one die in this senseless war. The truth is, I don't even really care who wins, I just want this madness to stop! If soldiers on either side kill my children, they may as well kill me. I want to leave Liberia. People that we know, who we used to be friends with, are slaughtering Gio and Mano friends because they are *Gio or Mano*. It's time to get out of here."

We had known each other since my family moved to Liberia. Don was always my teacher, always the expert, but he was no match for me today.

He looked at me as though he was seeing me for the first time as I prepared for a public argument on the Old Road. He had been supporting me financially and mentally, I wondered if he was tired of trying to hold his family and my family together and finally decided to just let go.

"Okay, well okay, it looks like you have made up your mind, but I'm telling you, Ahnydah, this is a mistake. You have eleven years here, you mean to tell me you going back to America and start from scratch?"

"Anything I have I can get back. I left everything I had in America to come here. The thing is, I cannot replace a child. Don, Zevah is grinding her teeth down and my children are terrified. I can't keep doing that to them, for what? Let the people stop fighting first."

"Only soldiers can get you to the Embassy, you know that don't you?"

"Yes, and you know everybody, you know soldiers. Help me get us to the Embassy."

I could see the veins popping across his broad forehead. He continued walking. Leading with his head, his strong chin jutted forward.

"Go home Ahnydah," he roared. "I will work on it. If I find out something, I will come and tell you."

I faced him squarely, knowing that he would do nothing of the sort, so I hedged my bets with, "Don, no matter what, tomorrow we are going to the Embassy."

"Sis, I see you are determined and you'll need to be. These boys ain't playin.'"

I took another breath and spoke the words that seemed to jump into my head and out from my dry throat. "Don, can Kizzie go, and take Manke with her?" Before he could open his mouth, I continued. "She's so little and happy, think what could happen to her if she stays. Don, she's just a baby!"

I hadn't left my home with the intention of taking Don's wife and daughter with us, but when I saw Kizzie combing Manke's hair it became clear that I had to at least ask. How could I take my children to safety and leave his daughter behind in this war and violence?

My suggestion struck a raw nerve.

"What? Stay the hell out of my family's god dammed business!" he yelled. "If you want to tuck your tail and run back to America with *your* mouth dragging the ground, I'll do what I can to help you, but you mind your own business. I decide what's best for them!"

I believe I had used all my "sister points" with my last comment. Oblivious to whatever scene we were creating on Old Road, I shot back, "Here you go thinking about yourself again! *You* are strong, but you have a *three-year old!*"

I lowered my voice and finally allowed the pent up frustration that had been on a low boil over the last two months spill onto him. "Let's be clear—if any Liberian on this road got the offer to send a small child to America *now* they would take it *and you know that!*"

I was shaking as I stood toe-to-toe with my hero, and continued in the softest voice I could manage. "When this thing is over you can send for your family Don, but in the meantime, don't you want your little girl safe from harms' way? Your ma and pa are old. When will they even see their own grandbaby?"

"You are scared and I understand that but I told you, I decide for my family, not you!"

We walked along and I took in the sights of the Old Road market where women were selling greens that had been kept too long to be considered fresh and feeling the palpable sadness in the air. I was silent, and spent.

"Look Ahnydah, we need to find a radio somewhere so we can call the Embassy and let them know you want to leave. Maybe they will send a Pajero truck for you and the children."

The discussion was over and I didn't press the issue any more. He was proud and independent and he loved and adored his little Manke, but he was not going to let me take her.

Barely fifteen minutes after my argument with Don on the Old Road, as we walked back toward his house, we met Roland. We greeted each other and when he asked how we were, I blurted out that somehow I had to find a way to get the children out.

There had been an uneasy distance between Roland and me ever since I had evacuated Yohanna. He had gotten drunk once and came by my house to threaten me. Sometimes he just sat and cried, and I listened uncomfortably as he talked about missing her. When he came, I tried to send him away with a token gift of rice, but even with all of his tears and pain, I never second-guessed my decision to send my granddaughter to safety. He would someday take comfort in the fact that a part of him was safe in America, even as he fought for his own life.

His response affirmed for me that once you make up your mind and stand in your intention, you get what you need and you never know where it will come from. He said, "Emah, follow me. I know where there is a radio to reach the Embassy."

I thought, is this a set up? Is he finally going to deal with me for sending Yohanna away without his consent?

I was suspicious—and had every reason to be—but there was nothing to lose. We turned around and walked back past the American Cooperative School and quite a distance further toward Congo town, finally stopping at an abandoned home that had once housed Wackenhut Security personnel. Looters had invaded the once lovely home with a huge front yard. Everything of value, including light and bathroom fixtures, was gone, everything except a few chairs and a direct phone line into the American Embassy.

Don called the Embassy and gave them our position and held the phone to my ear as a voice from the American Consulate's office said, "We will not engage hostile troops to come for you. If you and your family reach the Embassy, we will get you out. How you get here is your own business."

If I thought for a moment that getting to the American Embassy would be easier because of our American citizenship—that fantasy faded fast. The Calvary was *not* coming.

Biblically speaking, the ancient Israelites had gotten the call from God to exit Egypt, but as I recall, the trip through the wilderness, though ordained, was not easy. Nevertheless, the Israelites had prevailed, and we would too. I parted with Roland and Don at the intersection of Old Road and Chubor. Don told me to keep preparing for our departure. We would find a way to get my family out.

I was terrified. I knew we were leaving somehow, but I was scared to tell my children for fear that they would tell someone on Chubor or become emotional about leaving friends and pull against my already frayed nerves. Don had told me that our safest option would be to bribe Krahn soldiers to take us to the Embassy. What we were asking was dangerous, even for them, but they were the most loyal to Doe and had the most credibility. Helping Americans leave Liberia was surely a punishable offense.

Don promised to help me raise some money. I knew he had foreign contacts with cash, some who might have it stashed, but it was risky betting my family's escape on whether he could hustle up a significant enough bribe. Meanwhile, I remembered I had hidden $1,000 in final receipts from the most recent Red Cross Bazaar under my mattress. Shortly after I had written the Secretary General requesting an official leave of absence, the Red Cross Offices on Lynch Street closed. They closed headquarters before I could take them my final report and the final receipts from the Bazaar. I had naively thought I would simply hold onto the money until Red Cross offices reopened. At the time, we envisioned a Red Cross closure of a couple of weeks, a month at best. Now, after six months, it didn't look like the Red Cross was reopening anytime soon, and the money appeared to be a blessing in disguise.

All these months I had kept the money hidden under my mattress. Originally, there had been $1,200, but recently I had borrowed from the cache. Each time I borrowed money, I had written a promissory note and placed it in the envelope with the remaining money. I can't believe that under the circumstances, I actually struggled with the idea of using the Red Cross money—it wasn't mine, but I realized soon enough that getting my family out of Liberia alive trumped my integrity.

I tucked the money in my lappa and took it hastily to Don. He stared at me, amazed. He hadn't even known about the Red Cross money. Armed with $1,000, he went to make the deal for our flight.

One way or another, the $1,000 would serve us. Either Don would buy our way to the Embassy, or, if the soldiers didn't just take the money from him, I reasoned that we could use it to support our continued attempts to escape a more arduous exodus. Ultimately, we might have to go overland to Voinjama and try crossing the border into Sierra Leone—a viable, but much more perilous option.

AUGUST 7, 1990

My sense of impending doom had increased when the BBC reported the deployment of U.S. troops to the Persian Gulf for Operation Desert Shield. America's priority was protecting its oil interests in Kuwait.

My heart shattered into a thousand pieces because I knew, despite the American war ships visible from Mamba Point, all hopes for U.S. intervention to help stop the war in Liberia had sunk. This news fueled my paranoia about keeping our movements clandestine lest we face any retribution from Liberians angry over America's betrayal.

Soon, those ships would set sail and leave besieged President Samuel Kanyon Doe, who refused to leave Liberia, to 'settle up' with both the Charles Taylor and Prince Johnson warring factions.

I was on pins and needles. I still could not eat, and spent most of the day in my bedroom agonizing over how much of eleven years we could carry on our heads. I organized everything that the children would need for school, my curriculum vitae and a few treasured photos along with my business card holders. I planned to return, and I when I did, I wanted to be able to reach my contacts.

That evening, Don came to my house shortly before curfew to say that he had three Krahn soldiers willing to take us through the checkpoints and get us as close to the American Embassy as possible. He told me to sleep well and come to his house on the Old Road with everything we could carry on our heads the next morning.

"Kizzie and Manke are going with you," he said simply as he left.

How would I tell my children?

Baby steps, I thought to myself. I'll just tell them that we are moving back to Don's house in the morning.

That night, I carefully washed and soaked the last bag of dried red beans in my pantry. I awakened shortly before 3:00 a.m. to light the coal pot that we now used inside our kitchen and put the beans on the fire. It was early enough that I prayed that neither my neighbors nor marauding soldiers would smell food cooking. I wanted us to have a good meal under our belts before we faced the perilous day that lay ahead.

When I placed the steaming bowls of red beans and rice on the table and led us in Grace, it was nearly 5 a.m.. The children, initially groggy, happily devoured the heavy meal. My decision to leave them out of my anxiety had been wise. I remember looking across the table at Zefron. He had the annoying habit of smacking when he ate. This morning his smacking was a pleasant sound. Zevah was a girlie girl. She ate slowly, chewing her food carefully, while EliTikvah sat in her usual spot right next to Zefron, as he intermittently asked, "Tikvah, are you going to eat all your rice?"

I had no appetite.

"Emah, you will not eat your food?" queried a concerned Zevah.

"No, I'm not hungry. I will keep it for Chris."

The truth was the thought of food made me nauseous. *Would I really have the courage to do what needed to be done?* I covered my bowl with another to keep the food warm and placed it in the center of the table.

Chris had moved in with us after Binah's evacuation, and his presence had provided me a feeling of security and companionship. He had become like a son to me, and now, while we were exercising our prerogative of using the coveted American passport to beam us from Liberia, Chris, a Liberian National, had to stay.

We would be leaving him behind in a fully furnished home with a quarter bag of rice that he had helped me hide in the ceiling. Nevertheless, we would still be leaving someone who felt like family. I would ask him to share our home and food with Roland. I knew he would.

Chris, was well over six feet, and resembled former Chicago Bulls player Horace Grant. He balanced my packed leather suitcase on his head. It easily weighed eighty pounds. It held photographs, my journals, the few clothes that would have to do until we could get more, the children's school and immunization records, and the paperwork that documented my legal name change from Susan Peters to Ahnydah Rahm. Eleven years distilled down to eighty pounds.

The children packed their book satchels with their treasures. I threatened that whatever they packed, they had to either carry or give away on the road. I would come to regret not taking my own advice. As we walked through the gate of our home on Chubor Road, I refused to look back. Turning around would feed any lingering doubt that moving ahead and away was what must be done. Over the course of my life I will always remember that final walk down Chubor Road as a dark moment of personal loss.

As we neared Ma Seeton's, I knew the children would want to run down the road that led to her house to speak to Ma but they were silent.

Instead Chris asked, "You sure you will not go see de Old Ma one last time?" There was no way I could have looked at Ma Seeton as we left Chubor that day. I loved her. She was probably close to her 80's, and I suspected that her children in the U.S. were already working to get her out of Liberia. At least that's what I told myself. I hoped Ma would understand my leaving without saying goodbye. She knew that I would always put my role as a mother before every other alliance. She would have done the same. I had written her a note and put together a gift of rice that Chris would deliver. Tears slid down my face as we walked past the road that led to her house.

"Never mind yah," I heard Chris say. I was glad that he knew my heart.

One hour later

At Don's apartment, we waited for our military escort. Meanwhile a young Liberian girl, a nursemaid with two children whose Liberian parents were U.S. citizens, had also joined our group. Assembled in the living room were Don's wife Kizzie, his daughter Manke, our new traveling mate with her two charges, of maybe four-and-six years old, and Tikvah, who was six, Zefron, eight, Zevah, ten, and me. I mustered my courage to speak the words that would kill my dream. Taking a couple of breaths I said, "Children, I didn't say it earlier but we are leaving for America today."

Zefron frowned and then slowly smiled. "We will see Binah and Penemiel and Nookie?"

"Yes, soon we will see them and meet your grandma and your aunt Yvonne." EliTikvah played quietly with Manke, but Zevah burst into laughter, squealing, "My Binah and my Penemiel!" Relief washed across her round face.

"Chris, will you come with us?" Zefron said, who thought Chris was his big brother rather than his sister's boyfriend.

"No man, I will stay and mind the house. When things cool down, Emah can come back. Zefron and Zevah, ya'll take care of Emah an Tikvah ya'll hear? Tell Binah and them I say hello, yah."

My heart stilled, realizing that he who was being left behind to face God only knows what, was trying to make it easier for me.

When the van pulled up, our bags were loaded and we hastily said our good byes. I wanted to scream and cry. I wanted to hug Chris, but a hug was such a meaningless gesture now.

We left behind Kizzie's elder two Liberian children in Don's care. Roland didn't come to see us off, and I was happy not to bear the burden of guilt for leaving him behind as well.

Don introduced the soldiers. They were fierce-looking but barely past their teens. Don sat in front with the driver, and two others clung onto the sides of the van.

Inside the van, my children were excited. I had not seen their little faces this happy since before the first evacuation. I looked at the young woman, and the children with her, and admired her quietly facing the unknown. She had used the same phone as I had in Congo town to give the childrens' parents information to the Embassy, and they promised to verify the information if we arrived. We pulled off the Old Road and settled in to our ride. The first checkpoint was just before reaching Sinkor, and the soldiers that we had hired helped us blow through that checkpoint. We talked quietly in the jeep.

The second checkpoint was more rigorous. As we neared the Executive Mansion, it occurred to me that the closer we got to town, the more aggressive the checkpoint guards. This time they shouted at Don to get out of the jeep and answer questions. A couple of soldiers peeped into the windows of the jeep with their guns drawn, but when they saw only women and children, they waved us through. We were nearing Camp Johnson Road, a big retail area. Most of the Lebanese building supply shops and wholesale merchandisers closed their doors to front-door-business now. Our goal was to pass by BTC, Barclay Training Center, the barracks where Liberian Soldiers had sent their families, their wives and children for safety. Security, as it turned out, was more intense at BTC than near the Executive Mansion.

When we approached the checkpoint, our escorts jumped off the truck to talk with the sentinels. They met hardened Krahn troops who were protecting their own families. I was suddenly aware that at the previous checkpoints, Liberian English had been spoken with only certain words in dialect. Now I was aware and terrified by the fact that languages were being spoken that I didn't understand! However, I could still understand that the voices were angry and then pleading. Don jumped outside the truck, and the solders pounced, pushing and shoving him. Soldiers with guns trained on us forced us outside of the truck. Panic-stricken, I looked at Don whose eyes pleaded with me to stay calm.

Suddenly I heard Kizzie speaking frantically in her dialect. She exited the truck, taking control of the conversation. Thankfully, although she was Grebo, she understood Krahn, and later told us that she sprang into action because the soldiers were accusing us of being spies.

After a few moments of what sounded like a mixture of arguments and begging, she began to smile and talk with one of the soldiers in Grebo. He seemed able to understand most of what she was saying and Kizzie was forging a tenuous connection. Another rag-headed soldier with blazing red eyes stepped toward me, brandishing his weapon.

He challenged, "Mommie, why you going to the barracks, who sent for you?"

"General Julu sent for me, he is my *friend*." I said boldly. Speaking the word 'friend' in a certain way meant I was one of his women. I had no idea why I spoke General Julu's name other than I knew he was a well-respected general. I had never even met him and had no idea whether he was dead or alive. Once those words flew out of my lips, I was both surprised and terrified. I wanted to grab them in mid-air and cram them back into my mouth, but it was too late.

As the soldier glared menacingly, I threw back my head knowing that our lives depended on how fearlessly we lived these next seconds. Somehow, between Kizzie's Grebo endorsement, and my bodacious comment, the checkpoint guards allowed the adults back into the van, and finally waved it through.

Back in the car, after our narrow escape, we talked about which moment we thought had been pivotal in getting us back into the truck. Next to me, Zefron said quietly, "It was the Lord's Prayer Emah. I was saying the Lord's Prayer."

We passed the Barclay Training Center, the Central Prison, and finally reached the Monrovia Bakery at the bottom of the hill which lead up to Mamba Point, and ultimately to the American Embassy. The truck stopped abruptly, and our military escort told us that they would take us no further. Don gave them a look that made me think they had slightly reneged on the deal, but no one was going to argue with armed soldiers. We exited the van, unloaded our belongings, and they sped away. We were about two miles from the Embassy. We didn't need a clock to know that dusk was nearing, which probably accounted for our escorts' abrupt departure. Everybody picked up his or her bags, and we began climbing the hill. There was no traffic along the well-paved roads leading to the luxury homes and foreign embassies populating Mamba Point. In the distance, we heard gunfire.

Don was now the leader. "Once we start up this hill, we stop for no one, understood?" Everyone nodded in response. I took the rear position.

When I reflect on my walk toward Mamba Point, I know that I was still wrestling with doubts about leaving. My main concern was for my children, that they would be safe and reunited with their siblings and my family in America. I wanted that for them no matter what happened to me. Yet, I was leaving behind my dreams of wanting to create the best elementary school in Liberia, and eventually, establishing more day care centers for Market Women. I had wanted to spend my life working for the development of women in Liberia. *Now that I was leaving, all that was over.* I struggled with these opposing emotions as I ascended to Mamba Point.

I had routinely balanced huge buckets of water on my head in Kakata, but my neck muscles had never balanced anything as heavy as my eighty pound suitcase. I could have packed less, but after eleven years, I had an attachment to every item, every sheet of paper inside this bag. My neck and shoulders screamed under the weight of the suitcase. My children walked anxiously ahead carrying their own important essentials. Zefron carried the little drum that I had brought him from Kenya and his favorite short suit made of army fatigue cloth. Today he was dressed in black shorts and yellow shirt, his school uniform from Haywood Academy, while his sisters wore mid-length African print dresses. Don and Kizzie led our party of escapees up the hill. It would be the last time they would be together for years.

Random thoughts crossed my mind as I fought for the will to move forward. I knew if I set our suitcase down, I could never lift it to my head. The caravan moved further and further away. As I watched them move out ahead, I was tempted several times to just stop walking. *Oh God, I just need some help!* But I refused to call ahead.

On the deserted road to Mamba Point, I suddenly spied a scraggly looking man by the side of the road. Gunfire raged in the distance, and yet there he stood, almost casually, smoking. I was afraid of him at first and then felt a calming presence.

"I need help 'O,'"

"What you got for me mommie?"

I flashed the last five dollar Liberian dollar I had tucked in my bra.

"I got five dolla 'O.'"

He nodded. Lifting the load from my head, he moved swiftly ahead of me. I was lightheaded once he removed the suitcase. My head, neck and shoulders ached. It took several minutes to regain my balance and catch up to him. The distance between the others and me shortened.

I was more concerned with gauging the distance between us and the gunshots. As curfew encroached, there was no stopping. Finally, I caught sight of the Embassy ahead, and after a few more minutes, we stood at its gates. In case of separation, I had buried the passports of each of my children at the bottom of the bags they carried. I had tucked mine inside the waistband of my lappa. As we lined up at the gate, I removed the five dollar bill from my bra and paid the man who had so ably bore my burden. A line of people assembled outside the gate, many were Liberians with relatives who were American citizens.

"Emah, look at Soniyah!" Zevah tugged at my arm, grinning in the direction of the line where the young girl who had rescued her from Konola, stood. She had always told us that her father was an American. Her younger brother had evacuated with Binah and Penemiel. Her repeated attempts to get a visa to join her father and brother had met only denials from the Embassy. Just a few years older than Zevah, Soniyah had survived these past months by relying on her wits.

When I looked in her face, I saw both fatigue and fear but her optimism was a magnet. "I will go today Mistress Rahm. I will go to my Pa in America! I have everything I need to go today 'O.'"

I sensed this declaration was more her way of keeping her own spirits up than to convince us, yet there was still an aura of power about her. I hoped today would be her day. The Counselor who repeatedly denied her exit visa was a mean-spirited woman whom no one liked. She had a reputation for being a tough gatekeeper. Today there was no reason to deny a visa to anyone with a shred of evidence of U.S. citizenry. The war had already been more violent than anything ever seen in Liberia.

As I looked around me at the line of weary and worried faces, I suddenly felt self-conscious of the privilege that came with possessing an American passport. Several years earlier, I had pondered renouncing my American citizenship. I remember asking myself what difference it made since I planned to remain in Liberia and to own property. The continual renewal of my Liberian work permit and residency visa seemed burdensome. Ironically, it was my Liberian friends who convinced me of the value of retaining the much-coveted U.S. passport. Eventually, I also had the presence of mind to make sure that my children, born on Liberian soil, had a passport as well.

At this moment, I could not fathom our fate had I not heeded that advice. Now, my children and I stood with one foot inside the gates of the American Embassy ready to be "beamed up" and away from the poverty, ignorance, and what to me, was senseless bloodshed.

Our party approached the front of the line, anxiety welling up inside of me and spilling onto those around me. Tikvah held onto the top layer of my lappa as I wiped my sweaty palms on my blouse. It was dusk. We were technically disobeying the dawn to dusk curfew. The fear was palpable. There was a gated area across from the Embassy, and inside its confines were hundreds of Nigerians, Ivoirians, Ghanaians, and other foreign nationals who had fled to the Embassy for protection. Marines stationed around the perimeter technically guarded the gated outdoor area across from the Embassy; however they were still vulnerable themselves to mortar attacks and stray gunfire from either the Marines or rebels.

I was numb, yet I breathed deeply, relieved that my Zefron, Zevah, and EliTikvah stood at the threshold of safety. I could never have borne the pain of losing my children to the war. Yet even as I stood at the Embassy gates, my heart remained with Old Road and Chubor Road, and with the streets of Sinkor, longing for First Steps Child Development Center to reopen. My heart still saw a future in Liberia for my family, one that would allow me to drink orange Fanta from my front porch and watch my children mature, while I mastered my role as 'the Big Ma' for the family. My broken heart still lived in the Liberia that I had fallen in love with eleven years earlier.

Given the escalating violence, leaving Liberia was the only sane decision available to me. Yet even as we neared the gate, I knew that there were members of the Hebrew Israelite Community, some of them children the ages of my children, who had been trapped upcountry when Charles Taylor's troops had taken Bong County. Those children would face horrors that Divine Providence had spared my children. I said a silent prayer for them. Once I reached the States I would make sure that their families knew that no matter what it took, they needed to find a way to get their children out of Liberia.

The bottoms of my feet ached and the friction of the centerpiece of the rubber thong between my big toe was painful. Sweat dripped from my fingertips, and my armpits reeked from the wild scent of nervous perspiration, but at least we were at the Embassy gates. Reservations cast aside, I quietly accounted for all my children like a hen counts her chicks, and then I recounted to reassure myself. I knew that whatever challenges lay ahead for me, their world was full of promise; promise that I hadn't robbed them of in the pursuit of my own dreams.

As we inched forward, my thoughts wrenched themselves from the past and I stood timidly, fearfully, and with deep regret in the present.

I watched Don present his passport. Still defiant, he informed the sentinel that he was only escorting his Liberian wife and daughter for evacuation.

"I'll be remaining in Liberia."

"Yes, sir!" said the sentinel crisply, sneaking a second glance at Don.

I collected our passports, cautiously removing mine from my lappa.

Finally, the Marine sentinel looked in my direction and demanded a little too loudly, "Passports open please."

He authenticated each passport, matching the photo to the bearer and directed people inside the gates.

Then I heard the words that meant my heart could stop hammering, my anxiety could dissipate into the red dirt roads of Old Road Chubor, and a new life for me and my family was just a few days away…

"You may now consider yourselves in the United States of America. Please, follow me."

A placid scene

ALL THE DAYS ARE NOT EQUAL

I received a gem of wisdom during a troubling time by Prof Rabbieau, a Sierra Leonean friend. He told me to look forward because "all of the days are not equal." His wisdom is both poetic and true.

During my eleven-year sojourn in Liberia, a lot had changed in America. I left in 1979, at the height of the Black Nationalist Movement. James Brown, the legendary R&B singer, had Black folks singing "Say it loud, I'm Black and I'm proud!" When I returned I found that we were now called African Americans instead of Black.

I left America on the strains of progressive Black men calling women 'sisters,' and boyfriends and husbands calling their girlfriends and wives, 'my queen.' When I returned, I was shocked and appalled that young women actually responded to being dubbed 'bitches' and 'ho's.

In 1979, I had felt an impending explosion as we tackled racism in America, but instead of an explosion and descent into a racial clash between Blacks and Whites, that anger had imploded and sucked self-hatred back into the African American community. Initially awe-struck, I pondered, "How could a group of people moving forward at such a progressive pace in 1979, be catapulted backwards in a relatively short span of eleven years?" But then, I had just witnessed, what I considered, a monumental backward trajectory take place in Liberia, I understood.

Earlier in my book, I shared my experiences in working with women involved with deeply rooted cultural practices and who chose to modify, rather than discontinue female circumcision, despite serious--nearly fatal--health consequences. I think we can all appreciate the dilemma of our sisters. However, I recently searched Google for female circumcision and came across information on multiple websites about modern women in America and Europe that have begun to popularize labiaplasty. They are, in effect, opting to have their labias operated on by plastic surgeons to make their vaginas to look cleaner and neater. So in the lyrics of a song made popular by the late Billy Preston, "Will it go round in circles?"

It took me nine months to get my family fully resettled. My Aunt Connie helped me land a temporary job at what was then The First National Bank of Chicago. My sister Yvonne cosigned for me to move into a modest home. My children were enrolled in public school, and within two months, quickly lost their thick Liberian English accents. Unfortunately, EliTikvah tenaciously clung to hers a little longer. The entire first semester the teacher complained that my young one insisted upon speaking in a "foreign language." Eventually, even stubborn Tikvah succumbed and began speaking like the other second graders.

While I taught my children about America's racism, which was something that they had a hard time understanding, the streets taught them about gangs. They learned to deal with both. Somehow, with the help of God, my family, and my neighbors, I managed to get all my children through high school, one through college, and the others through various post-high school training programs.

Today, my eldest daughter is a wonderful mom to her three children and a licensed foster mother who has mothered many children. She is, more than any of her siblings, the highest embodiment of the Liberian personality--or as they say in Liberia, "Tha Liberian woman!" Her formative years were spent in Liberia and for her, like all Liberians, it is family first, last, and forever. She still maintains close ties with friendships that were built in Liberia and an even closer bond with her siblings. My children are all productive citizens, wonderful parents, and my very dear friends.

During the first few years after our return, survivor's guilt consumed me. I spent many sleepless nights trying to figure out how I could return to Liberia. I was unable to open letters from friends I had left behind. Currently, I am without a U.S. passport which prohibits me from traveling internationally and even across our border to Canada. Unless something changes within U.S. policy, a passport will not be forthcoming. I was officially "repatriated" from Liberia and immediately held responsible for thousands of dollars in airfare. I have petitioned to have the State Department waive that repatriation fee, but have been unsuccessful at the time of this writing. From my perspective, I wasn't a "stranded tourist," I was returning to America from a war with dependent children. I left in my wake an eleven-year body of work and since our government brought Liberian refugees to America for free, have I not earned my way home?

Some might say that it was mighty convenient for me to slip under an American umbrella when the going got tough in Liberia. However, I stuck it out for as long as possible, hoping for the tide to turn. As a mother, I, like so many other women, would not hesitate to do anything that would ensure my children's safety. I regret none of my choices, nor would I deny myself the experiences that made me the faith-filled woman I am today.

I believe my sojourn was part of my soul's journey. Besides the lessons learned about being true to my own heart, I realized that everyone has a right to manifest their own life's purpose. Female or male, dominant or passive, everyone needs to be who she or he authentically is, rather than someone who is pressed into a predetermined mold. Additionally, the reality of being away from the overt day-to-day racism in America, and seeing race issues on a global level was an eye-opening experience. In Liberia on Lynch Street or on the South Side of Chicago on St. Lawrence, I am witness to a kind of barbarism is hard to comprehend.

What divides people is never really about race or color, or perceived differences, but about resonating at a higher or lower vibration or level of consciousness.

My Sweet Liberian experience was deep and wide. Fortunately, through my connection with others that had similar experiences, we collectively continue to heal. Twenty years later, our experience in Liberia is the strongest tie that binds us, and we are almost never together without referencing it.

In 1847, Liberia declared itself a free and independent nation. Twelve of Liberia's presidents were born in the United States. The question of whether America was ready to elect a man of color as its president was always backward thinking!

We have ties to Liberia just as the Jewish people have to Israel. However, there isn't much in the African American tradition that celebrates that fact. The celebration of Kwanza, a made-up holiday created by Black Nationalists in the 60's to combat the consumerism of Christmas and advance a positive value system for its celebrants, has grown and has itself become highly commercialized. One wonders why African Americans don't feel the necessity to celebrate Liberian Independence day, June 26th, as a day of real accomplishment in African American History.

On January 2006, after fourteen years of civil wars, Liberians came together and elected Ellen Johnson Sirleaf, the first female president of an African nation. In her inaugural speech, she honored all women....

"And now, before I close, I would like to talk to the women--the women of Liberia, the women of Africa, and the women of the world. Until a few decades ago, Liberian women endured the injustice of being treated as second-class citizens. During the years of our civil war, they bore the brunt of inhumanity and terror. They were conscripted into war, gang raped at will, forced into domestic slavery. Yet, it is the women who laboured and advocated for peace throughout our region. "

---From Ellen Johnson Sirleaf's inauguration speech on 16th January 2006.

On the home front, I watched Barack Obama rise slowly, quietly, and recall the day that he announced his candidacy for President. There was something special about him. That still small voice inside me said, "Support him, he is the one, he will win." The voice I have come to trust has never been wrong, and so, from that moment forward, I told anyone who would listen, "Support him, he will win."

Initially, even my closest friends, former nationalists, civil righters, and militants were afraid to believe, but I always knew. Countless times, my excitement for his candidacy was met with, "They're gonna kill him, baby," and "This White man still hates us." I thought how dare we even consider denying Barack his destiny because of our fear of the past?

My ultimate revelation came on Tuesday, November 4, 2009 when Barack Obama, like Abraham Lincoln, another big-eared Senator from Illinois, became the 44th President of the United States of America. It dawned on me then that I had left America in 1979, sure that Liberia was the land of opportunity for my children, yet now, a man of color was the President of the United States.

I was finally home, where I belonged.

DISCUSSION QUESTIONS

1. Given life in America in the late 1970's, can you understand why some Blacks wanted to leave America?

2. Do you think that life in America has improved to the extent that Blacks living here should be content?

3. Who was Ahnydah when she arrived in Liberia? What were the pivotal experiences that shaped her idea of race in America?

4. Discuss the parallels between life as a slave in America, and life as an indigenous person in the Republic of Liberia as expressed in the book.

5. What do you think about Ahnydah's relationship with her husband?

6. Could you ever consider having a second wife or sharing your husband or wife with another partner?

7. Do you think it is possible for African Americans to return to Africa and live productive lives?

8. How do you anticipate children, who are taken to live in foreign countries, adjust when they return to their country of origin?

9. What are your thoughts about Ahnydah leaving the Hebrew community? Should she have returned and tried to make her marriage work?

10. Should Ahnydah's children feel more Liberian or American?

11. What is acculturation? Do you think Ahnydah realized she was slowly losing some characteristics that she wanted to maintain? What were they?

12. Would you ever consider retiring to Africa or another developing nation?

13. What are the consequences for people who become involved in movements that are considered counter-culture?

14. Given Ahnydah's options of trying to remain in Liberia or return to America during the war, what would you have chosen?

15. What were the pivotal points that influenced Ahnydah's growth in Liberia? What role do you think tribalism plays in a country's national development?

16. After reading this book, what is your perception on how people grow and develop into the person they become?

RECOMMENDED READING

A Brother In The Bush; An African American's Search For Self In East Africa by John Slaughter. Agate Publishing Inc, Chicago April 2005

A Long Way Gone: Memoirs of a Boy Solider by Ishmael Beah Farrar, Straus Gioux, March 2007

Black Rage by William H. Grier, Price M. Cobbs, Basic Books, 1992

God, the Black Man and Truth by Ben Ammi, 2nd Revised Edition, Communicators Press, 1990

Don't Let's Go to the Dogs Tonight: An African Childhood by Alexandra Fuller, Random House, 2001

The House at Sugar Beach: In Search of a Lost African Childhood by Helene Cooper, Simon Schuster, 2008

Liberia the Quest for Democracy by J. Gus Liebenow, Indiana University Press, 1987

Long Journeys: An Arkansas Family in Africa: A Scrapbook

of Memories and History by Sarah McKee Burnside, Phoenix International, Incorporated, January 2007

Mukiwa: A White Boy in Africa (Paperback), by Peter Godwn
Grove Press, 2005 originally printed in 1996 by Atlantic Monthly Press

This Child Will Be Great, Memoir of a Remarkable Life by Africa's First Woman President, HarperCollins Books, 2009

This Our Dark Country: The American Settlers of Liberia by Catherine Reef, Clarion Books, 2002

The New Ship of Zion : Dynamic Diaspora Dimensions of the African Hebrew Israelites of Jerusalem (Afrika Und Ihre Diaspora), by Martina Koenighofer, Lit Verlag, February 1, 2010

The Truth About Black Biblical Hebrew-Israelites (Jews: the World's Best Kept Secret) by Ella Hughley, October, 1982

Where We Have Hope: A Memoir of Zimbabwe by Andrew Meldrum Grove Press, September 2006

SUSAN D. PETERS

aka, Ahnydah (pronounced ah-NIE-dah) Rahm, brings a treasure trove of experience gained from 1979 through 1990 in West Africa, to her memoir, *Sweet Liberia, Lessons from the Coal Pot.* She worked tirelessly for the Liberian National Red Cross Society leaving in January 1989 when she and a Liberian friend opened a school, First Steps, Child Development Center, only to close its doors in May due to the encroaching war.

Stubbornly remaining after America evacuated its citizens from Liberia in June, she and her children were stranded as the conflict described by The British Broadcasting System as, "The bloodiest war in West Africa since the Biafran War," raged. Finally, on August 8, her family made a harrowing escape to the United States Embassy. Despite the carnage of the Civil War, she feels that Liberia will rise from its ashes due to the remarkable pride and the indomitable spirit of the Liberian people.

Susan resides in Chicago where she is working on her next book, *Broken Dolls.*

Visit her on the web at www.susandpeters.com

LaVergne, TN USA
18 October 2010
201266LV00004B/1/P